THE
LAST LADY
FROM
HELL

By

RICHARD G. MORLEY

DEDICATION

Thanks to Martie, my wife, who spent countless hours transcribing my hand written manuscript onto a laptop without swearing at me about my illegible writing. With all my love.

Thanks also to Bill Lewis a good friend and a great drummer for his insightful opinions, help and interest in this book.

I would like to dedicate this story to the memory of my great Uncle Leslie Greenhow. His sacrifice and the sacrifice of so many others must never be forgotten.

COMMENTS FROM THE AUTHOR

*"I have written too much history to have faith in it; and if any-
one thinks I'm wrong, I'm inclined to agree with him."*
Henry Adams, Historian, 1838-1918

"Hope and not loss of lives is what decides the issue of war."
B.H. Liddell, Historian, 1895-1970

World War One quickly became the forgotten war as it was followed so closely by the Spanish influenza pandemic (between 50 and 100 million died in two years), the world recession / depression, and then by The Second World War a mere 23 years later. Those that were in that struggle seemed reluctant to talk about it, no one wanted to speak of the glory of the battle and the honor of victory. That war was fought by a generation that went tight lipped to their graves save a few. They felt that the horrors that they had endured were best left buried as deeply as the friends they left behind.

My effort in this novel was to give insight into a small portion of the Great War by using my characters as vehicles and attaching a human element to history that is so often lacking in many text books. I have taken some literary license concerning some events and those alterations will be corrected at the end of the book; for those history buffs. I spent three years researching and writing this novel and hope that I have provided as good a presentation of events as is possible. In an effort to better understand the perspective of my characters I went to the areas of the Western front that I discuss and walked the battle fields. I stayed in Auchonvillers, Albert, Arras, and Ypres and traversed the existing trench system where so many died. I visited the Thiepval memorial where 70,000 names of missing British soldiers are chiseled into marble columns. I would recommend that anyone who has an interest in knowing more about The Great War visit this area of France and the many memorials and cemeteries honoring the fallen. You will be overwhelmed.

All of my main characters are fictional and several characters I chose to use in important events are also fictional. I will let the reader know which are historically correct and which are not at the end of the novel. My hope is that you the reader enjoy this story and come away with some new knowledge of a forgotten war.

PART ONE
ENLIGHTENMENT

Queens University, Kingston, Ontario. Fall semester, 2005

YOU KNOW HOW PEOPLE SAY the early bird catches the worm? Well, it's starting to look like a wormless day for me. I rushed across the campus in an attempt to make my sociology class on time. Bounding up the stone steps of Mackintosh-Corry Hall, I was glad to leave the chilly autumn air behind and turned left, running for the open door of Professor Kathryn Krull's class.

She was at the podium still arranging her notes. I had made it under the wire. She glanced up from the podium as I sat down.

"Ah, Mr. Way, so nice of you to join us," she said, to the sound of snickers from my classmates. She held up a hand to quiet the class and began.

"We shall be discussing the phenomenon that has affected virtually every society throughout the history of mankind," she announced. "That would be the phenomenon we refer to as war. We will be discussing the many causes, affects, and ramifications of war.

Why do they start? How could we have avoided them, if at all, and how can we avoid them in the future?"

War will always be a topic that can generate diverse opinions and with the Iraqi war, the Afghanistan war, and the global war on terrorism, the topic proved to be especially timely.

Professor Krull continued for forty-five minutes attempting to wet the thirst for knowledge of a crowd of college students whose thirst was, frankly, more suited for beer than knowledge.

Her parting assignment for us was to write a five-page paper incorporating our insightful thoughts on war.

"You have the freedom to use your imagination," Krull said. "I am expecting some interesting papers. Thank you and have a wonderful Thanksgiving."

We were about to break for Thanksgiving, so I had several days to think about and complete this assignment. Yeah! Something to be thankful for: a five-page paper.

"Holy crap, it's two-thirty!" I said, glancing at my watch. "I need to run again."

Bagpipe practice would start in thirty minutes and I had to run across campus and get my pipes at the dorm, only to come right back to where I was.

I ran out the door past some slower I-don't-really-have-any-where-else-to-go-now students, whose sole purpose in life, it seemed, was to get in my way and then slow to a snail's pace. I'm not paranoid. I believe they really are out to get me or at least screw up my day.

I had started playing the bagpipes several years ago in my high school band in Guelph, Ontario. We had a pipe and drum marching band and, despite the fact that I always felt that you became a music nerd if you played an instrument in high school, there was something about this instrument that was just, well, cool.

Maybe it was the *Braveheart* thing or maybe the Sean Connery influence, but when we got kilted up and played at a football game, the girls paid more attention to us than to the football players. Even the football players themselves had a curious appreciation of the bagpipers—not in a weird way.

I personally believe that the instrument stirs something ancient, something long-forgotten that lies deep within us. Whatever it was, I still didn't want to be late for practice.

As I hurried across campus toward the dorm, I began to ponder Professor Krull's assignment. It occurred to me that the pipes have, historically, been thought of as an instrument of war. Perhaps I could fit that into the assignment somehow. I bounded up the dorm stairs, waving to my pals as I flew past them. I grabbed my pipes from my room and flew back down the steps, two at a time.

"Going to get rid of some of your hot air, eh Brian?" one of my pals called. I just laughed as I ran out the door.

Practice was an hour long, and it took a full twenty minutes to tune all of the pipes, leaving us only forty minutes to play our tunes. We were able to squeeze most of our parade sets into those forty minutes, still leaving ample time to take a good beating from our taskmaster pipe major.

"Watch your cuts and holds, work on clean starts and stops," he barked. "Revisit the music—some of you are not playing the band setting."

That was very often the drill after every band practice. The simple fact was that the good pipers didn't need the lecture. It was the not-so-good pipers that should have listened, yet many didn't. Consequently, only a few would improve.

Not to sound conceited, but I am not a bad piper. I know there are others who are far better, but they only inspire me to do better. Actually, it's a good spot to be in—the middle that is. If you are the worst player, you feel like crap and everyone else either looks down on you or pities you. If you are the best, everyone expects perfection and looks more closely for any mistakes. Upper middle. That's the place to be.

"Hey, Brian. You going home?" a voice asked. It was Mike Hanniford, a good piper and a good friend. He was half Algonquin Indian, but he looked more like a full-blood. That made for a very interesting mix: pipes and a native, or first nation as we call them, would not seem to be a natural.

I snapped out of my mental wandering. "Yea, Mum and Pop are having a big Thanksgiving thing going on. You know, lots of family and food. What about you?"

"No, we don't really celebrate Thanksgiving," Mike deadpanned. "We're not that thankful since the white man took everything from us."

This unending ball-busting was Mike's style, and we could be ruthless to each other with off-color remarks. All in good fun—you truly only bust the balls of the people you like.

"You're just angry because your tribe invented the boomerang arrow and damn near wiped itself out."

"Frig off, eh!" he said laughing. "You frig off ya bugger."

"How about come with me to Guelph?" I asked. "Lots to eat and plenty of fun people. There's even a topless bar about four blocks away from my folk's house, but I think they are closed for Thanksgiving."

"Na," he said. "But thanks anyway."

"Come on," I insisted.

Mike considered the invitation for a moment. "When are you leaving, eh?"

"Soon as you're ready."

"Okay, then," he said smiling.

"Good deal! I'll meet you at my car in twenty minutes."

≈

Twenty minutes later I plodded across the parking lot with a large bag of dirty laundry—a gift for my Mother, who I knew would appreciate it. Mike was at the car, leaning on the front right fender of my classic 1979 Datsun B-210, with a sappy grin pasted across his face.

"Hey, don't scratch the fender with that boney butt of yours, ya frigger!"

"I was polishing it with my bum, ya freak," he said. This is going to be a long trip, I thought.

"Hey," Mike said. "I just got the latest issue of *The Voice* and thought you might want to read it over our break."

The Voice is a quarterly magazine for bagpipers and drummers.

"I've got this five page paper due, I doubt I'll have the time," I said.

"Well, I brought it anyway. Check out this cool cover."

I took the magazine, setting my bundle of laundry down, and was stunned by what I saw. The cover folded out to form a twelve-by sixteen-inch sepia tone photo that looked very old. It showed a piper playing on a makeshift stage in a classic piper pose—very straight with one leg cocked to one side. He was a handsome guy, and it was obvious he was trying to play pipes while attempting to hold back a smile. He was in full kilt, horsehair sporran, and a glengarry hat. To his right was another stage with four kilted men dancing around four swords laid out on the floor – the Scottish Sword Dance. It was a surreal scene, set against a background of a bombed out church and several trees that had been burned to stumps with a few charred and broken limbs remaining.

In the foreground was a large crowd of kilted soldiers sitting and cheering for the entertainment. This group of men was mud covered and haggard looking, but still appeared to have the spirit to laugh and cheer. Among them were a few men, with blank expressions and vacant stares, who seemed numb to their fellow infantrymen.

It was the most stirring photo I had ever seen, and I knew I had to learn more. I flipped the cover over and on the back a small-print caption read, "A kilted regiment enjoying some entertainment after the devastating losses of the Battle of Somme, WWI."

"Devastating" was the word that caught my attention.

Mike got into the Datsun and hollered, "Let's go!" The trance was broken, and I jumped in and tossed my sack of dirty clothes on the back seat.

≈

The three-hour drive was a blur filled with idle chatter and poor drivers. I couldn't stop thinking about that photo and the word "devastating."

Finally, we pulled into my parents' driveway and hopped out of the car, eager to stretch our legs. The house I grew up in was very modest, in a modest neighborhood in a modest city. Guelph is my idea of a nice city. It is well-designed—not too big or too small, yet plenty to do. Guelph is home to several universities and a good amount of industry, including a large brewery. It is nicknamed "The Royal City" because it was named after the ancestral family of George the IV of England.

My folks must have been waiting at the door because they came out almost immediately. Hugs, kisses, handshakes and introductions followed.

I couldn't wait to get inside to a computer and search online for "the battle Somme" and find out what the word devastating meant to the writer of *The Voice*. I went inside and got on-line. First I had to contend with the dreadfully slow family computer. It desperately needed some attention, not like the ones at school which are constantly cleaned up by an army of unpaid computer geeks.

Finally, I found a summary of "Battle Somme" on Wikipedia.

"A major offensive of World War One, led by Field Marshall Douglas Haig against German forces on the western front in the Somme Valley of France. Haig bombarded the trenches for seven days dropping over 1.6 million artillery shells. On July 1, 1916 at 07:25 the Hawthorn ridge mine prematurely went off followed by 13 more at 07:30 marking the beginning of the ground assault. Unfortunately, the Germans had plenty of advance warning and had fortified their bunkers, allowing them to weather the assault far better than was anticipated by the British. What ensued was the single most devastating loss of life for the British Empire in history. The first day of the Somme offensive the British suffered 56,000 casualties..."

I did a double take. Did I read that right? The British suffered 56,000 casualties on the first day of the Somme offensive? I was stunned. How could that be? As I continued reading, I discovered that the German machine guns did most of the work, cutting down the oncoming soldiers like blades of grass.

How could I have never heard of this battle? Fifty-six thousand casualties in one day. That was almost as many as the lives that were lost in the Vietnam War over 12 years. Devastating was exactly the right word to describe the losses, especially since the Battle Somme went on for five months!

The enormity of the losses in this battle stunned me. I was in a haze, enough to concern my mother, who was busy preparing for the family gathering.

"What's the matter, Brian?" she asked.

"Mum, have you ever heard of the Battle Somme in World War I?"

"Oh, yes, that was a terrible battle, so many died," she said. "Your great Uncle Leslie was killed there. He was a stretcher bearer."

I looked at her. "Really?"

"Oh, yes. More Canadians were killed in Ypres and the Battle of Passchendaele, but we lost a lot of good young men at the Somme."

"I need to know more about this time in history. I know so little about it!" I said.

"Well, dear, I just read in the paper yesterday that we have one of the last surviving veterans of World War I right here in Guelph at the Veterans Home. He's 109 years old and served for three years. I think the article even mentioned that he was a bagpiper."

"Do you think he would mind if I paid him a visit?" I asked. "I mean, he lived through this battle but may not want to remember such a horrible experience."

"Old people love to get visits from young people," she said. "It makes them feel needed and wanted especially if they can pass on something of value."

My Mother is a very wise person. She never received any higher education, but books can't teach common sense.

"It's too late now, honey, but tomorrow you should go talk to him."

I smiled. "You know how sometimes things just seem to come together, Mum? First there was Professor Krull's assignment about war, then I invited Mike on this trip and he just happens to bring *The Voice* along, and now I learn that there's a survivor of the Battle Somme right here in my town. I'm going to ace this paper!"

GUELPH VETERANS HOME

I ROLLED OUT OF BED at about half-past nine and banged on Mike's door on my way to the bathroom.

"Get up, we've got stuff to do!" I called.

On my return trip to my bedroom, Mike opened his door bleary-eyed with a severe case of bedhead. "What on earth time is it?"

"Nine-thirty," I said. "Get dressed. We're going to get something to eat and then go meet a piece of history."

"Holy crap!" Mike grumbled as he rubbed the sleep from his eyes. "Nine-thirty?"

We were downstairs by ten, not bad for a couple of college boys on a Saturday morning. My Mom was more than happy to fix a classic home-cooked breakfast, which was warmly appreciated by us starving students.

After going online for directions to the Veteran's Hospital we hopped into my Datsun. I brought along a tape recorder, a pad of paper with a trusty ballpoint, and the issue of *The Voice*.

≈

Within twenty minutes, we had arrived at the Vet's home and were walking up the front steps to the entrance.

All old-folks homes seem to smell the same, I thought as we walked through the door. It was a kind of antiseptic cleanser odor, mixed with the scent of urine that has been in a Depends far too long. Then there was the smell of old things, a combination of mothballs and passing years that clung to the possessions these old warriors brought with them in an attempt to make this final stop a little more tolerable. They were bits and pieces of their lives, simple reminders of a better time and place.

At the front desk, I asked the receptionist about the gentleman who was featured in the article in the *Guelph News*.

"That would be Mr. MacDonald," she said. "I believe he's in the TV room."

"Do you think it would be all right if we interviewed him for a university paper?" I asked, holding up my recorder.

"Oh, another paper, that's grand," she said brightly. "I know he loves the attention. Bear in mind, though, he is 109 years old and he tires quickly."

I nodded, proving my understanding, but neglected to correct her misunderstanding about my being with a paper instead of just writing one.

"So, you're Clark Kent now, eh?" Mike whispered as we followed the receptionist down the hall to the TV room.

"A harmless misunderstanding," I quipped. We entered a large room with twenty or so old armchairs, most of which were occupied by old folks. Some were sleeping, while others read the paper or chatted with their neighbors, who might or might not have been listening or even caring what was said. Very few, it seemed, were actually watching the television.

The receptionist walked over to an elderly man sitting in a large, high-back chair. His back was to the television and he was staring out the window, alone in his thoughts.

"Mr. MacDonald?" the receptionist called loudly. It appeared the old man's hearing was not what it once was.

"Mr. MacDonald, I have two young men here that are from a university newspaper. They would like to speak with you."

"Who? Where?" he asked, coming out of his daydream.

"Right here, behind you," she said waving us around to the front of him. "Boys, this is Mr. Ian MacDonald."

Mike shot me a scolding glance for allowing the newspaper ruse to continue, as we walked around the chair to see this very old man.

Ian MacDonald was neatly dressed with a white shirt, a tie and a jacket. His trousers were pressed and shoes shined. He had a full head of white hair, and his enormous ears conspicuously gave away his advanced age. With a wry smile, he looked up at me with clear eyes.

"Forgive me for not getting up, boys," he said. "How do you do?"

I had never met anyone over 100 years old and didn't quite know what to expect. "Very well, thank you," I answered.

He held a hand up to his large ears. "I can't hear very well, even with these bloody hearing aids, so I'd appreciate it if you would be so kind as to speak up."

"Yes, of course," I said loudly. "Good to meet you, sir. My name is Brian Way and this is my friend Mike Hanniford. We are from Queens University and I would like to interview you for my paper, if that's okay."

Mike shot me another sour glare.

"I'm happy to speak to you young men, I happen to be a Queen's alumnus myself—and you don't have to shout," he said cheekily.

My eyebrows shot up. This is getting better and better, I thought. He's an alumnus and a joker.

"I understand you were in World War One," I said fumbling for an opening. I was not a seasoned journalist and it showed. I had no prepared questions, no direction, and no thought as to what information I needed to glean from this fountain of knowledge.

"You haven't asked my name!" he barked, looking at me with a twinkle in his eye.

My face reddened, and I knew instantly the old man could see right through me.

"Well, I, uh, I'm sorry," I stammered. "I already know your name from the newspapers and the receptionist.

He held his hand up and chuckled. "I'm razzing you young man. What is it that I can help you with?"

I relaxed. This guy is sort of cool, I thought. How can someone be so old and still be cool? I was about to ask Mike this question, but he was focused on the television, watching a rerun of *Gilligan's Island*. To be fair, I knew I had a lot more interest in the information this man possessed than Mike, so I was happy to see that he was being entertained.

I turned back to Mr. Macdonald and noticed a small pin on his tie. It looked like a bagpipe.

"Is that a bagpipe on your tie?" I asked, pointing to it.

"Yes. Yes, it is.

"Are you a piper?"

"Yes, but I haven't played in many years. I don't have the lungs for it anymore."

"I'm a piper myself," I said.

He smiled and nodded, and an awkward silence took over. This is painful, I thought. Why is this so difficult for me? This man is living history. He possessed first-hand recollections of some of the most historically horrific battles in modern civilization. I needed to find a way to tap into these personal insights before this window to the past was closed forever. Then I remembered *The Voice* in my jacket pocket and took it out. I unfolded the cover photo and held it up before him.

"I understand you were at the Battle Somme."

Ian took the magazine and squinted at it. He reached into his pocket and removed a pair of thick reading glasses. He put them on and inspected the photo. As he looked, his expression changed. He stared intently for several minutes. It seemed that he was no longer looking at the photo, but was looking deep into it, recollecting something long forgotten or perhaps buried.

"Mr. MacDonald, sir?" I said quietly.

His eyes refocused and he said, "Terry Manning."

"Pardon me?"

He pointed at the piper and looked up at me with tired, sad eyes. "Terry Manning," he repeated.

"You know the piper in that photo?" I asked. I couldn't believe it was possible. What were the odds of that?

"Yes" he responded softly, putting the magazine in his lap. "He was one of the best pipers I ever knew. We were good friends."

The old man reached into the side pocket of his jacket and produced a beautiful, ornate white bone pipe and a pouch of tobacco. He packed the bowl as he continued to gaze down at the magazine. Then he lit a match and produced a large billow of sweet aromatic smoke. Ian drew deeply on the pipe and began to speak in a low hypnotic voice. I turned on the tape recorder and leaned in closer to hear him more clearly.

PART TWO

THE STORY

1915 – Queens University, Kingston, Ontario

[Transcribed from Ian MacDonald's recording]

I APPROACHED THE UNION ST. Athletic Field, which would later become the site of Richardson Stadium in 1919, and could hear the crowd loudly singing the Queen's fight song.

> *Oilthigh na Banrighinn a' Bhanrighinn gu bràth!*
> *Oilthigh na Banrighinn a' Bhanrighinn gu bràth!*
> *Oilthigh na Banrighinn a' Bhanrighinn gu bràth!*
> *Cha ghèill! Cha ghèill! Cha ghèill!*
> *(same tune as "The Battle Hymn of the Republic")*

"We must have scored a touchdown," I thought. It is traditional to sing this song after every score. This was McGill versus Queens, one of the biggest rivalries in Canadian higher education.

I was late for the kickoff, but I was really far more interested in the halftime show anyway. The pipe band in particular. I had received a partial scholarship that hinged on my getting into the pipe band and, later that afternoon, I was to be at band practice for the tryouts.

Queens University was known to have one of the best college pipe bands in Canada and I wanted to get a good look at them before the tryouts. The halftime show was the perfect opportunity for this.

There was a lot riding on my qualifying for the band and securing the scholarship. I came from a farming family on Wolfe Island, the largest of the Thousand Islands. We had limited resources and Queens University was very expensive. This was my only avenue toward a higher education.

It was a warm fall day, but you could still feel the crispness in the air. It had that smell of fall. A light haze hung in the air that muted the vibrant colors of the trees, like an impressionistic painting, everything blended together.

As I walked toward the bleachers, the halftime cannon went off, causing me to jump. What a wallop that thing gave. I was just in time.

On the sideline, I could hear someone yelling out orders, then the drums marked time and the pipes began playing. Out marched the band, looking fine and marching in perfect unison. Their playing sounded grand and was very tight.

The band wore full dress military attire: kilt (Royal Stewart Tartan), long tunics, glengarry hats, horsehair sporrans and white spats. The Royal Stewart tartan, an overall red with a cross hatch of muted green and thin white lines, has long been one of the most recognizable tartans, and it makes anyone wearing it look sharp. The thought of being in one of those uniforms and marching with this band gave me a flash of excitement, and I smiled at my mental image.

Most of the tunes they played were familiar to me. Most marching bands tended to have standard repertoires, including "Scotland the Brave," "The Minstrel Boy," and "Marie's Wedding."

≈

The Drum Major led the Queens band out to the field, followed by the pipes. Bringing up the rear was the drum section. The drums were powerful and precise. They sounded like one drum with the thunder of twelve. Supporting it all was the bass drum, huge and commanding. The drummer pounded out the cadence and signaled the band to start and stop with an air of total confidence. All the starts and stops were clean and crisp, not one pipe or drum sounded too soon or lingered beyond the last note, a sign of a good band.

The pipe major called for pipes down. The drummers snapped out rolls as the pipers brought their pipes down in unison and marched off to a single tap of a side drum. A well-disciplined unit, I thought.

I wanted to introduce myself, so I began to make my way around the stands to where they were gathered. But as I did, a knot of doubt formed in my stomach. What if I can't cut it? I had played pipes for years, but never in an organized band.

As I approached the group, the first person I came to was the drum major. He was a massive imposing fellow, well over six feet tall, and with his feather bonnet he appeared even taller. In his right hand he held a five-and-a-half-foot staff with an orb on top called a mace. It gave him an air of superiority, and grandeur, almost like royalty. The drum major must have weighed 250 pounds, but he carried his large frame with ease. He had a prominent mustache that came down each side of his mouth. He didn't seem all that happy—perhaps it was the effect of the mustache, which gave him the appearance of a perpetual frown. Maybe this is not the fellow to talk to first, I thought, but I took a gamble and introduced myself.

"Pardon me, sir," I said tentatively. "My name is Ian MacDonald and I'm a freshman at Queens. I have received a bagpipe scholarship and..."

Before I could finish my rambling announcement he spun around and glared at me. I swallowed hard. This guy looked mad. His expression was enough to make my knees start to knock.

"Perhaps I should speak to..." I began.

"What?" he bellowed. "A freshman?"

I feared he would roar "fe-fi-fo-fum" next, but to my immense relief, he smiled a broad toothy smile and said, "Yah mean fresh meat!" Then he roared with laughter at his own joke. Poor form, I thought, but wasn't about to call him on it.

"Congratulations!" he said. "What did you say your last name was? Was it MacDonald? Any relation to Al?"

"Yes," I said. "Alan is my older brother."

"One hell of a rugby player and an all-around good egg," he said, slapping my back hard enough to knock me off balance.

"I'm Dan McKee. Come on, I'll introduce you to the fellow you really want to speak with, our pipe major."

He turned and walked through the crowd of kilted pipers and drummers, which parted with his approach. Those who did not move, received a friendly poke with his mace which accomplished the desired result with no malice intended or perceived. He led me toward a lean, sharp looking piper whose uniform was the same as the rest except for a red sash draped across his tunic, and four chevrons or military type stripes on his sleeve. His face was youthful and he exuded the air of leadership and responsibility that was necessary to function as a pipe major. His ramrod posture helped to accentuate this authoritative perception.

"Terry," McKee bellowed, "We have more fresh meat, I mean another freshman." He laughed again deep from his belly. Poor form.

"This is Terry Manning our Pipe Major," he said by way of introduction. "Terry this is Ian Mactavish!"

"MacDonald," I corrected.

He slapped me on my back again even harder and laughed. "That's what I said—MacDonald." I wondered whether my brother liked this guy.

Pipe Major Manning looked at me with a raised eyebrow and an analytical gaze.

"Ian MacDonald" I said, thrusting my hand toward him. My father always said that you can tell a lot about a man by his handshake and the shine of his shoes. Terry had a firm, genuine grip. He smiled as we shook hands, but it struck me as more businesslike than friendly. I supposed that to maintain a position of authority, one must exercise a degree of aloofness.

"Be at Grant Hall, room 110 at 1600 hours. Bring your pipes and have them warmed up and ready," he said. "Nice to meet you." Then he snapped around and briskly walked into the crowd.

≈

My heart was pounding in my chest as the reality of the moment caught hold. This was really happening, I thought as I headed back to my room. I'm going to be a piper at Queens. The exhilaration was short lived, though, as I overheard two pipers discussing the latest news of the war in Europe. My thoughts turned to my older brother, Alan. Alan left ten months earlier with the first Canadian wave to fight for England. The reports coming back were mixed and my family had not received a letter for some time.

I glanced at my wristwatch. It was three o'clock. I had an hour to prepare for my audition. I walked up the limestone steps of Grant Hall. The buildings of Queens University are made of limestone, as is almost every building in Kingston, Ontario, which, as a result, had been tagged with the not very original nickname "the Limestone City."

My pipes were stored in a case that my grandfather had made for me when I was twelve years old. He was a real craftsman with cabinetry and his skill was evident in this velvet-lined case. I purchased a new set of Macgregor pipes when I was seventeen. Though they were slightly larger than my first pipes, they still fit snugly into the case.

I took the pipes from the case and practiced scales for the next forty minutes, as Terry had requested. Warming up the pipes and reeds before a performance diminished the tendency of this finicky instrument to go out of tune. The practice enabled the pipes to provide a modestly consistent tone.

≈

Being an all-wood instrument, except for the bag, of course, the bagpipes are often at the mercy of the elements. The blow stick, three drones, and chanter are made from African blackwood, a very hard wood that provides a maximum volume with minimal reaction to temperature or moisture changes. The chanter—the part on which the tune is played–has eight finger holes and a hard, double reed, which gives it plenty of crisp volume. The cane reeds, however, are more susceptible to temperature and moisture and can pull a bagpipe out of tune smartly.

When a solo piper is tuned and playing, one would seldom notice the tonal changes brought on by environmental factors. But get a band of twenty pipers whose pipes all react to climate at a different rate and you have tonal chaos. Therefore, it is essential that a band be tuned as close to a parade step off as possible.

≈

I could hear the sounds of pipes being tuned as I opened the large oak doors to Grant Hall. As I entered Room 110, the combined noise of twenty plus chanters being played up and down the scale blasted me.

Pipe Major Manning was keenly focused on the tuning and either didn't notice my arrival or chose not to acknowledge it. I preferred to remain anonymous at the time anyway. I moved quietly to the periphery, content to watch and listen. Tuning is an important process, and requires some time to complete. A good piper with a good ear and a ready band can, however, make the process move along at about three minutes per piper.

"You! Pipes up!" I was jarred from my thoughts to see the Pipe Major looking in my direction.

A thump of adrenaline coursed through me as I hurried to the center of the room.

"Blow up and tap off!" he barked.

The reed of a drone is softer and more flexible than that of a chanter, so it makes a sound with less air pressure in the bag. To silence the drones, you tap your hand on top of the drone opening and it quiets. I can't explain why it works, but it does. When all three are tapped off, you can blow more pressure into the bag and the chanter reed will sound.

I quickly blew up my pipes, tapping off my drones, and continued to blow evenly into the blow pipe to keep constant pressure. Manning stepped directly in front of me and made a sideways fist, with his pinky outstretched. To me it looked as if he were choking an imaginary chicken in a dainty way. My puzzled look was all he needed to see.

With his blow pipe still in his mouth, he continued to blow air into his bag. Between breaths, he commanded, "A! Give me a low A!"

Then it dawned on me what his hand gesture meant. To produce a low A, you cover all the chanter holes except the one covered by your right hand pinky. I blew harder and squeezed the bag until the chanter barked out a low A.

Manning did likewise and we played the same note for several seconds. Then he held up his hand with his middle three fingers outstretched to form the letter E. I was catching on.

I followed his lead as he continued up and down the scale while he listened for the difference between our reeds. They were obviously off, so he stopped blowing, as did I, and he held out his hand. No words were necessary. I pulled out my chanter and placed it in his outstretched hand. He put the chanter to his mouth and blew an E on the exposed reed. With his teeth biting down on the base of the reed, he pushed it deeper into its seat, sharpening the note. When he was satisfied with the tone he handed it back to me.

I reset my chanter, blew up, tapped off my drones and waited for his next command. I followed Manning's lead up and down the scale, now in perfect tune.

Then, without a word, he turned away and moved on to the next piper. This fellow has a great ear for tuning, I thought. Minutes later, with the last player in tune, Manning moved to the center of the room.

"Circle up," he called out.

I watched as all the pipers formed a circle so I followed their lead and joined in. An observant piper next to me noticed my slowness to respond to Manning's command and tapped my shoulder.

"Follow me," he whispered.

"Thanks, I'm Ian MacDonald," I said.

"Sean Lyons," he replied.

Sean was not a tall man, less than six feet, but he had a strong frame. Not a muscleman sort of build, but more like that of a farm hand or a mason. His jet black hair was short, in a crew-cut style, and his eyebrows were so dark, they almost looked penciled in. A five o'clock shadow graced his square jaw. I was thankful for the guidance from this obvious senior piper. What I didn't realize at the time was that I had been taken under the wing of one of the finest pipers in Ontario, and without question, the second best piper at Queens University next to Terry Manning.

The other pipers stood at the ready, heads up, backs straight. Their heels were together, but their toes were spread apart at a forty-five degree angle. Again, I followed their lead, and stood with my pipes up on my shoulder, blow pipe in my mouth and my chanter held in front of me.

Pipe Major stood silent and motionless in the center of the circle, his eyes fixed straight ahead. We waited for a command but none came.

Then, suddenly coming to life, Manning barked out his orders.

"Band ready, pipes up! From an E. "Going Home!"

Everyone blew up their pipes and played an E. Manning pumped his foot up and down three times and we began to play the tune. Manning made his way around the circle, listening to each chanter and adjusting the reed of those that weren't perfectly in tune.

Satisfied with what he heard, he had the band stop playing and called in big Dan McKee and the drummers to join the circle. He told McKee that he wanted the band to play "Scotland the Brave" twice, starting with a three pace roll. Dan acknowledged the request with a nod.

≈

In a concert or in practice, the pipe major usually calls cadence, but there are those occasions when the pipe major requests the drum major to call the tune.

On the street, the drum major calls cadence: "By the right! Quick march!" This command tells the marching band members that they should "dress right," or keep their line straight, formed on the member farthest to their right.

"Quick march" tells the band what type of march to expect, and the speed at which the cadence is called sets the tempo for the drum section which, in turn, sets the tempo for the tune and the speed of the march.

McKee stiffened. "Band ready!" he yelled. "By the right...quick march!" The bass drum pounded out its beat and the snares growled out their three-pace rolls. The pipers blew up, first striking in the drones then following with a short E before playing "Scotland the Brave."

I quickly noticed that Sean and all the veteran pipers were watching Terry Manning. Not the man himself, but his fingers. As his fingers moved, so did theirs.

Those in the circle who weren't focused on Terry's fingers were, like me, "new meat" and tried desperately not to look lost.

I noticed one fellow in particular. Lean, blonde, and well dressed, he was obviously well off. But most striking to me were his pipes. They were a piece of artwork with sterling silver engraved furls and tuning pins, even the chanter had a silver base. They must have weighed a ton, but to me they were the most ornate and handsome pipes I had ever seen.

≈

My thoughts were broken by a deep booming voice coming from behind an opening door. Into the room burst an imposing figure waving his arms and yelling.

"Stop! Stop! Stop!" he shouted over the deafening sound of twenty pipes and drums. The pipes groaned and whined to a stop and the drums tapered off.

"If you don't want to play together," the man said, "then leave and play solo on some street corner for two bits! Now, let's try it again, but this time together!"

Without hesitation, Terry snapped to attention.

"Gentlemen," he called out, "'Scotland the Brave.' By the right... quick march!"

The drums rolled and the pipes struck in and we started the tune again. I thought we sounded quite good. But halfway through the tune, the visitor apparently thought otherwise.

"Enough!" he wailed. The band stopped disjointedly.

"I expect better from you, Terence," he reprimanded. The man had a distinct Scottish brogue, which along with his deep, resonant voice, perpetuated his image. He carried himself erect, and with one thick eyebrow slightly raised, this gave him a strong commanding air of superiority.

He walked into the circle and surveyed the group, stopping his gaze only momentarily on the new pipers. Manning moved next to the man who stood waiting expectantly.

"Gentlemen, for those of you who are joining us for the first time," Manning said, "May I introduce our pipe instructor, Victor Matthews."

Matthews' eyes were hard and analytical. Scanning the newest pipers in the group, he took a quick glance at me and began to move my way. I braced myself and expected the worst.

"Name," he snapped.

"Ian MacDonald," I answered, almost too quickly.

"MacDonald, hold your chanter parallel to your body, squarely in front of you. Don't play it into your belly," Matthews said pragmatically. "And you're over blowing. Don't blow to hear yourself."

His appraisal completed, Matthews then moved onto the next newcomer. I breathed a sigh of relief, as inconspicuously as I could, lest he turn his attention back to me. Wow! I had expected a thrashing and instead got some great, sound advice on how to make myself a better piper.

Matthews went around the group giving critiques to pipers, mostly new, until he came to the fellow with the ornate pipes. The young man had taken his heavy pipes off his shoulder and was holding them more comfortably under his arm. He apparently had not noticed that everyone else was still at attention with their pipes up.

"Name!" Matthews barked, his eyes glaring.

"Patrick McDill," the young man responded, fidgeting uncomfortably.

"I don't recall hearing anyone call pipes down McDill!"

The reaction was swift. McDill's pipes popped back into the proper position, drones on his left shoulder, chanter at the ready and blow pipe squarely in his mouth. He stood at attention hoping he could recover from this blunder in protocol.

"Blow up and strike in!" Matthews commanded.

Now it should be noted that when a piper blows up a bag the drones will come in at different times. To avoid this unpleasant sound, a piper can strike the bag with his right hand. The strike should not be too firm, about as firm as one might slap a baby's bottom at birth. If done correctly, this slap jolts all three drone reeds and they come in at the same time.

McDill blew up and struck his bag, but because he was anxious under Matthews' constant glare, he slapped his bag just a wee bit too hard. The result was the drones coming to life along with a faint squeak from the chanter. It was not a godawful squeak—in fact, it would have gone unnoticed by the man on the street—but it was an affront to Victor Matthews' ear.

"Stop!" Matthews said. I expected him to unleash his fury on the young piper, but he didn't. Instead, he simply held out his hand and said, "Chanter."

McDill obediently unseated his chanter and handed it to Matthews. The pipe instructor looked at the reed with no change of expression, then he raised it, reed first to his mouth.

I fully expected him to blow out the scale or play a brief tune while adjusting the reed in its seat. Instead, he bit down hard on the reed as though it were a small carrot or sprig of celery. The crunch was clearly audible throughout the silent room, and it made every piper grimace and cringe.

Reeds were expensive. If you had a good reed, chances are you grew very fond of it. Many pipers even form a sort of bond with their favorite reed, and when it finally cracks or grows too weak to play, they will save it long beyond its usefulness.

Matthews spat out the broken reed onto the floor with disgust. McDill was stunned. His mouth dropped open, and I thought for a moment he was going to tear up and sob.

Matthews then reached into his jacket pocket and pulled out a new reed seating it firmly into the chanter. He handed the chanter back to McDill and said, "Blow up, strike in, and give me an E."

To his credit, Patrick quickly recovered and did as he was instructed. He struck in his drones, they came in cleanly with no chanter squeak. So far, so good. He blew harder and gave a squeeze to bring in the chanter reed and...nothing. A puzzled look came over his face, he blew harder and squeezed harder. Still nothing. Then he blew with all his might, growing visibly red in the face, his neck and cheeks puffing up like a bullfrog.

The chanter chirped momentarily, but his efforts were pointless. The reed was as hard as Victor Matthews' gaze.

The room was quiet and tense. The seasoned pipers avoided Matthews' gaze and were looking down at the ground. I sensed that they had seen this performance before and they knew what was coming next.

Matthews marched over to the door and hollered down the hall, "Sheila, Sheila Lougheed, please!"

Several moments later a young, attractive woman came in the door. I had seen her on campus several times before. She worked for the band as a scheduling secretary and a requisition officer while attending Queens for nursing. Sheila was about five-foot-five, with brown hair and large soft brown eyes that twinkled more often than not. She had a bold toothy smile and laugh that would erupt like a volcano, very loud with no inhibition. I was instantly attracted to her.

"Yes, Mr. Matthews" she pleasantly responded.

"Sheila," Matthews said, "this young man is having some difficulty with his bag pipes. Take them from him and play 'The Biddy from Slio' for us."

Her warm smile went flat as she looked at Victor Matthews with disappointment.

Matthews' hard voice softened with the request. "Please," he said.

Sheila gently took the handsome pipes from McDill, looking into his eyes briefly with an apologetic glance. Up to her shoulder went the pipes, and she blew up quickly and looked straight ahead, almost in a trance.

Three quick breaths and the bag was full of air and ready. She struck in the drones, and without any obvious effort began to play this snappy jig clearly and strongly. Aside from my amazement and appreciation for this talented piper, I felt badly for McDill and his obvious embarrassment.

Sheila finished the tune, clearly stopping and handed the pipes back to McDill. "Nice pipes," she said with a weak smile.

As she turned and exited the room, she gave Matthews a stern glare. She had obviously been used by Matthews before to humiliate cocky new pipers and did not appreciate the awkward position it put her in.

≈

Matthews walked over to the dejected McDill. "Weak reeds make for weak pipers, and pretty pipes a good piper do not make," he said, for the benefit of the whole room. "McDill, work on your lip and wind and do not shave that reed!"

As he turned and walked out of the room, he said loudly, "There is only one real musician in this room and he's leaving."

And with that parting slap he was gone.

McDill was visibly rattled, but to his credit, kept a semblance of composure. Terry Manning broke the uncomfortable silence. "Don't take it personally McDill, he did the same thing to me. Just become a stronger piper."

I wondered whether Terry was just trying to sooth Patrick or if it was true that he, too, had been on the receiving end of Matthews' hard lesson. But before I could think about it too much, Terry addressed the room.

"You new pipers will do just fine," he said. "You all know how to play so I'll suggest this to you now–don't settle for good enough. Learn the band tunes, and come prepared to our next practice."

Then he called, "Pipes down." With three quick drum rolls, all of us lowered the pipes from our shoulders and tucked them neatly under our arms.

"Dismissed," Terry said, and the band began to scatter.

≈

Sean Lyons, who had been standing beside me the whole time, leaned toward me and said, grinning, "That went well. I think Victor likes you, eh? Your reed is almost as soft as McDill's."

Whatever the reason, I had somehow avoided the public humiliation that had been doled out to McDill and received the message from Matthews loud and clear.

"I don't suppose the band has any stiffer reeds on hand, eh?" I sheepishly asked.

"I'll fix you up," Sean laughed. He went to his case and returned with a medium strength reed which he handed to me.

"Several of the fellows are going for a beer at *The Portsmouth Inn.* Why don't you join us?" *The Portsmouth* was a pub located on the edge of campus that was a popular hangout for Queen's students. It was known to be smoky, crowded, and boisterous. I happily accepted the offer. It was a quick walk over to this establishment where the atmosphere was loud and inviting as we opened the door.

≈

Dan McKee, Terry Manning, and Drum Sergeant Bill Lewis were already at the bar with a beer in their hands, so we wasted no time joining them. Sheila's laugh rang out above the barroom buzz and I felt glad that she had joined us.

The conversation drifted from politics and war, to professors and band business. The latter included some brief laughs at the expense of Pat McDill. I quietly realized that dumb luck alone had spared me from McDill's fate and felt thankful for that.

I complimented Sheila on her piping and innocently asked why someone with such obvious talent wasn't playing for the pipe band? The conversations of most of the group stopped and they all stared at me waiting for the response from Sheila that they all know too well.

"Girls aren't allowed in the pipe band," she said simply. "It isn't considered proper or lady like."

"It's a bunch of crap." Dan said quietly turning back to his beer.

"It is what it is," Sheila said with a shrug of her shoulders, and turned the conversation to a new topic.

I felt bad that I had broached the subject, but she seemed to be okay with it and I didn't mention it again. As I nursed my beer and watched this group, it occurred to me that somehow and by some stroke of luck I had fallen in with this elite group of talented band members. I knew that I had my work cut out for me if I wanted to remain in the inner circle.

KINGSTON, ONTARIO, 1916

My family hadn't heard from Alan in eight months and we feared the worst. Although we scanned the newspapers daily for any word on the fighting, he seemed to have vanished. That cold emptiness in our lives only made the onset of winter that much more harsh.

The winters in Kingston are normally bitter cold and, because of its location on the east end of Lake Ontario, the city has frequent snow and constant wind. Kingston rests on the western banks of the St. Lawrence River near the head, and is separated from the United States by a large island called Wolfe Island. There is a ferry service provided by the municipality of Marysville on Wolfe Island at the cost of 5 cents. The ferryboat is a sturdy old tub called "The Wolfe Islander". She can carry about six cars and fifty people and operates most of the year. However, in the winter the river freezes over and ferry service becomes impossible.

Because Wolfe Island is a large farm island, six miles wide and twenty-one miles long, it provides goods and services to Kingston and vice versa, so it is essential that there is movement between the two.

The three miles of water between the island and Kingston freeze to a thickness of several feet at times and provides an adequate, though nerve-wracking, ice highway for commerce. The danger of crossing the ice is offset by the need for trade, so the risk is equal to the reward.

Even though most people cross without incident, occasionally a truck or wagon falls through the ice which heightens the reality of the danger. But it is a risk accepted by those who chose to participate in this perilous practice.

I was one of those cavalier people who crossed the ice without reservations. Instead of a wagon or truck as my choice of vehicle, I had something much faster and safer. As a young man, I had constructed an iceboat. The boat was capable of carrying three people and some stores or one person and three to five hundred pounds of supplies.

The boat was well-suited for the St. Lawrence with deep skates for ease of passage over frequently snow covered ice. The skates were also longer than most and angled up high in the front to accommodate the uneven surface of the river ice. It wasn't uncommon to be whisked along by the brisk wind at as much as fifty miles per hour. On weekends, I would make runs across in my iceboat to visit friends, run supplies, or simply to entertain myself and clear my mind. You can't appreciate the bone-jarring, pounding exhilaration of racing across the ice at high speed until you experience it. The cold wind bites your face and your eyes water uncontrollably in protest. This makes it almost impossible to see where you're going while you're going far too fast to get there.

I made it a point to invite my close band friends out for a crossing. This was cheap thrilling entertainment. Bill Lewis, our drum sergeant, was the only one who seemingly couldn't get enough of ice boating. Bill, a wonderful fellow, seemed to be comfortable with a high degree of recklessness. The faster, the better for Bill. He was fearless and impervious to the cold. We would be clattering along at a good clip, thirty or better and a gust would catch us lifting the upwind skate off the ice and accelerating us immediately to well over fifty. This burst of speed would prompt Bill into letting loose with an uncontrollable series of whoops and howls. This behavior was well out of character for this normally reserved man and gave me some insight into what lay beneath the surface of my friend.

I grew to really appreciate this man as a friend and a person. One day we were getting ready to ice boat over to Wolfe Island. We were at the boat ramp at the bottom of Princess Street where there was always a crowd. Skaters, ice boaters and observers would gather at this launch site. The problem with rivers and ice is that the water is moving under the ice and can cause the ice to be deceptively thin in spots while remarkably thick in others.

We were just about to hoist the sail when a woman near the dock began screaming. The ice had given away and her daughter had broken through. The young girl was clinging to the edge of the hole, but the current was slowly pulling her under.

A crowd immediately gathered, but no one seemed to know what to do. Bill dashed from the boat across the ice at a sprint, he dove onto his belly and was sliding toward the hole at a good clip. His trajectory was such that he would pass just to the right of the hole and slide right by. As he passed the hole, he reached out with his left hand and grabbed the girl from the water. Bill rolled to his right, which catapulted the youngster over the top of him and clear of danger and they both skid to a stop fifteen feet away for the hole.

Bill had hardly come to a stop when he was up on his feet. He ran to the girl, snatched her up into his cradling arms and presented her to her astonished and appreciative mother.

The whole thing happened so fast that most people missed it and Bill didn't stick around for any praise. He returned to the ice boat and to my slack-jawed stare.

"What?" he said, as though his heroics were as normal as brushing his teeth.

Both Bill and Dan McKee knew my older brother Alan and would regularly ask of his whereabouts. This I appreciated more than either would ever know. Under their tough drummer facade, these men were old softies and dependable to the core.

≈

I had been accepted into pre-med and I was struggling with a heavy workload. Life became a juggling exercise between studies and bagpipe practice. This full schedule allowed for only one or two nights a week when I could escape to *The Portsmouth* for some socializing. I would savor these moments when I could just relax, no brainwork, no competitive piping, just good friends and beer.

I recall one evening when our socializing was rudely interrupted. The problem with pubs is that too much beer can bring out the worst in some people. It can provide an excuse for young men with high levels of testosterone to flex their beer muscles, not their brains, and such was the case this night.

A Queen's football player had taken a shine to Sheila, but was not getting the response he had expected. So he decided to prove his manhood by trying to pick a fight with Dan McKee.

It was pure madness. Dan was at least six inches taller and a good fifty pounds heavier. Beer can make a plain girl pretty, a big man smaller, and a small man bigger. Dan ignored the taunts, dismissing this fellow with no more than a sideways glance and a toothy grin. Dan's nonchalant reaction seemed to frustrate the drunken football player so he persisted with his verbal assaults. Several of his teammates were joining in the fun, spurring him on, which only emboldened the drunkard.

Finally, Bill Lewis, who had been carefully watching the event unfold, stepped between Dan and the big mouth. Bill moved to within inches of the fellow's face.

"Why don't you pick on someone your own size, Pal?" Bill asked.

The man took a step back, looked Bill up and down and said, "Well, Buster, it looks like you're about my–"

Before another word came out of his mouth, Bill unleashed a haymaker to the drunk's stomach. The man's eyes bugged out, he let out a groaning rush of air and sank slowly to the bar room floor gasping for the breath that had been so clearly knocked out of him. Bill stepped over the gasper and began moving toward the man's friends when Dan's big hand reached across his chest to stop him.

"Relax Bill," Dan said.

Terry, Sean, and I were closing ranks to help Bill but stopped with Dan's command.

"Look fellows," Dan said to the man's teammates. "You guys seem like reasonable gents. We came here to enjoy good company and cheap beer, so I'd like to extend an invitation for you to do the same. The next round is on me."

They looked at one another, for their allegiance to the gasper was short-lived and the prospect of a free beer was certainly more inviting than that of a pounding. They decided to join us and we ended up making some good friends that night.

I, however, was still a little rattled after the confrontation. Not being much of a fighter—just an occasional scuffle in the school-yard—the adrenaline was still pumping through me and my hands were mildly shaking. I was astounded as I watched Dan, Bill and the others laughing and drinking with their new friends. There was no sign of anger or hostility to be found. These men with whom I had the pleasure of associating were very special indeed. Their qualities would be put to the ultimate test in the not too distant future, as would mine.

PART THREE

THE REASONS TO JOIN

The First Canadian Expeditionary Forces, Ypres, Belgium

[Recreated from historical records]

I n the fall of 1914, with the outbreak of the war in Europe, the British Empire put out a request for help throughout England and all her realm.

Canada was considered under the crown so the Governor General of Canada turned to Sir Sam Hughs, the Minister of Militia, for help. Because Canada had only a militia and not a formal army, Hughs put out an urgent request to all young men to answer the call for help. Although it was a voluntary request it was answered resoundingly with thousands of men ready to protect the Crown.

Canada rapidly moved to prepare a large flotilla of transports and an enormous quantity of supplies and men. Training camps were set up near Quebec City where the men would receive some basic training, uniforms, equipment–including the notoriously unreliable Ross rifles–and an assignment to a specific unit or branch according to one's qualifications.

By September 21, thirty-two merchant ships had been converted into troop and supply transports. Two days later the ships were in port, ready to be loaded with 7679 horses, 70 big guns, 110 motor vehicles, 705 horse-drawn vehicles, 82 bicycles and over 100,000 sacks of flour.

Nearly thirty thousand men would also be on the ships. They were the First Canadian Expeditionary Force, consisting of 29,070 men and 147 officers. The men had trained for two weeks at Camp Valcartier outside of Quebec City and were ready for orders. The supplies had been steadily coming and all that was needed was to load the massive fleet in some organized manner.

When one considers the magnitude of such an undertaking, it is easy to understand that there would be some setbacks. In fact, it was suggested that Sir Hughs insistent, hands-on involvement had somewhat delayed the process. Regardless of the minor setbacks, it remains one of the most monumental achievements in Canadian history. Thirty-two ships, over 30,000 men trained and ready, and a massive amount of supplies were ready in less than six weeks from the initial request.

≈

Among those brave volunteers was Alan MacDonald, the oldest son of the MacDonald family and Ian's brother. He was an avid rugby player and a fine athlete. He had played in his first year at Queens and was considered one of the fastest and toughest lads on the rugger field.

Alan had been assigned to Princess Patricia's Canadian Light Infantry. At Camp Valcartier, the men were selected for areas that would suit their capabilities. It became obvious to Alan's superiors that he was remarkably fast and had a good mind for recall. He was placed in the communications corp. During his brief training at Valcartier, he was put through the rigors of military training along with classroom training in the area of communications in a theater of war. He became proficient in hardline telephones, signal light operation and, most importantly, the art of running while transporting information and reading a map of the trenches. Alan knew that his training would continue in England and he was ready for the challenge.

The word came down for the Canadian Light Infantry to move aboard their assigned ship *The Royal George*. She was a large vessel, some 525 feet length overall, with a beam of 60 feet. She was owned by the Canadian Northern Steamship Line since 1910 and had plenty of nautical miles behind her. Not a pretty ship, but a sturdy ship. She was to be home to 1,175 troops for the next two weeks.

In her holds *The Royal George* carried a combination of ammunition and flour—5,602 sacks of flour to be exact. The men often joked that if she were to be sunk by U-Boats all that would remain would be a giant floating dumpling with 1,175 men stuck to it.

As funny as that sounded to all aboard, the reality was that German submarines were indeed the single greatest threat to the convoy. Because of this, precautions had been taken by British Admiralty to protect the convoy with an escort of war ships from the "Grand Fleet," a term used by Brits in reference to their massive array of warships.

The escort was made up of seven warships: HMS *Charybdis*, HMS *Diana*, HMS *Eclipse*, HMS *Glory*, HMS *Magnificent*, HMS *Princess Royal, and HMS Talbot*. They took up positions along the convoy with the *Magnificent* in the lead and the *Eclipse, Diana* and *Charybdis* leading each of the three columns of transports. *The Princess Royal* was on the port wing, the *Glory* on the starboard wing and *The Talbot* brought up the rear. The convoy and escort was so massive it spanned over twenty-one miles long.

≈

On October 1, a message was read to the troops aboard each ship just prior to their departure from Gaspe Bay for the crossing.

*"On the eve of your departure from Canada, I wish to congratu-
late you on having the privilege of taking part, with the other forces of
the crown, in fighting for the honor of the King and Empire. You have
nobly responded to the call of duty. Canada will know how to appreciate the patriotic spirit that animates you. I have complete confidence that you will do your duty and that Canada will have every
reason to be proud of you. You leave these shores with the knowledge
that all Canadian hearts beat for you, and that our prayers and best
wishes will ever attend you. "May God bless you and bring you home
victorious."*

–F. M. ARTHUR, Governor General of Canada.

Alan wrote of this event in one of the many letters he sent
home. He told his family how excited he was at being involved in this
historic undertaking. He described how, as he stood at the rail of the
Royal George watching Canadian soil disappear astern and seeing
the convoy stretched to the horizon, he couldn't help the profound
sense of pride that came over him.

≈

With Canada behind the convoy and a vast and dangerous expanse
of open water ahead, the safety of the men and ships was in the
hands of the escorts. But, not to diminish the escorts contribution,
the true reasons that the crossing went without incident were poor
communications between British and Canadian Admiralties, poor
information forwarded by the German spies, miscalculations by the
German military, and just plain luck.

Rear-admiral Wemyss was in charge of the 12th cruiser squadron, of which *HMS Charybdis* (flag), *Talbot*, *Eclipse*, and *Diana* were
a part. But when the Canadian Minister saw only four cruisers to
protect 32 ships he made the statement that the convoy was inadequately protected and that the departure would be put on hold.
Instead, the news went out that the crossing was cancelled.

When the rear-admiral later explained that the escort was, in fact, made up of seven warships, the others waiting offshore, the Minister gave permission for the departure and the convoy left port on October 3.

This information, however, never reached the British authorities. On October 6, the British Admiralty sent word to Canada asking about the disposition of the fleet and the decision of the Minister. One can only imagine the surprise at Whitehall on learning that the fleet had been underway for three days. If Whitehall knew nothing of the fleet movement, then the German spies definitely knew nothing, a great advantage to the convoys safety.

≈

On October 8, the German Admiralty was informed by agents working in New York that a massive troop transport of twenty-three ships had left Canada on October 2 escorted by eight warships, a remarkably accurate account. The German military made an inaccurate assumption that the troops were battle ready and that the destination would be Boulogne, France and the Western Front. They rapidly dispatched their submarines to go to Boulogne and lay in wait to ambush the troop carriers that never came. On October 12, as the fleet neared British waters, all 30,000 men were called topside. *The Princess Royal*, a lion class battle cruiser, had dropped back to the aft of the convoy and then was called to action. Her bow rose up as her massive engines gave her full power, water was thrashed wildly to each side as she jumped to her battle speed of 25 knots. She flew up the center of the convoy with her band on deck playing "Oh Canada" and "The Maple Leaf Forever." Thirty-thousand men exploded into cheers as the British showed their appreciation for the sacrifices these men were about to make.

The original destination of disembarkation for the convoy was Devonport but because German U-boats had been spotted in the channel, the fleet went to Portsmouth in the southwest of Great

Britain. The troops were dispersed to four main training camps: Tid-worth, Kitchener's, Woodwich Common, and 1st East Surrey. The men would spend several months preparing for the difficult task of trench warfare. Then in early April, the First Canadian Division of the Canadian Expeditionary forces was sent to Belgium.

≈

The German Army had pounded through Belgium en route to France, leaving in its path unimaginable death and destruction. When the German war machine collided with the French Army, it was stopped by France's unexpected intense resistance. The French still retained some of the Napoleonic fighting ability that had made that country a formidable military power many years earlier.

And along with their alley, Great Britain, the French had not only stopped Germany, but had, in fact, pushed the Germans back into Belgium.

This created what is called a salient or bulge in the western front which was referred to as The Ypres Salient.

This area had special significance to both sides, it represented a success for the allies and a failure for the Germans and because of this there was almost continuous fighting through the war.

There were three major battles at Ypres, however, between these major events constant skirmishing was common. On 17 April this was the area to which the British Expeditionary Forces, or B.E.F., sent the Canadian troops. The Ypres Salient had been experiencing a lull in the fighting and it seemed a good spot for the untested newcomers. There were no major movements of troops by either side, so no large scale battle was expected. And, since the 1st Battle of Ypres had exhausted both sides in a costly and bloody stalemate, this period of relative calm was very much welcome.

For these new men the trenches were a brief novelty, but very soon they learned that if the basic rules aren't followed it could re-sult in deadly consequences. Every day the Germans would lob several obligatory shells into the trenches or spray the trench tops with machine gun fire. This action would immediately be answered with British shells and gunfire. The April rains turned the Ypres Salient front into a mud-filled hellhole. Life in the trenches, horrific as it was, now became even worse with a constant routine of emptying and repairing the water-filled ditches.

The trench systems were an early answer to the high volume of artillery delivered by both sides in the first six months of the war. To march an army across open fields toward a barrage of artillery and machine gun fire, the other main weapon of the Great War, would be complete suicide. Trenches were the only reasonable solution. Most trench systems included supply trenches, advanced trenches, and entanglement trenches. The entanglement trench was heavily fortified with barbed wire, meant to slow the advances of an opposing army. It was very effective and was widely used by both German and Allied forces.

The Canadians were being provided with hands-on training in trench life with a minimum of risk. They worked in the mud and water repairing the dugouts, bunkers, trench walls and even repairing the barb wire entanglements. Only occasionally would they form into small raiding parties and attack the Germans under cover of night. They would have to pass through the advanced trenches and through gaps in the barb wire so as to cross "No Man's Land," the area of shell-hole pocked land that separated the Allied and German advanced lines. It was a muddy, lifeless patch of dirt strewn with the dead and parts of the dead from a year's worth of slaughter.

The stink of death was overwhelming and unforgettable. Unfortunately, smell is a sense that can trigger memories, good and bad. The simple stench of a rotting animal on the side of the road years later could be enough to awaken horrific memories in anyone who might have been there. The smell was inescapable and left a prominent impression on these young men.

≈

THE SECOND BATTLE OF YPRES, 24 APRIL, 1915

Little stacks of sandbags,
Little lumps of clay,
Make our bloody trenches,
In which we work and play.

Alan Macdonald kept his head down. The entrenchments were not always that deep nor were the parapets that high. If one stood up to straight, the chances of having your head blown off were better than good.

Being in the communications corps of Princess Patricia's Light Infantry provided him with more than his share of danger. The outcome of a battle and in fact the lives of thousands of men could hinge on good communications. Alan had been well trained in the use of Lucas signal lamps and the handling of carrier pigeons as well as field phones and the new Fullerphone, but the bulk of communications relied upon the runner and Alan was a good runner.

As one passed through the maze of trenches, one could easily get lost, so, there was a system of numbered signs posted to help point soldiers in the correct direction. That is if the signs had survived the continuous shelling from enemy and allied artillery. Compared to the main trenches, the communication trenches were smaller and not as well constructed or maintained.

There were some twenty miles of trenches for every mile of Western Front, so a map of the trench system was a necessity. Unfortunately, if such a document fell into enemy hands it would be disastrous, so Alan was provided with nothing more than coded directions.

He glanced at the directions briefly. "Runner? That's a laugh," he said to himself.

The spring rains had turned the trenches into mud. Trenches were really just ditches that would collect the water that could no longer be absorbed by a barren landscape that had long since been bombed beyond recognition. The main trench floors were covered with duck boards, a series of batten-like boards laid out to keep the soldiers' feet above the water and alleviate the mud problem, unfortunately most communication trenches were dirt, now mud with no duck boards.

The mud was sticking to Alan's standard issue hob-nailed boots making the already heavy boots feel like lead weights. Running was out of the question, just walking was a struggle.

Alan headed for Bunker 153, an outpost in the forward trenches. He sniffed the rancid, rotten-smelling air like a hound dog looking to catch scent of its prey. Alan wasn't looking for prey, it was looking for him. He was sniffing for signs of the new killer: chlorine gas.

Chlorine gas in itself was not what killed you, but when mixed with water it formed hydrochloric acid. When the moisture of your eyes, mouth and lungs came into contact with the gas it created acid that burned your tissue in turn causing a long and painful death.

Two days earlier, on 22 April, the allied troops defending the Ypres Salient had tasted the first German gas attack of the war. The salient was defended by the French to the north, the Algerians (French Colonials) in the center, and Canadians to the south.

The Algerian forward spotters noticed a massive green cloud rolling along the ground coming from the German lines and assumed it was a smoke screen, so they readied for an attack. Instead, the lethal gas was upon them before they recognized the peril they were in. Many died an agonizing death where they had stood. Others ran, but that only kept them in the cloud longer and they also died. The result was a large gap in the allied line of which the Germans, not willing to rush into the dissipating gas, did not take advantage.

The Canadians, however, closed the hole from the south, braving the dissipating gas and preventing a German breakthrough.

Alan had seen the poor wretches that had encountered the attack. Many were blind. All were coughing foamy blood or had horrible labored breathing. This was a new, diabolical weapon that struck fear into the troops, yet the psychological impact it had was much greater than the actual loss of life it caused.

The biggest flaw in using chemical gas as a weapon was that it needed the wind for its delivery. If the wind turned, the weapon would turn on you. Also, the gas dissipated and diluted as it rolled farther away from the gas canister making the area of maximum potency unpredictable. Despite these drawbacks, gas would remain atop the list of things most feared throughout the war.

Before Alan left on this mission, a friend quipped, "There's no wind today Al, you can breathe easy." It was a saying that had become commonplace in the trenches with the advent of gas.

Alan continued to sniff despite the lack of wind. Gas artillery shells remain a danger so he had to keep his guard up. His hand instinctively reached to his side and he touched the gas mask that hung there. Infantrymen found that a wet rag held tightly to the face would cancel most of the lethal effects of chlorine gas, but runners were given the scarce masks because of the importance of their job. Even though the wearer of these masks looked somewhat like an anteater, the comical appearance was a small price to pay for protection against the gas.

Alan stopped again to recheck his directions and kick some of the mud off of his boots. His pause was interrupted by a series of bombardments hitting some fifty yards away. A shower of mud and debris rained down around him as he ducked instinctively and protected himself.

A helmet clunked down into the trench next to him and rolled several feet before it came to rest in the muck. Alan hoped it had not been worn by a fellow B.E.F. or C.E.F. infantryman just moments before. He waited another few moments collecting his thoughts and his composure before continuing his journey to Bunker 153.

Most bunkers were underground rooms dug below trench level and covered with corrugated metal roofs and sandbags. They could withstand a fairly good pounding, but a direct hit from large howitzer shell would more than likely be a disaster.

The bunkers did provide a welcome shelter and were often crowded with men looking for any relief from the trench. There were many bunkers placed throughout the trench system and they would regularly be filled in and dug again to lessen the possibility of the enemy attacking a known position.

Alan popped out from the small communications trench into a main trench. The floor was covered with duck boards. The duck boards were a welcome sight after the schlep down the muddy communications trench, so he stamped his feet to loosen the caked mud from his boots.

His feet were soaked and he had been well warned of the danger of trench foot, so he always carried three pair of socks stuffed into his tunic. It was a pointless exercise in as much as he was putting a dry sock into a thoroughly soaked leather boot, but it was a momentary reprieve and headquarters believed it reduced the incidence of trench foot.

Alan turned left and noticed a shell casing hanging from a stick protruding from the trench wall. A mallet was tethered to the shell. This was one of the innovations someone had come up with to warn of a gas attack. The brass casing made a fine bell sound when hit and carried well over the vegetation free terrain. There were also an abundance of empty casings so they were perfect for the job.

As Alan continued around the corner of the larger trench he encountered two soldiers sitting in a funk-hole. A funk-hole was a type of dugout in the sidewall of the trench. It was up and out of the mud and provided a place to sleep, rest or just dry out for a while.

Both men seemed to be resting with their feet toward each other and their backs against the walls. They were too still. Alan had seen this before. He knew they were both dead and he knew that gas was not the cause. The faces of the gas victims were contorted and their lips were purple and bloated and covered with bloody froth. No, these men had been killed by the concussion of a nearby artillery explosion. Sometimes when a shell exploded and you were below ground level, the explosion was so powerful that its concussion could crush one's internal organs and brain leaving no outward sign of injury. Such was the fate of these young men. Alan made a mental note of their location and would pass on the information to the stretcher bearers upon his return.

According to his directions, Bunker 153 was just around the next bend which was closer than he had estimated and he came upon the bunker unexpectedly. A sentry was momentarily startled by Alan's appearance and raised his rifle to the ready in a quick reflex move.

"Bloody hell!" he scolded. "You scared the piss out of me man!"

He was one of the Canadian Scottish, a kilted regiment of tough fighting men.

"I've got some troop and artillery movement information for your commander," Alan said.

The man turned and banged on the door in some coded knock. The cigarette that hung from his mouth dribbled ash down the front of his heavy wool tunic as he waited for the door to open.

"A runner for Sergeant Warner," he yelled at the door.

It slowly opened and a voice said, "Come in man, don't just stand there!"

Alan stepped through the doorway leaving the cool April air of France behind and entering the musty damp sweaty stench of a bunker filled with too many filthy soldiers and a smoldering coal brazier stove. The place was poorly ventilated at best and it was a wonder the bunch of them weren't dead from the exhaust of the coal burner being used for heat and hot tea.

Alan blinked his eyes to try to adjust for the sudden lack of light when the door closed behind him.

"I have a communication for Sergeant William Warner," he yelled into the darkness.

From deep within the poorly lit bunker came a strong, loud voice. "Warner Here! Make way lads!"

The men shifted positions to allow him to pass. A tall wiry man with a long stride moved through the group of wet and tired soldiers. His dark thick hair, along with a large bushy mustache, accentuated his already dark features. He looked to Alan as if he were a coal miner or a chimney sweep before the war. He led with an outstretched hand and a broad toothy smile. Alan quietly admired the look of the kilt that the man wore. The seemingly nonsensical refusal by some divisions to abandon the kilt for trousers in trench warfare only cemented the feeling that these were fighting men of an ancient order.

"I'm Sergeant Bill Warner" the man said.

"Alan Macdonald, sir," he said, handing Warner a sealed tube with some papers inside. Warner twisted the top off the canister as he walked over to a nearby candle for better light. They used candles because they would flicker and go out when the oxygen in the bunker was too low. From his pocket, Warner removed a pair of filthy spectacles which he smeared, in an effort to clean them, on his equally filthy shirt.

"Madness," he grumbled as he read the note.

Warner pulled his glasses off his rough leathery face and turned back to Alan.

"They risked your life to send me a message that nothing has changed! Fools! Guess what lads? We'll be here another night!" he shouted.

The men responded with a mock "Hip, Hip, Hurrah!"

"I love these men" Warner said looking sternly into Alan's eyes. "They ran with me into that green cloud of death two days ago and bravely fought back the Huns. Most are coughing and wheezing, they're underfed, overworked and are suffering the dysentery, lice and God knows what else and still they can kid around. I want you to send this message to Headquarters. We need R&R, we need better food rations—the rats won't even eat the crap we've been getting—and we need more rum!"

"I'll pass that along sir" Alan responded.

"Good! Now back with ya, and Godspeed. Oh, and the next time they send a duck board courier, make it for a reason! You can tell them that, too!"

He slapped Alan on the back and ushered him out the door.

They both stood in the sunlight stunned by the momentary change in lighting. Both instinctively took a deep breath of air.

"Not much better out here" Warner said with a cough.

The sound of bagpipes came from down the trench. Alan looked at Warner questioningly.

"Our piper likes to practice," Warner said with a chuckle, punctuated by another cough. "I believe he does it because it drives Fritz mad. They expect a charge every time they hear the pipes."

"My brother's a piper," Alan said,"but he's back home." Warner lit a cigarette. "Well, if he comes over here you tell him to be wary. They shoot the pipers first. They call us kilted regiments 'The Ladies from Hell,' you know! And the piper is considered the Queen mum," Warner said.

"I'll pass it on in my next letter home," Alan said as he turned and began a slow trot.

"Keep your head down, lad!" Warner yelled after him.

YPRES SALIENT, 24 APRIL 1915
German 4th Army, Pioneer regiment # 35

Gunter Bruner was tired. His job required hours of extreme concentration and it proved to be more stressful and exhausting than he had ever imagined. This was only compounded by the relentless pressure being put upon him by Oberst (Colonel) Petersen and the high Command.

But there was additional stress for Gunter. He was torn by his own personal, internal objections to his mission. Gunter Bruner was twenty-nine years old and had studied at Heidelberg. He was an accomplished chemist with a successful career at Bayer chemical a company founded in 1863 by Friedrich Bayer.

"A company responsible for discovering the wonder drug Aspirin is forced to use its resources to create something so sinister," Gunter had complained to closest friends.

Gunter had been chosen personally by Professor Dr. Haber who was tasked with setting up the Pioneer regiment #35. This was a regiment specifically formed to deal with the handling and dispersing of gas. The regiment had two battalions, each made up of three companies. There was a group of meteorologists, a group of specialists, and a telephone detachment and supporting troops in each battalion.

The attack had been planned for some time and it seemed now that the weather was the only determining factor. Gunter was in charge of two kilometers of the gas line. The entire gas attack was to take place over an eight-kilometer line and had to be released in unison. There were almost 6,000 canisters, a total of 168 tons of chlorine gas required to create a dense enough cloud to travel the several hundred meters into enemy trenches before it began to dissipate and lose effectiveness.

The dispersal procedures had been inadequately calculated and only briefly tested, but not to the satisfaction of Gunter and his fellow chemist specialists. There was quiet dissension among his group.

"We don't really know, fully, the potency of the gas," Gunter complained to a comrade. "And the rate of dispersal must be more properly calculated to take into account the speed of the wind and the type of terrain."

"Ja, the trenches are water logged as is the surrounding area of No Man's Land. As the gas comes into contact with water it diminishes rapidly. If we were to have a rain shower it would render the gas useless," his comrade responded.

"Just as well by me. I hate this weapon. It is dishonorable," Gunter said.

They were both fully aware of the outcome of exposure to this gas and were revolted at the idea that their intellect and skills were being used in such a base way.

≈

There had been some obvious miscalculations on the first attack of 22 April. It was essentially a test that had gone quite well, but the Germans could not take full advantage of the weapon because of a lack of working knowledge of its properties. Overly cautious, the Germans waited too long before moving into the "kill zone" allowing the Canadians to close the breach. Risking their lives in the face of such a horrific weapon was madness.

Outwardly his troops ridiculed the Canadian kilted troops—the "Ladies from Hell"—but inwardly Gunter knew that there was a deep respect for these fierce fighting men.

As the German troops moved into the gassed area two days early, Gunter and his specialists followed to document the results for Dr. Haber's weapon. They were revolted at what they found. The contorted bodies of the Algerian and French troops, their eyes puffed closed, lips red and bloated and their mouths flowing with a bloody froth were everywhere.

The Germans used three basic gas types. First there was Lachrymator, a form of tear gas, non-lethal, but effective in disabling troops for a brief period of time. Next were a group of gasses that were all lethal and debilitating. These included chlorine, phosgene (which damaged the respiratory system), disphosgene (which could dissolve the filters in gas masks), and asphyxiant gas (which displaced oxygen and caused suffocation). Even if initially survived, these gasses would cause slow death or long term damage.

Finally there was dichlorethylsulphide, a blistering agent commonly called mustard gas. It was inexpensive to produce, easy to handle and its ability to sink into trenches and linger for long periods made this the most frequently used gas throughout the war.

≈

The Fourth Army was standing ready for the word from the Pioneer's meteorologists and specialists. The next opportunity would not be lost to over-caution. This time they had increased the amount of gas canisters, thereby creating a far more lethal and long lasting attack.

The artillery was also ready to lay down an initial barrage short of the allied lines to cover up the approaching gas cloud. Then they would pound the back of the allied positions to prevent the troops from advancing from the rear as well as retreating from the front. It was a death trap.

The attack plan was to open a gap wide enough to send a large number of the Fourth Army troops through the center of the hole with enough room on each side to reduce the possibility of being flanked. Then they would push for the coast and cut off the allied supply lines.

≈

Gunter knew of the plan; it was no great secret. A lot was riding on the outcome of today's attack because this infernal trench war provided little movement in either direction. If the attack proved successful and allowed the Germans to advance, the gas attacks would increase and it would be the new weapon of choice.

But there are so many variables, Gunter thought to himself. He lit up a cigarette and took a long draw on it. As he exhaled the smoke, the field telephone rang causing both him and the telephone operator to jump.

"The meteorologists in the north sections say they have wind! They are asking for our observation," the operator relayed to Gunter.

The meteorologist who should have given the information was at that moment indisposed with a rather persistent case of the trots. Gunter looked over at the latrine and took another deep drag of his cigarette. As he exhaled, he realized that his smoke was drifting away in a north westerly direction. Perfect.

"Tell them that the wind is North westerly at three to five kilometers," Gunter said. The operator quickly passed the information along, then looked questioningly at Gunter.

"You don't have to be a meteorologist to watch my smoke float away!" Gunter said indignantly.

"They say they will begin the artillery barrage in twenty minutes if there is no change in conditions," the operator said. "Please give a condition report in ten minutes and in twenty minutes."

Gunter wished he had kept his mouth shut. He quietly cursed the sick meteorologist. He didn't need this extra stress. After all he had a 2.5 km. section of the gas line to tend to and he needed to ensure that the continuity of the release mechanisms were good.

"Get the damn meteorologist out of the crapper!" Gunter barked. "I have my own work to do!" He stormed off.

≈

YPRES SALIENT, 24 APRIL, 1915. TIME: 12:00

In flanders fields the poppies blow
Between the crosses row on row,
That mark our place; and in the sky
The larks, still bravely singing, fly
Scarce heard amid the guns below.

We are the dead. Short days ago
We lived, felt dawn, saw sunset glow,
Loved and were loved, and now we lie
In flanders fields.

Take up our quarrel with the foe:
To you from failing hands we throw
The torch;be yours to hold it high.
If ye break faith with us who die
We shall not sleep, though poppies grow
In flanders fields.
Lt. Colonel John McCrae MD C.E.F.

Alan kept trying to run, but it was pointless. He stomped his boots on an area of duck board that for some reason had no mud on it in an attempt to loosen the stubborn sludge from his hob nails. It wasn't that he needed to get back with any urgent news.

"This horse is heading for the barn" he told himself. Even though he had traveled the same path less than an hour ago, he pulled out his route directions and made sure of his position.

He recalled a chum who had gotten disoriented and wound up in an area of the front trenches that were so close to the German lines that he heard the German troops talking to each other.

"No friggin' way," Alan said out loud, determined not to have the same fate befall him.

He began to trot along the main trench then turned right into a shallow mud-filled communications trench, it seemed familiar. The short trench was slow going but it soon plopped him out into the main trench where he saw the two dead soldiers in the funk-hole. He looked down as he walked by them, he wasn't really interested in renewing the mental image of those poor souls.

"I'll send someone," he quietly said to the lifeless men. He picked up his pace again. He rounded a bend in the trench and was momentarily startled as he came face to face with a detachment of replacements clanging, talking, and smoking as they marched through the muck toward the Front.

"How is it up front today, mate?" one cockney fellow asked.

"Quiet so far!" Alan said, relieved to find he was not alone. He stood aside to let the men through. With all of the junk that was attached to them it's a wonder they fit down some of these narrow trenches Alan thought. As the voices and clanging faded behind him he felt alone again. Looking up at the sound of a passing reconnaissance aeroplane high above, he noted that the sky was a clear blue backdrop to his dismal surroundings. The sun was now high enough in the sky where it shone over the edge of the trenches. It felt warm and welcome on the back of Alan's wool tunic.

Alan knew this area of trench well and was feeling more at ease to the point where he allowed his mind to wander back to Wolfe Island. The warmth somehow triggered thoughts of springtime back on the farm with brother Ian. That was a good time of year. The cold winter was behind, the summer ahead, crocuses were up, and robins were bouncing across greening lawns. The world was coming back to life. Alan looked around at this bleak trench hoping to find some sign of spring, of life. He knew that if he were to look over the parapet all he would see was a country side gutted by countless artillery bombardments, snapped and limbless tree trunks, remnants of farm houses or churches and countless bodies strewn everywhere. All signs of normal life had been obliterated and the landscape had been reduced to a lifeless, unrecognizable scar. A small tuft of sod that was clinging to the upper edge of the trench caught Alan's eye and he stopped to look at its few blades of grass. The small patch of green invoked a slight smile as he marveled at its tenacity in hanging on to life. Alan's moment of reflection was interrupted by the buzzing sound of bullets overhead, like angry hornets. In the distance a German Maxim 08 rattled and growled as it delivered its deadly message. Alan picked up his pace.

Alan knew the main trench he was now in very well. Approximately 100 meters ahead of his position, the trench connected with the Yser canal where an advanced dressing station had been established some time ago. He would often stop there on the return run if his mission was not urgent. Even if it was a time sensitive mission there was a field phone located in the station and he could pass on information to his superiors more quickly from there.

There was a mildly selfish reason he looked forward to stopping in upon his return trips and that was because of a friendship that had developed with the chief surgeon, Major John McCrae. McCrae was from Guelph just outside of Toronto and the two men would kid each other with a good-natured rivalry between Queens and Toronto University. Major McCrae was always quick with a cup of hot tea, if there were no wounded to attend to, and he would sit with

Alan for long periods of time discussing matters of art, politics and religion. Their conversations were always civil and good-natured, McCrae not being one to make display of rank.

Dr. John McCrae was twenty years Alan's elder and looked at Alan almost as a son. He feared that this bright and energetic young man would become victim to this mad war that had devoured so many young men before him. It was a weight that became increasingly heavy day after day in McCrae's mind. He needed a break badly, but the wounded needed him more.

Alan was looking forward to a nice visit. Perhaps John would have some good news from back home. A hot cup of tea and some good company was a welcome thought. A slight breeze kissed the hair on the nape of Alan's neck, which along with the warmth of the sun on his back made for a comfortable combination.

Suddenly he stopped in his tracks, and tuned toward the front. The mild breeze was now blowing directly in his face at what he estimated was about four kilometers an hour. A chill ran down his back. It was an ideal wind for the delivery of gas. Alan spun and began to run toward the dressing station as quickly as was possible. This change in conditions was information that was of extreme importance, he had to get to that field phone. As he ran the last fifty meters through the muddy trench, he listened for the clanging of shell casing behind him, none so far.

YPRES, BELGIUM, 24 APRIL, 1915 TIME: 14:00

T he French, Algerian colonials and the Canadians had learned some valuable lessons from the gas attack two days prior. For example, the Germans would begin a large-scale bombardment of the rear of the area being attacked. This would, of course, trap the troops on the front between a death by gas and a death by artillery bombardment. The deadly trap also provided protection for the Germans against any troops moving up to reinforce those being slaughtered.

With this knowledge in hand, the French and British commanders decided that if a subsequent gas attack was to again be unleashed, the immediate response would be to have the heavy British sixty-pound guns return a counter attack on German artillery positions, and for the smaller French 75 mm field cannons, with their superior accuracy and rapid fire capability, unleash a concentrated attack on the areas suspected of being the gas release points. It was hoped that the plan would reduce the deadly firepower of the German heavy guns and disrupt the even-blanket dispersal of the poisonous gas by forcing it to dissipate more rapidly.

≈

Alan had made it to the field dressing station and, via field phone, had informed his superiors of the changing conditions and the possibility of another gas attack.

Preparations were being made rapidly to respond to any German offensive. French, British, and Canadian commands were notified and Sir Douglas Haige ordered their plan into action.

All guns were properly positioned and ranges set to coincide with the most recent reconnaissance. When the time came, they would be ready to respond.

Alan was well away from No Man's Land, but far from out of danger. The dressing station was about 600 yards from the front, which he knew reduced the danger of small arms fire to the point of being little to none. The heavy guns were, however, another matter.

Alan leaned outside the station against some timbers and lit a cigarette. Though the B.E.F. provided every man with twenty ounces of tobacco each week, sometimes it didn't seem to be adequate.

Major McCrae, a lifelong asthma sufferer, insisted that all smoking be done outside the station, and Alan was happy to respect his friend's wishes. He really didn't know why he started the bad habit anyway, perhaps it was a grown up pacifier. He snorted at the mental image of himself with a sucker in his mouth.

A group of infantrymen trudged past, down the main trench toward the front. They ignored him as they passed and disappeared down the long trench. Alan turned away and looked at the rows of crosses tightly bunched together in the Essex farm fields. This is where the dead were buried. Alan knew why there were so many crosses packed in such a small area. He had helped dig several V-shaped burial trenches. They were designed to accommodate a single soldier at the bottom, over whom two more soldiers would be laid and then three, and finally four across, stacked like cord wood. It was the most efficient use of burial ground, but it seemed less than dignified or respectful for these soon to be forgotten young men.

The sun was high in the cloudless sky. Alan looked at his wrist-watch. Though it was encrusted with mud he could still see the face, which read two o'clock.

"It's too nice a day for a war," he said to Major McCrae who had come outside and was jotting down some thoughts on a pad of paper.

"I hope you didn't just jinx us. Better knock on wood," McCrae said.

Alan smiled knowing that John McCrae was a deeply religious man and didn't believe in such superstitious nonsense. Nonetheless, he rapped his knuckles three times on one of the support timbers of the dressing station, just in case.

McCrae went back to his writing. One of the ways that he dealt with the stress and madness of his duties was to write poetry. It was like taking a shower and washing off some of the filth of the war. Perhaps, this was his pacifier.

Several birds flew by chirping in a spring mating ritual. It was amazing to see the resiliency of nature. McCrae momentarily looked up from his pad in admiration and appreciation of this small event, then began to write again.

≈

His pencil stopped. Alan stiffened. They had both heard it. Three or four distant thuds. The big guns were firing. The guns fired with a high trajectory and, because of this, the sound would reach the target area before the shell. The delay gave the soldiers several moments to take cover, but this was often futile because the big shells made big holes and cover wouldn't help except maybe for debris protection.

It was the lighter field guns that would scare the hell out of you. Whizz-Bang! That was their nickname for obvious reasons. Because of their lower trajectory, the round would show before the report.

Toward the front, the sound of clanging could now be heard. Alan threw down his cigarette and darted inside to the field phone to pass on these developments. McCrae joined Alan in the station ordering his team to make ready for the eventual flood of casualties.

The men sprang into action, setting up clean dressing and rolled bandages in the most accessible and efficient order. Morphine and ether were readied for the quick and dirty job of patching and passing along the wounded. Instruments were immersed in an alcohol bath.

In the midst of this flurry of activity, Alan realized that the group of soldiers that had marched by moments before were heading into a death trap. He had to try to warn them.

"I'll be back!" he yelled to Major McCrae, and ran outside and toward the front. Alan estimated that they hadn't gone too far at their slow and unenthusiastic pace, so he hoped it wouldn't take too long to catch up to them.

The first of the big shells hit about 100 yards south of Alan as he ran toward the men. Debris and mud rained down on him as he ran with his head down in a crouched trot. He knew that this area was about to become a madhouse of confusion when the main bank hit so he picked up his pace.

He saw them just ahead. "Turn back!" he yelled as a shell whistled down and hit to the north of him. "There's gas ahead! Turn back, now!"

The men needed no more explanation and began to run back at a far more enthusiastic pace, but it was too late. The area was being destroyed and only luck could see them through safely at this point.

Though Alan's ears rang from the explosions, he could still hear a massive volley of distant thuds. Many more were on their way. As he ran down the wide trench toward the Yser canal and the dressing station, the entire horizon to the west erupted with thunderous noise and huge muzzle flashes. The French, Canadian, and Algerian artillery were answering the German assault. Being close down range of the assault, the impact of these brutal weapons had a staggering affect. Even though these guns were hundreds of yards away, the reports of the cannons felt like someone was kicking Alan in the chest with each flash.

More German shells were landing all around. This was not a battle. It was simply survival. A low "woof" came from deep behind the German lines like a bark from some huge dog. It was a distinctive noise that Alan had heard before.

"Big Bertha," he said.

Big Bertha was the name given to a massive howitzer built by Gustav Krupp, and named after his wife. At seventy tons, the weapon was so heavy that it could only be moved by rail, and couldn't be brought very close to the front. But with the ability to deliver a 2,200-pound shell some twenty-five miles at a maximum elevation of eighty degrees, it didn't have to get too close.

Big Bertha's drawback was that it required a team of more than ten men to operate it, and it could be loaded and fired only about three times per hour.

From the ally's side, the French 75s were rapid-fire for field artillery. They had been designed in 1891 and were so successful as a close support weapon that they would remain the mainstay of the French military for the next several decades.

The 75 was capable of delivering sixteen-pound shrapnel shells at the rate of fifteen rounds per minute. Because the gun was designed to absorb most of its own recoil, it seldom had to be repositioned to remain on target. Its trajectory was shallow, unlike Bertha's, and it would skip a shrapnel shell up to chest height before it exploded and sent shrapnel in all directions.

This skip and explode property made it ideal for trench warfare because it would explode down as well as up and shower the Germans in the trenches with deadly shrapnel balls of metal.

Today, the French were using the 75s to try and hit the chlorine delivery canisters and disrupt and disperse the wall of deadly gas. The Germans were using Big Bertha to pass up the trenches and pound the artillery positions, and end the French and Canadian counter attack.

≈

In the middle of this barrage, Alan and a large number of retreating troops were desperate to stay alive. They were in the thick of it, safely down range of the gas for the moment, but right in the area of maximum bombardment by the Germans.

There was no longer any real reason for Alan to run. After all he could be simply running into an exploding shell. He decided to hunker down. There were several dugouts in the walls of the trench where he could take cover. The dugouts not only provided relief from the mud and protection from the rain, they provided shelter from shrapnel shells. Alan crawled into a deep funk-hole keeping his head down. The wide brim of his helmet provided modest protection against any shrapnel coming down.

Nothing much to look at anyway, so keep your head down and hope for the best, he thought. A number of the retreating soldiers ran through the system past Alan, apparently believing that a moving target was harder to hit. Alan knew better.

The explosions were so frequent and relentless that Alan could barely hear the men shouting and screaming. All he could hear was a loud ringing, occasionally interrupted by the yelling of men who still believed that they still had some control over their destiny.

A gut-wrenching explosion went off so close to Alan that it sucked the air right out of him. As he gasped for air, he flashed back to the two dead men in the funk-hole earlier that day. He began to lose consciousness, and a wave of fear came over him.

"Oh God, no," he whispered. "Not like them!"

Any semblance of daylight was blotted out and replaced by a gray cloud of dust and smoke. He fought hard to hang on, gulping for what little oxygen was still available, only to find that it had been completely replaced by sulphur, burnt gunpowder, and the stink of death, so thick he could taste it.

A high-pitched squeal in Alan's head began to replace the screams and crying of men. His peripheral vision was beginning to close in as he strained to look around. What little he saw through a closing gray tunnel vision was a confused scene of men and parts of men in various states of death and dying.

Then, for some reason, the images faded and were replaced with the vision of a robin hopping along a lush green lawn. Alan felt soft warm breezes caressing his face as they were blowing off the end of Lake Ontario and up the foot of Wolfe Island.

Shock was setting in and his mind was defending itself against the horrors of the moment. The pleasant recollection of spring was now replaced by a white light of increasing intensity. The squeal in Alan's ears was now a soft buzz. It was the last thing Alan was aware of.

YPRES, 24 APRIL, 1915.
The Carnage

The fuzzy image of a man's face was coming into focus. He was trying to say something, but nothing was coming out of his mouth. It was like watching a silent movie. His face was dark and smeared with dirt and soot, and he looked to Alan like a coal miner or a chimney sweep. The haze behind him was being interrupted by what seemed to be men running in all directions. The man's mouth was asking a question, his teeth seemed so white in contrast to his blackened face.

Alan tried to read his lips.

"Are you all right?" the man asked again.

Why is he asking me that? Alan wondered. This was the first, modestly clear, cognitive thought that had run through Alan's head in at least forty minutes. As Alan began to recognize his surroundings, or what was left of them, he realized what had happened and the background images began to make sense. His hearing was partially returning and he became aware of the rattling of machine guns and the pops of the Enfield rifles being interrupted by the explosions of the ever-falling artillery.

He preferred the temporary deafness that had accompanied his close call with a Krupp 5.9-inch shell, known by his comrades as a "Crump."

The man with the dirty face was checking Alan's arms, legs, and torso. Alan recognized him now. It was his friend John McCrae. He brought his face close to Alan's and yelled, "Do you know who I am Alan?"

"Yes, John," Alan responded, dazed.

"Can you move your arms and legs?" McCrae asked.

"I think so," Alan said.

"Then do it for me!" McCrae commanded.

Alan painfully moved his extremities for the doctor.

"You're one lucky bugger, Alan," McCrae said. Then with a pat on Alan's shoulder, he turned and ran into the confusion to attend to the wounded.

≈

Alan was lying in an awkward position. On his back, he felt like a sheep in a ditch. He moved his arms and legs around and made an effort to roll over onto his stomach. With a great heave, he pushed himself into an unsteady upright position which caused a wave of searing pain to run through his body. He thought he might pass out, but fought to hold on. Lucky bugger, eh? He thought.

His first step was unsure and he almost toppled over on the rough terrain. His gate was that of a string puppet, a Pinocchio, as he walked in a strange, animated manner, trying to regain his balance. Alan's equilibrium was returning slowly as he walked in a zigzag pattern. He tried to establish his location, but everything had changed.

"The sun," Alan said aloud, testing his hearing as much as his senses. "It's setting in the western sky, that's the way back."

Now he knew which way to go, but, before he could start his retreat, Major McCrae reappeared.

"Al, I need you to help with the wounded. Bring them back to the dressing station," McCrae ordered.

Confused, Alan looked at John and then at the landscape around him. There were men everywhere. Some were crawling, some running, some writhed in pain on the ground. Others lay dead in the mud. He recalled what had happened and how he had gotten there. The devastation slowly sank in, and brought him back to the present. Despite his own pain and unsteadiness, he knew he was needed.

Alan went to the first and closest man he saw. Following orders like a mechanical man, he grabbed the wounded lad under the arms and tried to help him to a standing position. The wounded man let out a howl that would curdle blood as Alan brought him upright. A passing ambulance corps stretcher bearer yelled to Alan.

"Put him down you fool! He has no feet! His feet are gone!" Stunned by the revelation, Alan looked down at the fellow's legs and indeed, his pant legs were bleeding and tattered with no sign of feet.

"Tourniquet his legs and carry him out!" the stretcher bearer commanded. Alan quickly took out his pocket knife and cut the pant leg off at the knees. He used the material to make tourniquets which helped to slow the bleeding greatly.

Having grown up on a farm where he had to slaughter chickens, pigs, and cows, the sight of blood was nothing new to Alan, but this was different. He fought a wave of lightheadedness at the sight of the soldier's shredded legs, but he did what he knew he had to do.

The other advantage of growing up on a farm was that he was no stranger to physical effort. As a youth, Alan and his younger brother, Ian, would compete when carrying bags of grain. He could carry two 100-pound bags with ease and run from one barn to another in an effort to show up his younger brother. The soldier weighed about 170 pounds and went up and over Alan's shoulder with relatively little effort.

He trotted down what was left of the duckboard path with his wounded cargo and arrived at the field dressing station in several minutes. The scene was total chaos, with McCrae yelling out orders. Two orderlies grabbed the wounded man from Alan's back and yelled, "Go get more!"

The allied artillery was barking and flashing behind the dressing station up on a hill, and wounded were being brought in at an alarming rate. Alan returned to the trenches. He ran back to the area he had just left minutes ago and found that the scene had not changed except for the presence of a medic who was busily moving from man to man tying up tourniquets, bandaging wounds and administering morphine.

Alan ran over to a man curled up in a fetal position who the medic had just finished with. He bent over and was about to grab the man for transport when the medic reached over and held his hand against Alan's shoulder stopping him. Not a word was said. He simply shook his head then pointed to another. The medic had been trying to help those who could be saved and heavily morphine dosing those he knew were doomed. Alan passed over the poor soul who was slipping into a quiet sleep of death and picked up the fellow the medic had indicated.

It wasn't long before Alan lost count. He became like a machine carrying out of this hell hole the broken remains of every mother's sons. He didn't lose himself in deep thought about man's inhumanity to his fellow man. In fact, he didn't think at all, he simply did what he was told with mindless perseverance.

The more men that ran through the trenches toward the front to meet the battle, the more wounded Alan had to carry off. He was carrying a soldier on his back when a shell landed in the trench behind them knocking the ungainly duo to the ground. Alan clambered to his feet and began to hoist the wounded man up onto his back again when he realized that the young man was now dead. He had absorbed the force of the explosion along with a deadly dose of shrapnel and, as a result, Alan's life had been spared. Alan left him in the mud and went back for more wounded.

≈

Time seemed to be inconsequential as the battle raged on. The gas had done its dirty work and had dissipated, yet the Germans couldn't take advantage of the attack by pressing forward because of the continuous bombardment by the French, British, and Canadian artillery.

The steady stream of soldiers moved up to meet the battle and the steady stream of wounded returned to move through John McCrea's dressing station. It was dark now and the horizons to the east and to the west were alive with great muzzle flashes. The artillery rounds would explode with a blinding flash, like a huge camera flashbulb, leaving a momentary imprint on Alan's eyes and exposing the panorama of mud and wounded. He would begin to move toward the outline of a wounded man and then wait for another round to flash and light his way.

There were still so many wounded in the area that it seemed his job would never cease. He kept moving toward the wounded man and noticed the dim lantern of the medic as he kept up his marathon of mending the broken bodies.

Alan's foot kicked into something in the darkness and a howl was heard from right beneath Alan's feet. He toppled over a wounded soldier and landed partially on top of him producing another howl.

"Sorry," Alan said as he tried to right his equilibrium. The lamp swung around to dimly illuminate Alan on top of the soldier he had just tripped over.

"I'll have the litter bearers take him. He's stable," the medic hollered. "There's someone over the top who's calling for help. See if you can do something!"

Alan knew that the trench system provided modest protection against the bombs and machine guns, and to leave them would be suicide. Yet, between the explosions and constant growling of the Maxim MG08s, the wounded man's pleas rolled over No Man's Land and into the ears of all in the outer trenches.

Alan took a rough bearing on the sound of the man's cries and waited at the edge of the trench peering into the darkness in that direction. All he needed was a flash from an explosion to get a visual on the wounded man.

He hadn't waited long before a shell, about fifty meters away, lit up the dismal panorama with a ghostly white flash. The picture was imprinted on Alan's eyes. He saw the man. He quickly scrambled up and over the parapet stumbling and running over the uneven terrain in the direction of the fallen soldier. Another flash from an exploding shell froze the landscape in front of Alan for an instant and he clearly saw the wounded man four meters ahead of him.

He dove ahead and landed on his belly in the muck as an observant machine gunner hosed the area where Alan's frozen image had been moments before.

"I don't even have a gun! I'm just trying to save this man!" Alan yelled in frustration to an enemy gunner who couldn't hear or even understand his angry rant.

He crawled over to the moaning man and tried to quiet him. It was no use. The fellow was in agony and was beyond caring. Alan fished around in the dark until he found a small stick of wood about an inch thick and four inches long. He rolled it up and down his muddy tunic sleeve, cleaning off most of the mud and pushed it into the man's mouth crosswise.

"Bite hard on this and be quiet!" Alan yelled in the man's ear. He did as he was told. Alan looked around to get his bearings and took a deep breath.

"Now's as good a time as any," he told the wounded man. "This may hurt a lot, but I'll have you to safety in no time!"

The man looked up at Alan, his eyes wide with pain and piercingly white compared to his mud-caked face. "Thank you," he snorted through the tightly clenched piece of wood in his mouth.

Alan grabbed the man under his arms and began dragging him backward toward the forward trenches of the allied forces. The artillery was being kind for the moment. Alan was being protected by the veil of darkness. Only the sweeping Maxim machine guns, randomly firing at ghosts, presented a threat. Alan continued to trudge backward sweating profusely from the combination of physical and mental stress.

The night became oddly quiet for a moment, and the loudest sound Alan could hear seemed to be the pounding of his own heart as he struggled with his load over the uneven ground.

Thump... thump... thump... Alan knew that sound. It wasn't his heart pounding. It was the distant report of German artillery guns firing. He knew there would be only seconds before he saw the flash of explosions from incoming shells. He had to increase his pace.

The first explosion was several hundred meters to his left, toward the Algerian forces. The flash momentarily lit up the countryside just enough for Alan to see that the trenches were only two meters away. He tugged at the man's armpits, but he would only drag so fast and Alan was beyond exhaustion. The next explosion was to his right, well into the Canadian trench system, lighting up the area behind Alan as if he had back lighting on a theater stage. He was at the trench's edge.

≈

The sniper had been watching No Man's Land for some time. He was a patient man. That was the secret of a good sniper. He had seen the entire journey of Alan Macdonald over the fifty meter stage. He knew the bravery that was involved in Alan's actions, and admired the man from his hidden position 100 meters away. With each flash, he watched the stop action picture show progress, but now it was almost to an end.

He thought back to his boyhood, when he and his father would hunt deer in the Black Forest near Baden Baden. He recalled the beautiful buck that they had been watching for fifteen minutes. The buck was protecting his small herd, trumpeting and charging at a pack of wolves before eventually defeating the vicious animals. The buck was wounded but victorious, a magnificent animal. While the boy was marveling at the courage and strength of the buck, his father took aim and shot him dead. The boy looked at his father, stunned.

"He was something to be admired," the father said. "This is not personal, my son, it's just hunting."

An exploding shell flash silhouetted Alan and the wounded man at the trench edge, and the sniper fired.

"It's not personal, my friend. It's just hunting," he murmured, as he pulled the bolt back and expelled the spent hot shell. He quietly hoped that he had missed.

≈

Both men tumbled down the embankment of the forward trench. The medic ran to help Alan with the wounded man and to congratulate this remarkable hero on his impossible retrieval.

The wounded man had dropped the wooden stick from his mouth and was howling loudly, no longer being concerned about making noise. Alan lay face down on the muddy floor of the trench.

The medic drew closer with his lamp.

"Hey, buddy, nice job," he said hopefully. In the dim lamplight, he could now plainly see a hole in the top of Alan's helmet from which blood was oozing and a small puddle of blood was forming on the ground around Alan's head.

The medic closed his eyes for a moment. He was already emotionally dead from the endless horror he saw every day, but he knew this would be yet another bad memory that he would have to try to forget later on in life. He turned his attention to the wounded man that Alan had saved.

PART FOUR

THE JOURNEY

"The RMS Olympic, Ol' Reliable

[Transcribed from Ian MacDonald's recording]

C amp Valcartier had been two weeks of modest training. We did our daily calisthenics, learned basic infantry concepts artillery, some trained for cavalry, some trained for engineering and some just trained as infantry or rifles.

We were infantry, although we were trained to perform as stretcher-bearers and given basic first aid. Although we were not expected to carry rifles into battle, much to Terry's disappointment, we were expected to be able to use them should the occasion arise. So we, along with a group of fifty other trainees reported to the rifle range for rifle etiquette, bayoneting, and target practice.

Sergeant Mac MacLellen was our instructor for the day. He was a stocky, barrel-chested redhead and stood about five-foot-nine. We immediately liked him because he wore the kilt of the Canadian Scottish Regiment, consisting of a hunting Stewart tartan along with the khaki hose and puttees wrapped around his ankles above his hobnailed boots.

He looked and acted every bit the rough-and-tumble career fighting man, although at fifty years old we questioned his being, perhaps, a little long in the tooth.

"This, my fine young men is the Canadian model 10 Ross rifle. It weighs nine pounds, fourteen ounces and is sixty-and one-half inches long. It fires a .303 caliber bullet and is bolt action, with a clip of 5 cartridges. A steady infantryman can hit a target at 100 yards. Should your target somehow get closer, you have a detachable 10-inch bayonet fixed to the muzzle with which you can convince your target to stop."

We all laughed nervously, but Mac was all business, showing us how to break down the rifle, clean it, and reassemble it in lightning fast speed. He put on a great show until the time when he was to demonstrate marksmanship.

"Gentlemen, from a standing position, one places one's foot in front t'other in a wide stance. The butt of the rifle should be placed firmly into your shoulder while you stand sideways to your target, like so."

He took up the classic rifleman stance. "The muzzle should be supported by your left hand and that hand should have the rifle strap wrapped around it to steady your aim. Look down the sights, align them on your target and squeeze, not pull, the trigger."

It should be noted that at this time in Canada, there were no allowances made for left handed people. If you were a southpaw, you were taught in school to write with your right hand and function as a righty in all aspects.

We all waited for Mac to impress us with his marksmanship and braced for the inevitable crack of the gun but all we heard was click – nothing. We could see Mac's jaw flex as he pulled the bolt back to toss the misfired shell out and replace it with another. He steadied again and... click... nothing.

He didn't look back at us, but you could see his eyes looking left and then right while his face reddened and his jaw flexed more profoundly. He reached up and cleared the chamber again only the cartridge did not eject properly. He was visibly shaking with anger as he dropped to one knee and slammed the butt of the gun on the ground. The shell popped out of the chamber.

Trying to regain his composure, he chambered another cartridge and, again... nothing! Then, in a wild display of outrage–and with a barrage of remarkable curse words–he heaved the rifle with all his might at the target.

We all watched in awe at this stunning performance while the Ross arched high into the air and came down 50 feet down range. This time it went off with a loud crack, causing Mac and the rest of us to hit the dirt.

"Those friggin' shit sticks will end up killing more Canadians than Germans!" Mac barked. He thoroughly abandoned his composure as he raised himself to his feet.

The rest of us looked on in disbelief. If our lives depended upon this rifle, perhaps we should reconsider our joining the CEF. Fortunately the Ross would be replaced with the far superior Lee Enfield Rifle by the time our troops reached the trenches of the Western Front.

≈

Our Canadian training had not all been that noteworthy and was, thankfully, behind us quickly. Another Canadian Pacific Railway rattled us toward Halifax at the end of the two-week training period to an awaiting troop transport ship bound for England.

It was late afternoon when our train finally arrived near the Halifax Harbor. We were directed to assemble several hundred feet from the station. So we dutifully filed out of the coaches. The brief walk was welcome after hours of being cramped into a noisy coach car. It was a cool afternoon. The sea breeze easily countered the weak attempt of the spring sun to warm us up. The pungent smell of the sea had an almost recuperative effect, a smell of life and death. We drew the salty aroma deeply into our lungs to clear the stink of too many men being transported for too long in too close quarters.

Before us a massive ship was docked with long, steep gangplanks reaching up to the top decks high above the dock side. It was the biggest vessel I had ever seen and it was painted in the most remarkable paint scheme imaginable. The entire hull, some seventy feet from gunnel to waterline, was painted in a bizarre pattern of geometric shapes, all having brilliant contrasting colors. Blues, yellows, greens, oranges, reds, and whites were splashed in these seemingly nonsensical patterns.

"What the frig is that?" asked Dan McKee.

Sean said he felt seasick just looking at the boat. A nearby deck hand overheard the comments and approached the group offering up his educated insight.

"Well, Lads, that is your ride to England. She is the RMS Olympic," he said with a distinct Irish brogue. "She measures eight hundred eighty-two and-a-half feet in length overall with a beam of ninety-two and-a-half feet." He swept his arm along the length as he described the ship in solemn terms. "The four stacks or funnels stand seventy-five feet above the top deck. She's one of the fastest cruise ships at twenty-four knots, with the power of two large steam engines developing fifteen thousand horsepower each, and one low-power turbine developing sixteen horsepower. She was launched in 1910 at Harland and Wolff's Belfast yard as one of the largest luxury liners ever built and had been converted to a troop transport just recently. She can now carry as many as seven thousand troops in one crossing."

We all looked from him back to the ship nodding our heads in quiet appreciation.

"What about this peculiar paint job?" I asked.

He looked left and right as if to ensure that the coast was clear, then leaned toward us.

"It's the dazzle paint job," he said conspiratorially in a loud whisper.

Our puzzled expressions told him he needed to provide additional explanation.

"All the strange shapes and the angles with the bright colors create confusion," he said.

"Confusion for who, the fish?" Bill Lewis asked.

"No smart guy, the Germans," the Irishman said. "With this pattern, the U-Boats can't tell which way we're going or how close or far away we are! It makes it bloody hard for them to judge when launching torpedoes at us and it works like a charm."

A small crowd had gathered around this well-informed gentleman as he rattled off the statistics pertaining to his ship. He said the HMS Olympic had also been outfitted with small cannons whose function was to blast the U-Boats out of the water.

Again, we all nodded with appreciation. The anti-submarine guns did provide a degree of comfort and the paint job was certainly optically confusing. The fact that the ship was several times faster than a U-Boat was reassuring. But because hardly a day went by without the newspapers reporting yet another sub attack, we weren't completely sold on the safety of our crossing.

A sergeant was calling out orders to the multitude on the dock and it appeared that it must be time to board, so we gathered up our knapsacks, our Ross rifles, and webbing. By the way, webbing was the nickname for what was known as the Oliver pattern of straps that criss-crossed you and from which hung a shovel, a canteen, mess kit, a number of tools, some useful, some not, and a pouch for ammunition. The ammunition was useful in case your Ross rifle decided to fire properly. All in all, about 35 pounds of rubbish was attached to the webbing. Problem was when you walked you sounded like the donkey of a pots and pans salesman. We, of course, also had our pipes and drums to transport, which added to the weight and made for a laborious trek up the steep gangplanks.

We were directed to our quarters below deck and were surprised to find that, for a luxury liner, the accommodations were anything but luxurious. In her transformation to a troop transport, Harland and Wolff had stacked bunk beds into the small cabins of the upper decks and had turned steerage into a massive dormitory of endless cots, hammocks and bunks. My group claimed a small cabin with six bunks in it and settled in for our weeklong crossing.

THE CROSSING

As the giant ship prepared to cast off, Terry Manning tried to muster up an impromptu band to play on deck as we left the docks and harbor. Once a pipe major, always a pipe major. We grabbed our pipes and joined him. The drummers were less enthusiastic and had to be coaxed into joining us with promises of copious amounts of whiskey.

On the upper deck, we could see the tugboats far below, like Lilliputians trying to tug Gulliver. They moved us slowly away from the dock. Terry quickly tuned our chanters and then rapidly tuned all the drones. He had a great ear and could move through the small band tuning so quickly that it was really remarkable. Our old instructor, Victor Matthews would not have approved of his haste, but we were in tune and playing in less than ten minutes.

The tugboat hands waved their hats when they finally figured out where the piping was coming from.

A crowd stood on the docks and saluted as we played "Going home". The people of Nova Scotia or New Scotland have a profound appreciation for the bagpipes and were obviously moved by the performance and, of course, the sacrifice that all aboard were accepting.

The pipes and drums are most conspicuous and attract attention anywhere they are played, as evidenced by the number of our shipmates that had assembled around us on the aft deck. They were smoking, sipping whiskey and generally taking in the moment, perhaps thinking about the uncertainty that lay ahead.

Further up the ship, near the bow, we could see several figures dressed in white and sporting white hats. They had also noticed our performance and one of them headed toward us with a determined gait.

We continued to play "Rowen Tree" as this stocky man in the white uniform arrived and stood conspicuously on the periphery of the crowd of interested shipmates. We finished our set and neatly stopped to a raucous display of approval by the crowd. The uniformed man strode over to Dan McKee who had, as drum major, been calling out the tunes.

"First Mate John Spader" he said, introducing himself.

"And?" McKee asked, raising his eyebrow. He towered over the first mate who may have measured but five-nine.

Spader was not intimidated in the least. "The Captain requests your band join him at the captain's table and he would be honored if you would perform for the men before the meal."

Dan turned to Terry Manning. "Pipe Major, what say you?"

The Pipe Major outranks the Drum Major and so the question was deferred to Terry. Terry responded positively without hesitation. Sean Lyons suggested that for two drinks we could be coaxed to play longer, to which Spader laughed and said he'd pass the suggestion along to the Skipper.

≈

That evening in the dining room, the drummers seemed more enthusiastic. Perhaps the prospect of good food and free whiskey served as a motivator.

We all circled up to Dan McKee's directions and played for almost a half-hour. The crew and men loved the performance and spurred us on with hoots and hollers for more. Hunger and thirst, however, seemed to compel us to end our show and join the captain for our well-earned payment.

First Mate Spader escorted our small band to the captain's table and formally introduced us to Captain Bertram F. Hays. He was a pleasant English gentleman–very fit, with a smooth, confident demeanor.

He was about six feet tall and lean with close cut gray hair and a pencil mustache, a very handsome fellow.

"Gentleman, thank you for joining me this evening and welcome aboard the RMS Olympic," Hays said as he stood with his hat tucked neatly under his left arm. "I enjoyed your performance immensely and hope to hear more of the same on our voyage. Please remain standing and we'll have a toast to the Queen."

We all scrambled for our glasses.

"To the Queen," he said, raising his glass high.

"To the Queen," we responded. The whiskey was warm going down and helped put us at ease.

"Gentleman, be seated and please introduce yourselves, I must know more about your group."

As introductions were made, I watched how the ship's crew treated this man. They had an obvious profound respect for him, and he for them. He had an unmistakable air of authority, but it was tempered by a charming social grace that had obviously been perfected after many years of dealing with wealthy, upper crust cruise ship passengers.

"Allow me to offer another drink," Hays said waving his hand at the glasses on the table. A steward rapidly responded with a flask of the amber liquid.

Most of us had come from modest backgrounds and were not versed in the social graces. We watched the Captain and followed his lead–except, of course, for the drummers who grabbed rolls and began to heavily butter them without regard for social niceties.

Terry sat next to the Captain and they were chatting about the ship. Sean and I were next to each other and were idly talking about nothing important while trying to eavesdrop on the Captain and Terry's conversation. The ship was Captain Hays' favorite subject and he spoke of it with fondness, as though it were a family member.

Perhaps the second glass of whiskey had gone to my head and common sense had retreated, for I spoke up at that point and said, "Captain I noticed this ship looks a lot like the Titanic."

As I recollect, I believe I was trying to be somewhat of a smart aleck to make my comrades laugh.

Captain Hays took on a somber tone. "Yes, that's very astute of you to notice. The Olympic is, in fact, the sister ship of the ill-fated Titanic. The difference is that the aft deck of the Titanic was covered or enclosed and the LOA was a mere nine inches longer than the Olympic."

The table had become silent and every ear was now tuned to what the Captain was saying.

"This ship has been in service for five years and has made hundreds of Atlantic crossings without incident. After the Titanic tragedy, the White Star Lines took the Olympic out of service. No one would set foot on her, even after they doubled the life boats. She remained empty, so they sent her back to Belfast for extensive renovations. It took over six months to add several layers of bulkheads increasing the water tight compartment twofold. They also saw fit to add a double hull to her, increasing her beam by two full feet. This ship has, in fact, a stronger hull than most of her majesty's battle cruisers." He paused to let this information sink in.

"That, along with the doubling of the lifeboats, seemed to ease the fears of the traveling public. We had the 'unsinkable Molly Brown' join us as a publicity stunt." Hays looked out over the table with a wry grin. "She is, by the way, a wonderful woman with the remarkable ability to see only the good in life. She is, in fact, an infectiously happy person."

The faces of most at the table had gone from looks of concern to smiles of amusement.

"You are, gentlemen, on a remarkably safe ship," Hays said. "The unfortunate reality is that safety is very often realized in the wake of tragedy."

That night, I lay in my bunk, unable to sleep and thinking about the sister ship of the Olympic. That horrible night when so many lives were lost or forever changed. The story was widely known, of how the men on board demanded that the women and children take the far too few lifeboats and save themselves.

What a helpless feeling those poor men must have experienced, being in a situation where the requirement of the moment took over and they had to ask themselves to—and willingly did—sacrifice their lives for strangers. Mass heroism and sacrifice in the face of death just seemed to be remarkable to me as I imagined myself on board the Titanic that night.

Little did I realize that I, and so many others, were being unwittingly swept along by similar tides of misfortune. There were going to be sacrifices far greater in number and for a purpose far less gallant or tangible than that of the men of the Titanic. I pushed the thoughts from my head, remembering what my father had once told me: "Don't burden yourself with unproductive thought."

Amid my snoring comrades, I finally fell asleep.

≈

The seven days aboard the Olympic went by surprisingly fast. It was easy to meet people and commiserate, as we were all in the same boat—both literally and metaphorically.

Our practice sessions on deck had attracted other musicians both pipers and drummers. Mike Brill from Toronto, a drummer with a slapstick sense of humor, joined us. Balding and bulky, he could change his expression from a broad toothy grin to a sinister scowl and back to the silly grin in the blink of an eye. You could seldom take him seriously, except when he was playing the drums.

Another addition to the group was a medical student from McGill University by the name of George Cohen. George loved the pipes, as evidenced by his unbridled enthusiasm. Often, Terry would have to tell George to slow down his playing as he had a tendency to race ahead of the group in a tune. For the most part, he was a good solid piper and a fine addition to our group.

At first, George was a bit shy and standoffish and, being Jewish, he was a curious phenomenon to pipers. After all, Scots and Irish, even the occasional Englishman played the pipes, but, a Jew was most unusual. He was rather short and prematurely bald with abnormal amounts of hair on his back and chest–even his fingers were hairy. I had my doubts about his fitting in, but he would later prove to be a great friend and beloved member of our group.

≈

Near the end of our voyage, the coast of Ireland came into view far ahead on the horizon. It was a beautiful spring day, and, for the most part, we had had fine weather for our trip across the Atlantic. The sea had a sort of haze that hung over it, almost a light fog that would deposit dew on your eyebrows and eyelashes as the Olympic churned on toward Great Britain.

We had assembled on the aft deck for our mid-morning practice and had just finished our tuning when the Olympic let go with a deafening blast of her horn. The noise caught us completely off guard, and we collectively jumped about a foot in the air.

"Must be some kind of signal to Ireland," Sean said. It was a ridiculous notion as we were still too far away from the coast for anyone to hear us.

As I was pondering the horn blast, Dan McKee called, "Band ready!" I snapped to attention with my mouthpiece squarely in place and began to fill the bag so as to be ready for the strike in.

"The Minstrel Boy Set!" Dan yelled. "By the center... quick, March!"

Before the bass drum could pound out cadence, we were all startled by two loud booms. It was cannon fire coming from the bow of the ship. When the Olympic had undergone renovation in Belfast, Harland and Wolff had installed two anti-submarine cannons. They were not very large guns, only a three-inch bore, but they were capable of causing substantial damage to a U-boat.

The crew, however, was ill-trained and if they hit a sub, it would have been more by luck than skill. We all ran to the rails and moved forward for a better look.

"There it is!" someone yelled pointing off the port bow.

Several more cannon blasts were followed by three large splashes, well short of the sub.

The U-boat had fully surfaced, and you could plainly see the white hat of the captain along with three other sailors standing on the tower. U-103 was painted in large white letters on the tower and could be seen until the U-boat turned toward us.

Another man yelled, "A torpedo coming right for us!" The streak of bubbles and steam that followed the weapon made it easy to spot its direction and speed.

U-103
N55 30.0 LATITUDE
W010 40.0 LONGITUDE
[Recreated from historical records]

Claus Rucker was the commander of the U-103. He stood very erect and appeared much taller than a man barely five-foot, eight inches. Perhaps it was his white hat perched atop his head of white hair or maybe his authoritative demeanor. Whatever the case, the perception was undeniable.

Next to Rucker was his first mate, Hans Schwieger, a young man of 23 who had been on the water for only a year. He had done very well to achieve first mate in just one year, but he had ambitions of being commander soon. It was really just a matter of time, inasmuch as he was the younger brother of the famous Captain Walther Schwieger.

Walther Schwieger had been the commander of the U-20 which on 7 May, 1915 sank The Lusitania, killing 1,119 of the 1,924 people on board. This attack on an unarmed civilian vessel was widely considered the most infamous maritime crime committed during the war. And even though the world unanimously condemned the attack, the *Kaiserliche Marine* (Imperial Navy) looked upon Schwieger as a hero. Hans was planning on capitalizing on his older brother's fame.

As the U-103 glided over the uncommonly smooth seas at her long range cruise speed of twelve knots, Rucker leaned over the rail of the conning tower and admired his U-boat. He recalled his first command on an old kerosene burner. Those ships belched billows of black smoke out of the stacks and gave your position away.

Rucker yelled over the sound of the wind and sea, "We have at least 10,000 miles of range remaining."

Schwieger nodded. "We could go to New York Harbor and back and still have reserve fuel," he said.

"Perhaps we should, I have relatives there," Rucker replied with a broad smile of yellow, smoke stained teeth.

The diesel-powered U-103 was a Mittel U class of *unterseeboot*. She carried sixteen torpedoes and had an eighty-eight millimeter deck gun for weaponry. Her length overall was two hundred ten feet, and she could maintain a maximum speed of nearly seventeen knots on the surface, and just over nine knots submerged.

≈

Captain Rucker breathed the cool salt air in deeply through his nose, hoping to flush out the ever-present smell of diesel that was inescapable inside the U-boat. His lips were pressed tightly together, giving him the appearance of having just a slit for his mouth.

Rucker's full concentration was on the horizon through his binoculars. This was the hunt. Something caught his eye and, without lowering his glasses, he tapped his first mate on the shoulder pointing in the general direction of his sighting.

Schwieger swung his glasses over to the area for confirmation. He saw a distant plume of smoke, not yet visible without the aid of glasses. He nodded.

Rucker flipped open the cover of the communication tube and gave a hard blow then leaned close to hear the response. A loud whistle sounded at the helm.

"Jawohl," came the reply from the helmsman. Rucker looked at his water compass and barked the new course into the tube. "Steer 210 degrees," he ordered. The 103 was now on a perfect intercept.

Turning to Schwieger, he said, "Have the men come up for fresh air in groups of ten for fifteen minutes each. We may need to submerge for a while and I want them to clear their lungs and heads."

Eager to show his command qualities, Schwieger asked, "Should I request full speed sir?"

Rucker's tight-lipped expression softened slightly. "We don't know what we're running toward young Hans. If it's a dreadnought or destroyer we could simply be rushing to our own demise. Once we've identified our prey, we'll make our move."

Schwieger tipped his head in recognition of the captain's good judgment and quietly chastised himself for such a poorly thought out suggestion. Instead of impressing the captain with good command judgment, he proved he was not yet ready. Two hours later they were still miles away but they had determined that their target was in fact The Olympic. With four large stacks topping off her unmistakable profile, there was only one other ship that it could have been, and she sank many years earlier on her maiden voyage.

It also appeared that The Olympic's deep-water escort had steamed off to intercept and protect the next transport on their route segment, while the next escort had not yet arrived to continue the relay process. The timing was perfect. The Olympic was a sitting duck, an easy target, almost too easy.

Rucker knew his prey well. He knew that her speed was far superior to that of the 103, so there was some cause for stealth. He gave the order to prepare to dive. They would now move in for the kill. Hatches were secured and ballast tanks were filled as the U-103 readied herself for submerged operations.

Although the engine room was aft and separated by two hatches from the main operations area, the noise of the two diesels was enough to require orders to be shouted. When they were shut down and the boat switched to electric power, the lack of constant noise was a welcome relief. But the noise would be replaced quickly with excessive heat. The large engines were cooled by sea water when in operation but now there was no cooling being provided so the residual heat had nowhere to go in the tight confines of the sub. The temperature of the engine room quickly topped one hundred degrees, which proved too much for the engine crew. They sought relief forward with the others, but soon everyone was sweating.

≈

Rucker had set a course for a port-side intercept as the sub quietly slipped below the surface to periscope depth. He had moved to the periscope viewer and was looking at the Olympic through the eyepiece. Despite the dazzle paint job, Rucker had already determined the speed and direction of the target and intended to surface some five hundred yards from the planned shot.

The Olympic would require the most conservative approach, because Rucker knew it would take more than one torpedo to sink her. He believed, as did most U boat commanders, that the best shots were made from the surface. The speed of the target, its trajectory, ocean current, and closure were all parts of the "solution," the equation that had to be applied prior to each shot.

A surface shot also required little to no solution for the torpedoes' path. Torpedoes were propelled by compressed air that was heated to the point of steam. This process enabled a greater charge to be pumped into its storage tank extending the range and increasing the speed of the weapon. The sub had several electrically propelled torpedoes, but they were much slower and better suited for submerged attacks. Rucker had already decided that the wet-heaters, as the steam-driven torpedoes were known, would be used for this kill.

The captain wiped a drip of stinging perspiration from his eye and refocused on the movement of his prey.

"We shall surface in two minutes," he said. "What is the status of the torpedoes?"

Schwieger stood several paces away and drew close to the captain. "The forward torpedoes are charged and loaded and the tubes are flooded for firing," he said. He hesitated before adding, "But the aft tubes are experiencing some problems, sir."

Rucker stiffened. "What kind of problems, First Mate Schwieger?" he asked in a frosty tone.

Hans paled. "The gate on the port tube is only partially open and refuses to cooperate. The starboard side is not porting the air properly, preventing flooding, and–"

"And this is the first I hear of it?" Rucker barked, cutting him off.

The first mate was speaking more quickly now. "Sir, I saw no need to bother you as the mechanics said that the tubes would be ready five minutes ago."

Rucker took a deep breath and raised one eyebrow. "In the future, First Mate Schwieger, make every effort to keep the captain informed in such matters and he will determine whether in is unimportant or not."

He then turned away and peered into the periscope. "We shall just have to sink her with two fish."

≈

The temperature in the forward part of the sub was well over eighty degrees, so when the captain gave the order to surface all were looking forward to the welcome addition of the cool sea air, despite the danger associated with the impending battle.

As the U-103 broke surface the diesels clattered to life in anticipation of the switch from batteries. The conning tower broke surface and, after allowing a minute for the excess water to drain away, a sailor climbed the ladder to open the outer hatch.

The opening of the hatch was not a job that seasoned crewmembers often volunteered for. You simply had to do it once to understand why. As the junior seaman ascended the ladder and opened the hatch, a cascade of water drenched him, splashing on the floor below.

Rucker and Schwieger were standing well clear of the anticipated shower area. Claus donned his white hat and quickly climbed the wet ladder into the light of day, with Hans close on his heels.

A quarter-mile away they saw the Olympic. The ship was enormous even at the distance. Her hull cut through the water with such ease and grace it was easy to appreciate the beauty of this marvel of the sea.

Rucker shook his head slowly. "It is with regret that I shall send this fine vessel to the bottom, but there are perhaps six thousand soldiers aboard who will be killing our young countryman on the battle field and I have my duty."

Hans nodded, never taking his eyes off of the massive ship. "It must be done," he said somberly.

"Prepare to fire the port side on my mark," Rucker commanded. Hans called the ready command to the helmsman through the communications tube.

They were lined up for a perfect portside strike. Ruckers' plan was to unleash the first torpedo forward of mid ship and the second aft of mid in hopes of rupturing a boiler and causing massive explosions in the engine room. They were almost at the firing point when two white puffs of smoke blew through the wind over the Olympics' bow. There were two loud reports followed by two splashes about a hundred yards short of the sub.

Hans anxiously asked, "Should we dive sir?"

The captain still looked through his binoculars and was obviously unimpressed. "No. They are untrained *dummkopfs*. If they were to hit us it would be pure luck. Prepare to fire. Mark one. Fire one."

The first mate relayed the order and the first fish was away.

"Correct the heading to 180 degrees and prepare the number two." Rucker watched the first torpedoes white trail of bubbles as it sped on a perfect trajectory for its intended impact with the Olympic's hull. Young Schwieger grabbed the captains left forearm in disbelief.

"DO UNTO OTHERS..."
[Transcribed from Ian MacDonald's recording]

The Olympic lurched forward, billowing smoke from its stacks, as the two fifteen thousand horsepower engines were pushed to their limit by Captain Hays and his crew.

The torpedo was heading directly for the mid ship of the Olympic and was closing far too quickly.

We were collectively knocked off balance and stumbled to the right as Hays applied full left rudder. Our eyes were locked on the approaching steam trail of the torpedoes as the great ship listed over to the starboard in a desperate attempt to reduce its eight hundred eighty-foot profile.

Captain Hays called for full aft on the port engine and maintained full ahead on the starboard. The port propeller shuddered and cavitated as it reversed its direction against the onrushing water.

More quickly than I or anyone else had imagined, the Olympic turned toward the torpedo and we all watched with relief as the steaming tube of death passed along the port side of the ship and harmlessly away to our stern.

We collectively gave a cheer, and some of the men were even slapping each other on the back for making it successfully through our first brush with death. Then someone noticed that instead of turning away from the submarine and speeding away, we were continuing our left turn toward it. Several of us looked back at the bridge. We could plainly see Captain Hays and his officers at the helm.

"Why aren't we turning away?" Sean asked. "A U-boat only travels at about twelve knots, that's half our speed. We can easily out run it." It was a good question to which none of us had a good answer, but we were about to find out Captain Hays' intention.

The Olympic continued her high speed turn powering back just slightly so as not to overshoot. The men on deck had gone from noisy jubilation to quiet trepidation as they saw the Olympic steam toward the deadly U-103 at high speed. Her low profile slithering across the water was clearly in sight.

We could see its Captain and his men, who, it dawned on us as well as them, had hesitated a moment too long in determining Captain Hays' intention. Now they were scurrying below and closing hatches. Huge plumes of water blew into the air as the U-103 began to vent its air tanks and replace it with water to make ready for an emergency dive. It was clear now that the Olympic had every intention of ramming her and the tables had fully turned.

The deck of the Olympic was awash with men, all silently watching, unwilling participants in this life and death event. U-103 was a mere fifty yards away with Hays aiming squarely for her mid-section. The U-boat, however, was sinking fast and the churning, frothy water was quickly rising around the tower as she desperately dove for safety.

As we watched the 103 disappear beneath the waves, the crowd let out a frustrated moan. Twenty yards ahead of us was now empty water where the U-103 had once been. What was unknown to us, and even to the U-boat crew, was that the Olympic drew a solid forty feet of water.

We stumbled forward as the Captain demanded all engines full reverse from the engine room. The ship would normally take hundreds of yards to slow from twenty knots to ten knots. However, the maneuver was not intended to slow the ship but to thrust another fifteen feet of bow down into the water.

The Olympic shook from a loud and distinct impact far below the surface of the water. We could feel it through our feet. We all knew that the Olympic had tagged the U-103.

Running to the rails, we began to scour the water to the aft for debris of the U-boat to confirm the collision. Suddenly, Bill Lewis pointed and yelled. "There! Some life vests and oil!"

The water to our aft erupted into a boiling cauldron of oil, debris and bubbles. We broke into a spontaneous cheer at the knowledge that the Olympic had taken out one of these German demons of the deep. In fact, the double hull of the Olympic had cleanly cut the U-103 in half and quickly sent her to the bottom with little damage to the RMS itself.

I looked up to the bridge and could see the Captain looking aft with his binoculars. He lowered them and gave some orders to First Mate Spader who saluted him and marched away.

Moments later, as the ship slowed to a crawl, the deck hands began to man the life boats.

"Hey Ian, you think we're sinking and they forgot to tell us?" Sean asked, half in jest.

"I hope not," I said and looked at the others to see if anyone else found this a little unnerving. Dan McKee stretched out his mace and stopped a deck hand as he was running by.

"What's cooking pal?" he asked.

"The Captain has ordered us to lower boats away and retrieve survivors," the young man said. McKee raised his mace and allowed the deck hand to proceed on his way.

"Well, I'll be damned," Dan said.

The water astern was thick with oil and flotsam but, amid the floating debris, we could see men flailing in the icy waters. As the Olympic sat steady waiting for the completion of the rescue mission, it dawned on me that we were sitting ducks for any other German

U-boats that might be in the area. I noticed First Mate John Spader nearby and mentioned my concerns to him.

Spader smiled and said, "The Captain is a good Christian which compelled him to retrieve survivors. He is, however, not a foolish man and had ordered us to radio for British Naval assistance which is less than fifteen miles away steaming toward us at twenty-eight knots." He excused himself and walked off.

We were left there to discuss the wisdom of putting the ship and ourselves at risk to save the very people who had just tried to kill us.

"I'd leave them," Dan said. "Nothing personal, it's just war." Bill Lewis and Terry Manning both surprised me by siding with Captain Hay's decision.

"Besides," Bill said. "We stand a chance of getting some valuable information from our guests."

As our argument about Captain Hays' move continued, I was relieved to see three British battleships clearly in view on the not too distant horizon. They looked like three giant knights charging forward on their steeds, their stacks billowing black smoke and their bows sending cascades of water thirty feet into the air on either side as they cut through the seas at battle speed.

The first of the survivors were being escorted aboard and we all clamored over to catch a glimpse of our enemy. They were soaked and slimy with oil.

These were young men, our ages, looking very scared clutching to woolen blankets, shivering and keeping their heads down, lifting them only occasionally to steal a glance at their captors or saviors, a topic for another discussion. The enemy, I now realized, looked very much like any of us, not evil or sinister as I would have liked them to look.

"Why do they want to destroy Europe?" I asked my quiet friends. I was hoping that someone would give me a good reason to hate these men. It was much easier to wish them dead when they were just the hard cold U-103, now they had faces and looked frightened.

"Don't look so tough now, do they?" Terry commented. I nodded.

Captain Hays had joined us on deck as the last of the survivors were brought aboard. He stepped forward as the final two men came up the ladder. The first was a young man with a stocking hat. He was taller than the second man but, somehow seemed shorter. His head hung down in defeat.

The second man had a white captain's hat on with a soaking wet dress jacket hanging awkwardly askew. He stood straight and looked taller than the young man ahead of him, although he was not.

Captain Hays stood before this man and the two exchanged a long, silent stare. Finally, the U-boat Captain stood slowly to attention and saluted Hays clicking his heels as he did it. Several moments later Hays returned the salute.

Never taking his eyes off the U-boat Captain, Hays ordered a blanket for his enemy and had him escorted below to be cleaned up and given dry clothing. We sensed we were witnessing an ancient protocol that followed a battle, when one leader would submit and the other would honor his submitting. We looked on silently in awe and respect.

LIVERPOOL DEBARKATION

We disembarked The Olympic the next day in the dingy port city of Liverpool. Tired, but exhilarated after our voyage from Canada, we looked forward to joining our fellow countrymen on the Western Front.

The Olympic was being tugged into the dock, where crews were standing by to inspect the hull to determine the extent of the damage from the collision with U-103 and begin immediate repairs. The hull had not been breached, so the repairs were hoped to be minor. There were also several members of the Royal Navy waiting to escort the ten surviving crew members to a proper place for interrogation.

Terry Manning, always ready to play his pipes, hurriedly organized a marching band for our debarkation.

We marched off The Olympic in a two-man file playing "The Maple Leaf Forever," leading a mass of men down the gangplank to a large crowd of cheering Brits on the dock. There was a brief discussion between our Canadian officers and British officers, which was followed by an order to Terry to have the pipe band lead the men through town to a temporary billet area about three kilometers march from the dock.

Terry called out the tunes, Dan set the cadence and we were off, like pied pipers leading children through a town of cheering onlookers. It was a brisk march on solid ground, a welcome jaunt after a week at sea.

Our billets were in small tents, six men per, and the accommodations were spartan, but as we were only to be here for twelve hours, it was considered a brief inconvenience.

≈

The next morning we were awakened at the crack of dawn, lead through some calisthenics and fed a quick breakfast consisting of coffee, porridge and buttered toast. Then we gathered our gear and made a quick march to the rail yard where we boarded the troop transport bound for East Sandling training camp. This was not the old Kingston Pembroke Line. We were packed into boxcars with wooden benches nailed to the floor enabling every seated occupant to experience the true feel of the rail.

It was a bum-numbing seven and a half-hour ride that was further enhanced by the rattling and clanking of the old boxcars and the billows of black coal smoke that belched from the laboring engine and enshrouded the cars behind.

The day had gone from sunny and warm in Liverpool to cool and rainy as we approached East Sandling. Someone had opened the door and we were quickly made aware of how damp and chilly it really was. Around the camp were fields filled with recruits being lead through various training endeavors. They were climbing over barriers, crawling under barbed wire, shooting and bayoneting straw-filled German soldier uniforms.

As we all jumped out of our boxcar, one Sergeant barked out that this was standard weather for the time of year, so we had better get used to it. We formed into long lines by regiment and ordered to cue up in front of a tent for our assignments.

Assignments were generally given with consideration of one's life experience, qualification, and education. Because the men in our band had some higher education, the probability that we would be ordered to be a sapper or an infantryman was low.

As our group approached the table in the tent at the end of the line, we could hear a fellow asking a series of questions designed to help them place you in the position you were suited for. I looked past the shoulder of the man ahead of me and saw that the fellow sitting at the table was a small man with thick hair and enormous bushy eyebrows.

"Name, religion, education, qualifications," he growled out mechanically in a thick Irish brogue.

"He's a leprechaun, or perhaps a troll," I thought cheekily. But before I could sort it out for myself, it was my turn.

I had been reciting the information for three men ahead of me and was going to impress him with my efficiency. "Ian Macdonald. Protestant. First-year university. Bagpiper," I said.

The leprechaun never looked up as he scribbled the information onto a form. But as he was writing "bagpiper" on the form, he stopped and looked up at me with one great eyebrow raised.

"Did you say bagpiper?" he asked.

"Yes, sir. We–"

"We?" he interrupted. "How many is 'we?'"

"There are four pipers, and three drummers at hand with more–"

"Stay where you are!" he interrupted again. "I'll be back." He sprang from his chair and left the tent. I looked at Sean and Terry who were also bemused by this little fellow's odd behavior.

Several minutes later he returned with an officer in trail. The leprechaun's chest was all puffed out and he was beaming as though he had found his lost pot of gold.

The officer with him was a pleasant looking man, very distinguished, tall and lean with silver grey hair and a fine mustache. His uniform was neat and fit well, but he had a cane and walked with a noticeable limp. Upon his uniform breast hung an impressive number of medals including, as I noticed right away, Her Majesty's Medal of Valor. This was a man of considerable distinction.

The leprechaun barked, "Attention!" We snapped to attention and saluted as we had been trained to do at Valcartier.

The Officer limped over to me, saluted and then thrust out his hand.

"At ease lad. I'm Camp Commander Donald Hicks, and you are?"

"Ian Macdonald, sir." I noticed a small medal on his uniform that was a gold bagpipe.

"I understand that you are a bagpiper and that there are others?" Hicks queried.

"Yes sir," I said proudly.

"Wonderful news," Hicks said. "We sorely need pipers."

Terry Manning stepped up and interrupted.

"Beg your pardon, sir," he said. "We came all this way not to entertain the enemy but to fight them."

Hicks slightly raised one eyebrow, a warning to Manning to remember his place.

"And you, my impetuous private, are who?"

"Pardon me, sir, I meant no disrespect," Terry said, realizing his breach of protocol. "I am Private Terry Manning, Pipe Major of Queens University Pipe Band."

"Private Manning, I applaud your enthusiasm in wanting to engage the enemy. And I guarantee that you'll get more than a belly full of the western front soon enough. Furthermore, you must leave it up to your commander to determine where you will be most useful," Hicks said in a cool tone.

This was a mild dressing down by Hicks which served to correct Terry's rambunctious nature without real humiliation. Many other officers would have been a great deal more harsh.

"The British Army is prepared to offer each of you pipers and drummers a position of distinction among your fellow troops," Hicks continued. "And along with that position of distinction you will receive an extra penny per day above that of an infantryman."

We all glanced at each other.

"You will be doing a great service to the Crown. You are truly needed for your talents," he said. "I, myself, am a piper and was wounded in the battle at La Bassee last year, thus my limp. I will tell you this: The troops will hold you in great regard and, in fact, they will protect their piper before most of their officers."

It seemed we had little choice. Terry said, "We request tents in the same area."

Hicks raised his eyebrow again, but smiled slightly.

"Done. I neglected to mention that you may be required to perform other important duties as well as piping and drumming. You will be trained as stretcher bearers and instructed in field dressing techniques," Hicks said. "Now if there is nothing else, gentlemen, I request your presence in my tent at seventeen hundred hours this eve, and bring your equipment. Until then, Corporal O'Reilly here will assign you your tent. Good day."

We snapped back to attention and saluted our commanding officer. He returned the salute and exited the area limping along with his cane.

≈

The leprechaun–Corporal O'Reilly–turned out to be a decent fellow and escorted us to our respective tents giving us an in-depth tour along the way. We pipers settled into one tent and the drummers in another. Even though pipers would fight to defend their drummers, and vice-versa, there existed a playful riff between the two groups. We would constantly lob friendly insults at each other. Off-color references about one's familial lineage or mental capacity were simply forms of endearment.

The accommodations were meager and the tents seemed oddly colder inside than out. The British military had provided a small coal stove in the center of each tent with a pipe going up through the roof. It was wholly inadequate and threw off only enough heat to warm something within one foot of it.

As we later learned, it was valuable for heating a pot of tea and could dry out a pair of soggy hobnailed boots by morning if the boots were placed close enough. We could also put a basin of water on it to provide warm water for shaving and washing.

The fact remains that "the little stinkers," as Dan McKee called them, were better than nothing at all and could operate on just a handful of coal or coke. Our uniform was that of the 48th Highland of Canada and of course, we were kilted.

It would have been difficult to get the men to follow a piper who was not wearing a kilt. The 48th's tartan, Stewart of Fingask, was overall red with cross hatch blue and green, white and yellow. It could be easily seen by the men on the battle field. Unfortunately, it was also easy to pick out by the enemy.

There was also the practicality issue of a kilt in the battle field, especially when one was "regimental," or without undergarment. Sliding bum first down a muddy trench would instantly enlighten most kilt enthusiasts as to their short comings. Nonetheless, the true Scots and descendants of Scots believed that the kilt was the dress for battle and that it gave the wearer an ancient aura of distinction.

As day one at East Sandling training camp was closing rapidly, Terry was sitting on his cot oiling his drones with bore oil and glancing periodically at his pocket watch.

"He said seventeen hundred hours... that's five-thirty, right?" Terry asked anyone who might be listening. Civilians don't think in a 24 hour clock.

"That's what I heard," Sean said while lying on his cot looking vacantly at the tent roof. I smiled to myself at Terry's impatience. In the next tent, I could hear the drummers working on some routines, tapping their sticks in unison on various pieces of wood.

George Cohen was wrapping hemp around the stocks of his drones in an effort to stem the leakage of air from his bag. Hemp is a thin string that pipers use to wrap the chanter base, blow pipe base and all the drones where they go into the bag. I was working on a tune with my practice chanter, an instrument that looks and sounds like that of a snake charmer. It has a soft reed and creates a fraction of the noise of a highland bagpipe chanter. The tune was "Tumbledown Mountain," a snappy four-part jig that had a fair degree of difficulty because of the number of embellishments throughout.

I should explain that because the bagpipe is a continuous wind instrument, pipe music includes embellishments to create separations between the notes and enhancing the tune overall.

D-throws and doublings, taorluaths, grips, strikes, and leumluaths are just a few of these embellishments known as grace notes. They all consist of a series of rapid finger movements which must be performed in a precise manner and, if executed correctly, can provide the necessary nuances that create and make a tune.

"Slow down your taorluath, Ian. You're blurring it," Terry said, as I continued to practice the tune. I took his advice without objection and practiced my taorluaths over and over again with greater deliberation.

≈

"It's time to go to the commander's tent," Terry finally announced loudly, while looking at his pocket watch for the last time. We all stopped what we were doing, including the drummers in the next tent, and gathered up our equipment for the meeting with Hicks.

The sun was dropping in the southwest sky and the camp was becoming cooler by the minute as we marched over to Commander Hicks' tent with our pipes and drums. The camp was alive with men milling about chatting and smoking outside their tents. They were waiting for the dinner bell which would not sound for another half hour and were killing time.

"Hey, how about a tune?" someone shouted, while others chimed in as we walked by them.

"We've got to see the commander first. We'll play later," Terry shouted.

As we approached Hicks' tent we could see him standing out front craning his neck to observe our progress.

"Come in gentlemen," he said, moving inside as we neared. "I realize it's a little late for Tea, but I took the liberty of having our cook set up some with crumpets. I also have some brandy for those who prefer some spirit."

I noticed Bill and Dan eyeing the brandy and ignoring the pot of tea and plate of crumpets.

"Thank you for your hospitality Commander, hot tea would be just the ticket to take the chill off," Terry said.

We poured ourselves some tea and helped ourselves to crumpets. Both Dan and Bill showed great restraint in following Terry's lead and did not head straight for the liquor.

It was purely a social visit that Hicks wanted and he kept it that way by steering the conversation away from politics and the war. It was, however, an inevitable topic as we all continuously pressed him on his experiences in battle.

He acquiesced, finally, and in a low monotone voice began to recount his experiences on the Western Front. Staring blankly at the ground he rambled on about the unthinkable carnage. He made it clear that through no actions of his own he came out of the battle alive.

"I piped my platoon over the top only to watch the lion's share of my men drop before they got fifty feet. Each wave of men ran into German machine gun fire, charging over the bodies of their fallen comrades only to fall themselves fifty feet closer," he said. "Wave after wave advanced fifty feet at a time leaving most of them dead in the process until one of our Grenadiers took out the nest with a well-placed bomb."

A grenadier was the name for a man trained in throwing a grenade. It was later changed to "bomber" at the insistence of the Royal Grenadiers.

We all sat motionless, fixed on this man as he walked us through his own valley of the shadow of death. We were almost afraid to breathe. Hicks' voice weakly cracked as he explained that at the end of the day the British gave back all their ground to a massive German counter attack. The commander's eyes welled up as he stopped talking and took a heavy sigh.

"Somehow I was spared," he said softly, his head hung down as he sat staring at the tent door. Hicks shook his head as if to clear those thoughts from his mind and faced away from us.

"I believe a brandy is in order gentlemen," he said regaining his composure. We reverently stood and joined him in a toast to his brave lads gone west. There was no talk of glory and adventure, only the realities of the battlefield from a man who knew. We were all touched by his reluctant recounting of his experience and did not pursue any further information regarding the subject.

"Now, gentlemen, if you will indulge an old piper and your commander, I request the honor of joining you in several tunes for the camp before dinner," Hicks said with a soft grin.

Happy to escape the somber environment that had developed, Terry gladly accepted his request and we pipers went outside to tune. The drummers stayed inside the tent to make another run on the crumpets and brandy.

"Leave me enough for a bedtime nip," Hicks warned with a smile.

Whenever you tune pipes, it is impossible not to attract attention, and the inevitable crowd began to mill about waiting for the entertainment to start.

"Front and center, drummers!" Terry commanded in his loud and clear parade voice. The drummers ended their attack on the liquor and snacks and clambered outside with their equipment.

Hicks glanced at Terry and said, "You have command ability, son, I see officer in your future."

Terry puffed up slightly but pretended to ignore the comment. "Circle up!" he called.

The crowd was quite large and growing by the second. Hicks suggested we march over to a large field near the mess tent to better accommodate the number of men amassing. We formed up a line, two abreast, and marched out to the command of Pipe Major Terry Manning.

Hicks gimped along in the line without aid of his cane, but I could tell he marched with considerable pain.

The crowd parted as we marched to the clearing and then followed us until we circled up again. Terry called the band ready. "'Scotland the Brave,' 'Rowan Tree,' and 'Cockney Jocks,'" he ordered. "By the center, quick, march!"

The bass drum banged, the snares rolled, the pipers struck in the drones and the crowd went wild. Any pain that Hicks had been feeling was now gone, he was in the piper's trance and getting high on the opium of a cheering crowd. It turned out that Commander Don Hicks was quite an accomplished piper and despite his pain kept up with us younger pipers. We played for three-quarters of an hour before we were saved by the bell–the mess bell.

Terry called pipes down and dismissed the band for dinner. The men were fired up and the mess was loud and raucous. We all sat at the commander's table. It was the same food as the rest but it was an honor nonetheless.

That evening, as we turned in, I couldn't stop thinking about Don Hicks' vivid account of his horrific experience at La Bassee. I had never heard of such senseless slaughter and the realization that I had been so naive about war was now haunting me.

≈

Reveille came too early and we all scrambled out of our cots and into our uniforms as quickly as our early morning clumsiness would allow. We were ordered to fall in and were marched out past rows of tents onto a large field.

It was still quite chilly, maybe ten degrees Celsius, and the early morning darkness provided no hope of warmth yet. We formed up in huge lines, maybe fifty men in each and at least ten rows deep. Five hundred bleary-eyed men lined up for calisthenics at four thirty could not exist without plenty of grumbling. That grumbling was extinguished by the loud shouts of our drill sergeants who insisted on making us do this exercise called a squat thrust, among others. You would bend down, put your hands on the ground before you, thrust your legs out as to be parallel to the ground and then reverse the process to a standing position. It was an unsettling exercise for those that were kilted because inevitably you would be mooning the row of men behind you, which would conjure up any number of reactions from the groans of disgust to whistles or cat calls.

Most of us were in good physical condition and the morning exercises were not much of a challenge. However, George Cohen, our med student piper, was not very physically fit, having come from a well to do family that considered manual labor to be beneath their class and status.

George's lack of enthusiasm and inability to perform the exercises quickly caught the attention of our loud and very angry drill sergeant, Sergeant Balls. Yes. Balls. Perhaps his name was the source of his endless anger. Not knowing his first name, we decided it must be "Harry" and referred to him as such among ourselves.

"Sergeant Harry Balls" would root out weak soldiers and hound them mercilessly, pushing them to the mental or physical breaking point. Public humiliation was his favorite pastime and George Cohen was his favorite victim. I suppose that one could make a case that Balls was just trying to weed out those that were unfit for the battlefield or that he was trying to make better men out of all of us, but I believe he simply enjoyed bullying people and abusing his authority.

He would routinely reward George's poor performance with K.P. or latrine duty. Latrine duty was particularly bad because the latrine was simply a multi-holed outhouse and could get rather messy. Every week new holes would have to be dug and the old ones filled in with lye and dirt.

Balls badgered George relentlessly, until one day after a particularly ruthless dressing down in front of the men, Dan McKee decided to take action. Dan had become fond of George's dry sense of humor and easy-going demeanor and was weary of Balls' attacks on his friend.

As we were all on the practice field, bayoneting German scarecrows and belly crawling under barbed wire, Big Dan told Sergeant Balls that his presence was needed in the latrine to break up a scuffle between two men. Bill Lewis and Sean Lyons were nowhere to be seen, which led me to believe that something was afoot. Several minutes later, Balls returned a pale and shaken shadow of his former self. The training seemed smoother for George after that day and Balls noticeably kept his distance from our little group. I queried Dan on several occasions, but he insisted that nothing out of the ordinary and taken place, so I left it alone.

One evening on leave, Bill Lewis and I were on our fourth pint of ale at the local pub, when I asked him about that day. The beer had loosened the lock of secrecy and he explained how Dan, Sean and he had grabbed Balls, flipped over the cover to the latrine pit and held him by his ankles over the hole. Dan then calmly explained that he was going to be in deep shit if he didn't lay off George Cohen. He was held aloft over the stinking pit until he agreed to all the conditions required by Dan. I was mid-swallow and spit out a full gulp of beer when Bill revealed the truth about that day. He pounded me on my back as I coughed uncontrollably and said, "You didn't hear that from me."

As I slowly regained my ability to breath, I glanced up toward the bar and noticed Dan McKee giving us a sideways look, with a knowing smirk on his face.

LEAVING EAST SANDLING

We Canadians had somehow been mistakenly thought of by our British counterparts as an unruly lot of rascals with an overly developed affection for alcohol and an inability to follow orders well. We had, however, proven on the field of battle that we were ruthless, fearless fighters who the British were quite happy to have on their side. Because of our proven battlefield merits, our shortcomings were overlooked or, at least, tolerated.

Terry Manning was still very enthusiastic about putting the training behind us and getting down to the business of war and he let Commander Hicks know it regularly. Hicks, after some consideration, had decided to accommodate Terry's request. After all, we were already accomplished pipers and drummers, and we quickly mastered the requirements of stretcher bearing and field dressing.

The British Expeditionary Forces were hungry for men and the pipers and drummers continued to be of special interest. It appeared that our small group was going to see the Western Front. Hicks had made clear to us that we were going to be split into two groups consisting of two pipers and one drummer. Our orders would direct us to the regiments that required our services on the Front.

It was mid-June 1916 and the weather had been more hospitable than normal. East Sandling and, in fact, all of England was lush and green and for the last several weeks had been enjoying what could only be described as delightful conditions.

The drummers were grumbling about Terry's insistence on an early departure as they were enjoying the fine weather, but I could tell that they were every bit as ready to serve and were simply grumbling because they thought it was their obligation to maintain the drummer image.

When the orders were received Terry, George and Dan were assigned to the 1st Newfoundland regiment, part of the 29th Division of the British 4th Army. Bill, Sean, and I were going to join the 36th Ulster Division and be attached to a regiment upon arriving in France.

≈

On 24 June we joined a Battalion that was being sent to the coastal town of Seaford, England, where we were to board a troop transport to France to connect with our respective regiments.

It took the better part of a day to reach Seaford where we were billeted overnight in a large barn commandeered for just such a purpose. It was moderately comfortable but still smelled of livestock which bothered several of the men. To me it was a comforting smell that brought about a feeling of homesickness that I had not experienced up till then.

The next morning we marched to the docks, which was a thirty-minute undertaking. There, we were called by regiment for our ship assignments. Because we were not really attached to a regiment in Seaford we were assigned to the smallest group, which was in turn assigned to the smallest vessel. Out on a smaller dock sat our transport, The David Richard, a sixty-five-foot, single-engine steam freighter that was in dire need of a paint job and perhaps a good bottom scraping.

We made our way through the crowded front street and out to our ride along with the 140 other men, most of whom were either Scottish or Welsh and belonged to the British engineering division.

"Not quite The Olympic, eh?" Dan remarked as we neared the boat.

Terry looked warily at the old vessel and, with misgivings, simply responded, "Indeed not".

"Doc" George had gone on ahead of us all and was bombarding the boat's salty crew with a barrage of questions faster than they could answer.

"How long is the boat? When was she built? How many hours to cross the Channel? How many miles across is it?"

In an effort to save the crew from George's unending questions, Terry produced his pipes and interrupted. "I don't suppose you fellows would like to hear the pipes?" he called out.

"Hey, that would be grand!" one fellow replied, eager to get away from this inquisitive passenger and get back to work. One weather-worn crewman asked, "Do ya know The Black Bear, lad?"

"I do," Terry responded, "and it always sounds better when played after Scotland the Brave." The crusty old Scotsman cracked a smile on his leathery face exposing the fact that most of his teeth were missing and winked with a nod of appreciation at Terry's choice of tunes.

The crew seemed to liven up the pace as Terry played tune after tune and thirty minutes later we were shoving off. As lines were cast off, Terry played "The Skye Boat Song" and "The Highland Cathedral." Lovely, haunting lullabies that drifted across the entire harbor. For the short span of time that the tunes lasted, everyone, from crewman to passenger, seemed to stop and listen reflecting on the moment. The pipes carry well over water and have an almost mystical effect when combined with that element.

The David Richard steamed slowly out of the harbor and faded into the morning fog, ushered by two tunes that, sadly, would be played by Terry at the graves of hundreds of young men over the next several years.

≈

The straight-line distance from Seaford, England to Le Havre, France is approximately seventy-five nautical miles and with a smooth sea, the David Richard could maintain a modest ten knots making the "milk run" in a little over eight hours. Even though the weather was ideal, the Channel had continuous chop adding some time and discomfort to the crossing. The English Channel is very different from the Saint Lawrence River, which is all I had to measure it against. So I was somewhat surprised to find that you cannot see the French coastline from the shores of England, at least not from Seaford. The narrowest part of the Channel is twenty-one miles across up in Dover and on a clear day it is possible to see France! The Saint Lawrence, being my only reference as a waterway, has a modest current, but again, I was surprised to find that the Channel has no current.

"It's simply a body of water between Europe and England," one crewmember responded when George Cohen continued his incessant questions.

"Why don't we cross at Dover? This route is four times longer," I asked.

"Too close to the sub bases in occupied Belgium and we would be too easy a target up there," the crewman said. I think he was getting tired of the questions because he took a deep draw on a dirty old clay pipe and blew large a cloud of smoke at George and me sending us into coughing fits. When we caught our breath, he had moved up to the bow and was trying to look busy.

Terry, Sean, George, and I stood along the bow rail and let the cool breeze and light salt spray mesmerize us for quite some time. The morning sun was drying the salt spray quickly on our faces leaving an odd crispiness to our skin. It somehow felt natural.

"I should have joined the Navy," I said.

"Does Canada even have a Navy?" George asked.

I thought for a moment, but did not know the answer.

"I wonder how deep it is here?" George asked not waiting for an answer to his previous question.

Dan wandered up just in time to hear George's question and said, "Doc, if it's over your head, what does it matter?"

The drummers had been staying to the stern of the boat, and I believe a flask may have been keeping them occupied, but now the warmth of the mid-morning sun drew them forward.

≈

We were headed south-southeast into choppy two- to three-foot swells created mostly by passing vessels. In fact, the number of ships that were coming or going was astounding. Troop and supply ships of every conceivable size, Hospital ships marked with a large red cross and, of course, the patrolling British Navy, mostly Eclipse Class and Astraea Class cruisers.

Every few miles we would pass a Naval Ship slowly cruising with a large tethered observation blimp in tow. Men stationed in the blimps, which were several hundred feet in the air, could see the dark shadow of a sub a mile away and then the Destroyers would be alerted and a quick response would follow. The measures that the British Navy took were not excessive considering the remarkable success the German's were enjoying with their U-Boat attacks. The English Channel was, indeed, a target-rich environment for the enemy.

"Looks like a lonely job," Dan said as The David Richard slowly passed a ship with a blimp high above it.

"I'll bet he has a million dollar view," Terry said.

"How high do you think that thing is?" George asked.

"Always with the questions, eh Doc? Let's just say it's over your head," Dan said with a friendly smile.

≈

It was a slow crossing, but not a boring one and the time passed relatively quickly. About an hour and a half out of Le Havre we started to see the vague image of the French coast. As we drew nearer and the coast became clearer we could plainly see the beautiful bluffs and white beaches with no sign of the war anywhere. The pristine coastline was in stark contrast to the port city of Le Havre.

Like most points of commercial transfer, Le Havre was well used and had long ago lost any quaintness that it might have once possessed. The necessity of moving goods required a utilitarian environment and as a result the port had nothing more than that which was required. The waterfront buildings, which seemed far too close to the docks and harbor, were brick and stone and wore the soot of centuries of coal and wood smoke. The inner harbor was a madhouse of activity with local fishing boats motoring or sailing in and around the constant flow of transports.

I couldn't help but wonder why there weren't wrecks everywhere but, somehow through a maritime mutual respect, the vessels avoided collision. The larger ships moved to the southern end of the harbor for the deep water and the smaller ships, those with relatively shallow draft, went to the northern and older part of port.

The David Richard moved to the northern docks and the captain adeptly turned the boat hard to starboard in a turn into the dock. Then he reversed the engine of the single screw ship at just the right time, about three-quarters of the way through the turn, and the vessel snugged into the dock as pretty as you please.

The crew had moved into position on the bow and stern and cast out lines that the dockhands tied off. The David Richard was a well-oiled machine and we were duly impressed. We had not been invited by the commanding officer to disembark yet, so we waited and chit-chatted, watching the hustle and bustle of activity ashore.

A British officer stood on the dock with a large clipboard. He seemed to be of some importance because our commanding officer jumped ship and, after exchanging salutes, seemed to be getting a full briefing.

The officer was a rather tall man, around six feet, lean and fit with a strong jaw and a kind face. He was obviously all business, but seemed to carry out his orders without being officious to his fellow officer.

Our commanding officer returned to the ship with the officer and gave new orders to all men on board.

"Lieutenant Owen McDonnell will be directing deployment," he said. "You will follow his orders. Thank you."

"Short and sweet," Terry said under his breath.

"A man of few words," Bill agreed.

"Gentlemen, my name is Lieutenant McDonnell," the officer said. "Please listen carefully as I am not inclined to repeat myself. We should have one hundred-forty men from the British engineering division. You will please disembark the ship and follow Sergeant Kelly to my right."

A tall dark haired man had joined Lieutenant McDonnell and we assumed this was Sergeant Kelly. The Scots and Welshmen filed off in an orderly manner and disappeared as they followed Kelly.

"That leaves you six," McDonnell said looking at us. "Manning, Lyons, Macdonald, Cohen, Lewis and McKee, correct?" We nodded.

"Front and center men! Follow me!" McDonnell turned and walked down the dock. We grabbed our kits and instruments and clambered down the narrow gangplank to follow the lieutenant like a bunch of ducklings after the mother duck. He had a long stride and covered ground far more quickly than we could with our gear.

He turned and waited for us at the side of a four-story brick hotel. "How many pipers and drummers have we?" he asked.

"Four pipes and two drums, sir" Terry responded.

"Good. Two pipes and one drum will go the First Newfoundland Regiment, and the same to the 36th Ulster Division, of which I am a part."

It had been agreed upon sometime earlier that Terry, George and Dan would make up one group and Sean, myself and Bill would make up the other.

"I must say as an aside that we have needed some inspiration up front," McDonnell said, his voice betraying an Irish lilt that he had thus far done a good job of stifling. "It's been too long since the pipes have led us into battle. Ypres, last year, if my memory serves me. We had a total of five pipers, of which two were killed..."

I interrupted him. "You say you were at Ypres last April?"

"Yes, son, Hellfire Corner we called it. Why?"

"Did you happen to come across a runner by the name of Alan McDonald? He was with the Canadian First Division. He's my brother."

The lieutenant's expression turned into one of sympathy. "If you have not heard from him or received word about him, then I fear the worst. After all, we suffered three thousand casualties on 24 April alone and a total of six thousand by 3 May, mostly Canadian."

I deflated instantly. Bill drew near and put his hand on my shoulder, "We'll find him. Don't worry." I understood that Bill meant we'd find him alive, but he didn't say that exactly, and I didn't believe it exactly anyway.

McDonnell stiffened up and brought his clipboard around in front of him. "Manning, Cohen, and McKee. You will be going to the Newfoundland Division. There's a lorry waiting for you."

Sergeant Kelly had returned from directing the miners and was now available to insure that the lads found their way to the New-foundland Regiment.

"Kelly, if you would be so kind as to show these men to their transportation," McDonnell said. "You other three will be staying with me."

Our eyes all met as the reality hit that our small group was being split up. I knew, as did the others, that this could be the last time that we see each other, but no one seemed to want to be the first one to say good bye.

Finally, Dan stepped up to the plate and grabbed Bill by the arm. They embraced each other in a handshake that required both hands. I think that both men would have felt uncomfortable had they hugged, so their handshake seemed to become almost an embrace. We all followed suit with double-handed handshakes and exchanged quiet words of encouragement and promises of being reunited soon, a promise that we could only hope to fulfill. Then off they went following Sergeant Kelly. Only George looked back and waved.

≈

"Off we go lads," called McDonnell, interrupting the moment. He began to walk away briskly. Sean, Bill, and I followed him down the busy dock and up a narrow street off the waterfront.

"You fellows drink coffee?" McDonnell asked. We all nodded in an affirmative manor. "Good, you're in for a real treat, I know just the place."

Bill made some comment about the possibility of beer instead, which the lieutenant chose to ignore. We turned down a small alleyway where several tables and stools were parked on the sidewalk in no particular order. McDonnell turned into a little shop that smelled of sweet pastries and strong coffee.

"Bonjour, mademoiselle. Je voudrais quatre cafés, s'il vous plaît," McDonnell said, in what seemed to us to be quite good French. The young lady behind the counter seemed to understand his request. We were duly impressed.

The lady, thirty to thirty-five years old, was very attractive and flashed a broad smile directed at the Lieutenant, then she looked at us and raised her eyebrows while staring at our kilts with a slight smile. She soon produced four of the smallest cups of coffee I had ever seen, about a quarter of the size of a normal cup. The dark liquid in the cups seemed to be thicker than most coffee and had a strong roasted aroma that you could almost taste. "Merci," McDonnell said, tossing two francs on the counter.

"How much is that in Canadian money" I asked.

"I think that's equal to a little over one dollar," he said.

"Holy smokes!" Sean blurted. "How can anyone afford to drink coffee at those prices, especially when the cups are so tiny?"

"This is espresso—very strong. I think you'll find it's all the coffee you'll need. Take my word for it," McDonnell said.

Bill dropped a couple of cubes of sugar into his small cup, added some cream, and took a sip. "Wow! That's strong!" he announced. He smiled showing as many teeth as possible. "Have any of my teeth rotted off?"

We all laughed at his joke and cautiously sipped our coffee. It was indeed the strongest cup of coffee I'd ever had and it packed a good punch, too. The smooth, rich coffee kicked in right away and I felt that everyone, including myself, was talking and moving faster as the caffeine sped into our bodies, increasing our metabolism instantly.

Lieutenant McDonnell began to explain what was in store for us in the near future. "Gentlemen, you are going to be welcomed into the 36th Ulster Division and, although you are not Irish, I know my men will treat you all as part of our group."

"Why are we not with the Canadians or the Scots? Why the Irish?" Sean asked, not because he had a problem with the Irish, but because he was curious.

McDonnell's eyebrow lifted "You were won in a game of cards," he said frankly.

"To the victor goes the spoils," Bill said idly.

"Exactly" McDonnell said. "You fellows are a scarce commodity. Most of your fellow Canadians are still defending the Ypres salient and you are bound for Haig's big push. There was a question as to who would get the pipes and drums, so it was settled that a friendly game of chance would determine who was the lucky regiment. Perhaps you've heard of the Luck of the Irish? Well, much to the chagrin of several pompous British officers, the Irish luck prevailed."

"You said something about a big push? What's that?" Sean asked.

"Douglas Haig, Commander of the British Expeditionary Forces, has come up with a plan for a major offensive in the Somme Valley. Word has it that there will be thirteen British and eleven French divisions arriving within the week. The intention is to push the Germans back and break through the Western Front," McDonnell explained. "The Germans have been pounding Verdun with a vengeance for weeks and Haig believes that because of the resistance by the French, the Huns will be forced to draw troops away from the Somme area in an effort to fulfill their threat to 'bleed France white.'"

≈

We had all finished our espresso and knew that any more than one would have been too much, so we all stood after McDonnell had briefed us and left the shop. We were lucky enough to be billeted in a small hotel called "de Hotel Vert". The hotel had ten small rooms and all three of us bunked in one of them. There was one large bed and a cot. Sean and I took the bed and Bill happily snored away on the cot.

I was sleeping remarkably well when there came a rap on the door. "0600 hours men! Rise and shine, in fifteen minutes, we march."

We all jumped out of our bed things and strapped on our kilts that had been hanging neatly on the door to keep the pleats crisp. On went our hose, the hobnail boots, our puttee wraps and flashes. We tucked in our shirts, clipped up the sporran and chain, plopped our glengarry hats on our heads, used the chamber pot, and we were ready. We grabbed our gear and hustled down a narrow set of stairs into a crowded lobby.

The place was alive with uniformed men all moving toward the small front door and filtering out into the street. We had come to somewhat of a logjam at the bottom of the stairs and were unable to move due to the large volume of men.

In the midst of the crowd, we could see Lieutenant McDonnell barking out directions and trying to keep the masses moving. He spotted us and waved.

"Make way for the pipes and drums on the stairs," he shouted, and the sea of soldiers parted slightly allowing us to pass. McDonnell ushered us outside.

"I need you lads to help me assemble the men outside. If they hear the pipes, they will move faster into the street," he said. "How about 'Wearin' o' the Green?' That should awaken their Irish souls." Then he turned and marched back into the Hotel Vert to resume his directing duties.

Sean, who was still waking up, shrugged and said, "Let's tune up and play then."

Our hobnail boots were not well suited for the rounded tops of the cobblestone streets and we had to be somewhat careful not to slip and fall as we formed a three-man circle. We tuned quickly and began playing "Wearin' o' the Green" and "Wrap the Green Flag Around Me," and before you knew it the narrow street was teaming with Irishmen from the 36th Ulster.

The air outside was still cool from the night before, but the late spring sun had risen and was warming up the small city rapidly. Because the buildings crowded the sides of the narrow streets, there was a natural amplification of our small band which not only brought the men out for assembly, but also caused many of the local residents to throw open their window shutters and lean out to investigate the commotion.

After playing the set three times through, Sean stepped in and we stopped playing cleanly. After a second of quiet, the crowd erupted into appreciative cheering and hooting. We were all taken back slightly by the energetic response we received.

Bill leaned in and said, "Very passionate fellows, these Irish! Let's not play 'Scotland the Brave.'"

We smiled at each other realizing that the passion could be easily reversed to produce an angry mob. Sean suggested instead that we play "God Save the Queen," which made us burst out with laughter.

Lieutenant McDonnell strode over to us "Nice job boys! I do believe you've awakened the entire town. By the way it would be wise to avoid 'Scotland the Brave' and 'God Save the Queen' for this lot."

We were unnerved by the remarkable coincidence of his suggestion. He laughed and admitted that he had been trained to read lips
as an operative in MI-6, the military branch of the Secret Service.

Getting serious once again, he said, "Men, we will be marching
these new members of the 36th Ulster twenty-five miles today. Every
half-hour you'll be expected to play some tunes, about ten minutes
worth. Lewis, you will be expected to keep a street beat the entire
time. Single taps to the left foot will suffice when you tire. Every two
hours, we will take a fifteen minute break for water and personal
needs, after which we will form up and continue, understood?"

"Yes, sir" we replied in unison.

"You will be responsible for calling cadence and setting the pace,
a steady three-mile per hour march will do. You are their band and
they know it, they have been trained well and will follow your lead,
so let's form up!" McDonnell saluted, then turned and walked over
to speak with some fellow officers.

There were over five hundred men in the street forming up behind us. My heart was pounding heavily in my chest as I looked at
this mass of men forming up behind us to follow our command. It
was a huge responsibility, but Sean showed no sign of trepidation.

Then I realized something very important that was missing,
something we needed to know. I called over to Sean. "Where the
heck are we supposed to be going?" I asked. "Shouldn't we know
that?"

Sean looked at me slightly stunned at the realization. "I have no
friggin' idea," he said. "I'll ask."

McDonnell laughed openly when Sean asked about directions.
"Not to worry lad I'll be marching off to the right of you when we
come to an intersection. I'll un-shoulder my Lee Enfield and hold it
horizontally, waist level, pointing it in the direction that I want you
to go, I'll keep us on track. I've marched this route many times." Sean
returned and shared the comforting information with us.

≈

Soon it was time to go. McDonnell's face went stern and he began to bark out commands at the top of his lungs.

"Form up, troops! Form up! Five to a Line! Behind the pipes and drum! Three pace separation! Step to it!"

To be heard above the chatter and bustle of five-hundred men was quite a feat, but remarkably his voice carried above all the other noise. The men responded quickly and quieted down immediately, it was clear that they respected this man and were willing to follow his command without reservation.

In less than a minute, the troops were lined up five abreast and spaced properly one hundred lines deep. McDonnell returned to the front of the formation, off to the right of Sean. Sean was on my right, which was proper for the Pipe Major.

"Well, then, they're ready Pipe Major. Make your commands loud and clear," McDonnell said.

Sean suddenly took on a serious air. He took a deep breath and loudly hollered. "Mark time by the rolls! Step off to the street beat! By the right, quick, march!"

Bill performed three rolls on his snare drum. As he did, the whole formation began to march in place, marking time. Then another three rolls, followed by the street beat, and the entire group stepped off in unison, left foot first, to begin a march from which many would never return.

With McDonnell to our right holding his Enfield forward at a forty-five degree angle, we began to play a set consisting of "The Minstrel Boy," "Wearin' o' the Green," and "Kelly, the Boy from Kellan." Five hundred men in a thousand hobnailed boots pounded the cobblestone streets, echoing throughout Le Havre as we exited the port town. It was a spectacular moment. We felt invincible.

As we left the city and entered the countryside of France, we got down to the mundane business of marching. Between our playing every half hour, there was not much to do except admire the lush beauty of rural France and think. Out in the open countryside on dirt roads, the noise of the marching men was diminished and I could hear the chirping of sparrows and the laughing of farm children as they chased each other in a game of tag.

I looked around at the rolling hills, no smoke, no sound of artillery. No sign of war. An old man stood aside a stone wall with a cane steadying himself. He came to attention as best he could, holding a long salute as we passed. I wondered what war he had been in that gave him his obvious appreciation for the sacrifices yet to come by our passing group.

I was thinking far too much. Perhaps if the war was closer, the marching would be lessened and I wouldn't have as much time for pondering.

My thoughts were interrupted by the sound of engines coming up from behind.

The honking of an air horn from the first lorry sounded like the warning of an angry goose, as the driver came up on our left. It was a convoy of lorries filled with crates and provisions bound for the Front. Most of the trucks had field cannons in tow, that looked to me to be perhaps thirteen or eighteen pounders. I could never tell the difference.

Several lorries in the rear of the convoy were ammunition caissons and were kept about fifty yards apart from the convoy and each other. I noticed that most of the ammunition drivers seemed tense. The last one, however, seemed nonchalant and relaxed. As he drove by, I saw Dan, Terry, and Doc with stupid grins, saluting us as they sat on boxes of explosives. Sean and I looked at each other to verify that we hadn't just imagined the scene. Bill continued to pound out the street beat. He looked straight ahead and simply said, "Idiots!"

McDonnell had also seen them. "You know those fellows?" he asked

"Yes, sir," Sean said. "They're also pipes and drum players. They are friends of ours."

"Oh, yes," McDonnell said. "I do remember them from the dock. They should have chosen a less hazardous ride and someone should have taught them how to properly sit when wearing the kilt."

"I believe that was intentional, sir," Sean said.

Another convoy was approaching from the rear. They came dangerously close to our marching men, but somehow avoided hitting anyone. Again they had field cannons in tow, but this time two or three guns were attached to one another.

These guns, when being used in battle were generally pulled by teams of horses. The animals were far better suited for the rough terrain of the battlefield and were more versatile than a lorry or tractor under those conditions. Horses were taken to the front mostly by rail, so as to insure that they would be in top condition when needed.

We had been told at East Sandling that the outer trenches were large and could accommodate a team pulling field guns at a full gallop. They would regularly drill the artillery units in training trenches and I must say that it was thrilling to watch them pounding through the gullies flailing mud and dirt in every direction at break neck speed.

Our drill instructor had told us the ability to shift field artillery from one position to another was critical and could alter the outcome of any battle. "They're always good for a show," the D.I. would say with a snaggle-toothed grin.

"Good for a show," I repeated as my thoughts popped out of my mouth.

"That's right" McDonnell said. "They're headed for the big show."

PART FIVE

TOWARD THE SOMME

The 1st Newfoundland Regiment

[Transcribed from Ian MacDonald's recording]

Terry, Dan, and Doc had been assigned to the 1st Newfoundland Regiment. However, "The First" had started the 25-mile march a day earlier. So, the three men were put up in a small hotel for the night and had orders to report the next morning to the transportation coordinator to get a lift to the 1st Newfoundlanders.

Left on their own for the evening, the lads felt that some exploration was in order. It was not so much their desire for local knowledge as it was their thirst for beer that motivated them. At 1800 hours (6 p.m.), they set out on this quest for beer. It didn't take very long before they stumbled upon a sidewalk café where people were chatting and drinking. They decided to make this their first stop. It was a small café with flower pots hanging outside and wrought iron chairs and tables on the sidewalk.

The three men grabbed an empty table and sat down carefully so as not to wrinkle the pleats on the back of their kilts. A garçon quickly appeared and took their order, having no problem with the English language.

When the beer came, the garcon asked for payment. "Six francs, s'il vous plait," he said.

"That's about a buck-and-a-half," Doc said. They were shocked at the price of beer. Saddened by the realization that, at these prices, a soldier could never afford to become inebriated, they resolved themselves to a short night.

The waiter saw the long looks on their faces and suggested they try the house wine at one franc for three glasses. Canadians are instinctively good with math and can smell a deal a mile away, so they switched to wine and the evening was snatched from the clutches of defeat.

As the three went from café to café and countless conversations with locals they learned more about their host city. They were informed that a cliff separates the city into two halves, the upper and lower city. The city was founded in 1510 and became a major port of trade. The literal translation of Le Havre is "the harbor". It is situated at the mouth of the Seine River and opens into the English Channel.

Because it was built in the 16th century, the streets were narrow and not well suited for modern motor lorries, so the front street of the harbor, being wider than most, became the road that was most heavily traveled. All of this information and more was being accumulated along with plentiful amounts of wine and food. Sadly, what none of them could know at that time was that 28 years later Le Havre would be completely destroyed in the assault on Normandy in 1944, leaving nothing standing of the ancient city.

A corporal rapped on their door at 0700 hours announcing the time and that a mess would be provided between 0730 and 0830 at the Front Street military depot. Doc sat up and groaned, lying gently back down holding his head. Terry had the same sort of reaction, but big Dan McKee seemed to be impervious to the morning after effects of copious amounts of wine.

"Let's go Eh, it'll do you some good to get some coffee and chow into your gullets," he said.

"I bought the wine yesterday, so why am I paying for it again today?" Terry complained as he carefully climbed out of his cot. He found the washbasin and poured a large portion of the water pitcher over his head. The Doc produced some aspirin and the three men tossed back two pills each and set off to breakfast.

The B.E.F. had set up a large tent with rows of tables and benches. At one side of the tent was a long table with the cooks on one side and the soldiers on the other side being served breakfast. The order of the day was scrambled eggs, a side of bacon, toast and porridge. There were also several large pots of coffee and tea.

Just the smell of cooking bacon seemed to make one hungry, so they quickly moved into the queue and loaded up with food. After a good breakfast, they were indeed feeling better and all agreed that the next move was to find the transportation depot before they were listed as AWOL.

≈

Dan took the lead in asking directions and before too long they were at the supply depot. A very officious corporal, who seemed to be in charge, or at least in the know, studied their orders and informed them that there were two convoys leaving in one hour. He said they should hop on one of the motor lorries carrying provisions bound for Bolbec, a city about 25 miles northeast.

"How do we find the 1st Newfoundland Regiment?" Terry asked, feeling much better than he did two hours earlier.

"My paperwork indicates that they are attached to the 88th brigade of the 29th Division, and that they will be moving out by rail this evening. Simply ask someone when you get to Bolbec for the 88th Brigade of the 29th Division," the corporal said dismissively.

Dan McKee leaned across the desk of the corporal and said in a low growl, "Write it down on a piece of paper."

The corporal looked up at the big figure hovering over his desk and took a dry gulp, his Adam's apple slid conspicuously up and then down. He quickly grabbed a piece of paper and a fountain pen and scribbled out the necessary information handing it briskly to McKee.

Next Dan, who had not moved, said, "Point in the direction of the convoy."

The corporal rapidly raised his arm and pointed in the general direction. Dan smiled a broad grin beneath his full mustache and patted the corporal on the head as he would a good dog. Then the three all turned and left the silent corporal allowing him to regain his composure.

≈

Down near the docks the convoys were being loaded by hand which required hundreds of men armed with hand trucks and strong backs. There was one fellow standing in the middle of the loading area with a clipboard in his hand yelling out orders to men as they wheeled crates past directing them to deliver their load to the correct lorry. It was a chaotic scene that was somehow being organized by this supply depot maestro.

Terry decided that they should stay out of the way until the activity subsided a bit so as not to disrupt the work in progress. For half an hour the men sat on three crates that were being ignored until the maestro, after craning his neck around and standing on a small box suddenly stared right at the three kilted soldiers.

"There they are! Bloody hell! I've been looking for those crates for 20 minutes." He quickly verified his statement by checking the numbers on the crates with the numbers on the clipboard. The trio hopped off the boxes as a swarm of men with hand trucks charged toward them.

"Put them in Lorry #107 men," the maestro ordered.

"Hey!" Dan yelled above the noise of the depot. "What lorry do you want us in?"

The load maestro looked puzzled for a moment. He glanced at his clipboard, then back at Dan. "Who are you and why would I want you in one of my lorries?"

"We're attached to the 1st Newfoundland Regiment and have orders to hop your convoy in order to catch them in Bolbec before they move out tonight," Terry volunteered.

"I have room in the rear two lorries of the second convoy. I must warn you, however, these vehicles are designed to carry boxes, not men, so it will not be a comfortable ride."

The Maestro then looked at his clipboard, made some notes with his pencil, and turned his attention back to directing the loading of his convoys.

The three friends fetched their equipment and made their way to the second convoy in search of their ride. A total of ten trucks were lined up, the last two were spaced about 100 feet back from the rest with the same distance between them. Each lorry had two eight-pound field cannons, in tandem, between them. They approached the fully loaded Lorry #112, the next to the last in the line, and noticed that no one was aboard.

"Let's make ourselves at home," Dan suggested. They threw their things in the back on top of stacks of crates and proceeded to build a more comfortable riding environment by laying out bedrolls and backpacks.

Then a voice came from the driver side of the lorry. "Ello? Wot 'ave we 'ere?" An unshaven, scruffy-haired head was peering over the boxes at the lads. The driver. He smiled at them and exposed a mouth full of crooked yellow teeth.

"Makin' comfy, eh?" His cockney accent was almost undecipherable. "Make 'er comfy, bumpy, not too lumpy." The driver continued to expose his snaggly smile.

The cockney often speak in rhymes and often the rhymes are abbreviated to just the last words in the rhyme. This makes it almost impossible to understand the meaning unless you're cockney. For example, "Make 'er cumfy, bumpy, not too lumpy" could eventually be abbreviated to "not too lumpy," meaning make yourselves comfortable.

Doc smiled back, shrugged his shoulders and said, "Thanks." The other two asked what the driver said.

"I have no idea, but he seemed happy, so I just said thanks," Doc confided.

The driver diverted his attention to a large man in coveralls that was standing in the front of the truck.

"Neutral!" he yelled to the large man, confirming the truck was not in gear.

"Crank 'er " the driver yelled as he pulled the choke to the full on position. The large crank-man grabbed the engine crank and with one mighty yank, spun the Renault six cylinder engine to life. The driver eased off on the choke and the engine clattered and ticked at a comfortable idle RPM, while producing a faint cloud of blue smoke rising up between the floorboards. The driver then squeezed the large rubber ball on the end of the air horn, signaling to the cranker that all was well. The large man moved on to the next truck.

The driver was diligently checking his equipment, first the oil pressure gauge, then he pulled back on a large emergency brake lever located outside the cab on his left side and ratcheted back to the full on position. He then shifted the truck into first gear with a noticeable amount of grinding and gently let up on the clutch, the engine began to bog down as the lorry tried to move with the brake holding fast. Satisfied that the emergency brake was functioning as well as could be expected, he was ready to move out with the rest of the convoy.

"Ang on, lads," he yelled. "'iss ain't no breed'n Rolls."

"We're ready," Terry responded. The driver popped a half chewed unlit cigar into his mouth, ground the Renault into first gear and let out the clutch. The lorry lurched forward. The cockney double-clutched the truck into second gear with far less grinding and the lorry picked up speed in order to keep up with the convoy that was already well ahead.

The Renault, like many trucks of its time had almost solid rubber tires and no shock absorbers, so when run over the cobblestones of Front Street, it provided a ride that could only have been rougher had steel wagon wheels been used instead of the rubber.

The crates hopped with every large bump and shifted unsteadily as the lorry moved through town. The three passengers eyed the stacks of crates waiting for the poorly secured cargo to tumble.

"What's in the crates?" Terry asked as he steadied one crate.

"Flyin' pigs, mostly," the driver called back over his shoulder. Terry assumed it was more cockney jibberish.

"What is it again?" he asked, hoping for a different, more recognizable answer.

"Rum jars, toffee apples 'n flyin' pigs," the driver reiterated flatly.

"Did you say, rum? Mind if we crack a jar for the road?" Dan asked.

The driver craned his neck around with his eyes wide open – "If you wanta blow us all to 'ell! Bloody 'ell, do I look like a bleedin' wet nurse? Toc, Emma, flyin' Pigs–trench mortars!" he accentuated the trench mortar part.

It was common on the western front to employ trench slang for everything from toilet paper to ammunition. Soldiers often used the alpha numeric system in reference to items, for example, Able, Baker, Charlie stood for A, B, C, and so on. The trench mortar was abbreviated to TM, or Toc Emma.

The three immediately tensed and considered jumping off, even at 25 miles per hour. The driver glanced back and saw the concerned looks on their faces.

"No need to fret, gents. I bin transportin pigs for o'r a year and I kin say wifout reservation, none 'ave blown yet," he said. "In fact, it's almost unnerd of – it's bloody 'ard 'nuf to get 'em to pop off when we lob 'em at Fritz."

He broke into a roaring laugh at his attempt at humor. The fellows weren't terribly amused with or comforted by his joke.

"Well," Doc said, "I suppose if he's made it this long without blowing up, the odds are he and we will probably make it this time too."

It was the sort of statement that was meant to be reassuring, and the others nodded unconvincingly. Then the lorry hopped over a rut sending the crates of ammunition up and down with a crash, fraying the nerves of the three passengers and dashing whatever meager confidence had been building.

The Convoy was passing a division of foot soldiers ahead and swerved to the side of the road honking their horns to alert the columns of men of their passing.

"Wha?" the driver cried out, "A bleedin' pipe band, I'll be flogged!"

Terry peered over the crates and out the front windscreen, and saw that it was Sean, Ian and Bill Lewis leading the 36th Ulster Division.

"I'll be a friggin' farmer," Terry said. "It's our classmates! Let's give them the business as we pass."

As the lorry passed the front of the division, the three sat on the back crates saluting. That in itself wouldn't have been much of a razzing, but they sat with one leg propped up on a crate and because they were all regimental, their family jewels were there for full inspection by their comrades. As they moved away, they began to laugh uproariously until they were almost pitched out the rear of the lorry as the Renault's hard tires found yet another rock on the road to Somme.

After what seemed like an eternity, the truck followed its convoy off the road and into a large encampment near the railyard of the town of Bolbec. The boys jumped out at the earliest possible opportunity, leaving the caisson without so much as a word to the driver.

"I hate long drawn out goodbyes," Doc chuckled as he put some distance between him and the ammunition truck.

"I need a stiff drink," Terry volunteered.

"Me too," Dan agreed, "but let's find home first." He spotted a military police officer nearby, easily recognizable by his red cap. "We'll see if carrot top knows anything."

The MP did know and helpfully pointed them in the direction of the 29th Division. "Look for The Blue Puttees," he said.

Although they had no idea what he meant by that statement, the three walked off in the direction he indicated. The encampment consisted of several large fields filled with hundreds of tents lined up in neat rows. It was obviously a well-organized and disciplined division, evidenced by the precision with which the entire camp was constructed.

Unknown to the three men was the fact that the year before this division had seen some of the hardest action against the Turks in Gallipolli. This battle-hardened group had sustained over thirty thousand casualties in that one fight alone and the mettle of the men in this encampment had been tempered by the flames of hell.

Before long, the boys located the 88th Brigade and the 1st Newfoundland regiment. The head of the regiment was Colonel J. P. Kelton, a tall, handsome man with dark hair and a full mustache. Because he was a head taller than most, he was easy to pick out of the throng of men. What made him and his regiment unique, however, was that they all wore legwraps, or puttees, fashioned from blue broadcloth instead of the standard issue khaki, hence the nickname The Blue Puttees.

"Not as bold as your kilt, but yes, it does stand out," Kelton said, noting the interest the men had in the puttees. "I'm Colonel J. P. Kelton and I'd bet you three are our pipes and drums." He had an easy confidence about him which translated into a natural leader.

"We are your band, albeit a small one," Terry said, saluting, along with Doc and Dan.

"Looks like I have some competition" Kelton said, sizing up big Dan.

"Dan McKee, sir! May I introduce Terry Manning and Dr. George Cohen!" The three snapped to attention.

"At ease, gentlemen. You will be just what the doctor ordered. The men have needed a morale booster since the Battle of Gallipolli, and your presence is most welcome," Kelton said. Then turning to George, he asked, "So you are a doctor?"

"Just a nick name sir," Doc said. I'm in med school back home."

"Ah, I see. I'll have some sappers pitch a tent next to mine. I plan on using your talents to the maximum and I know you will enjoy working for this regiment. A better group of men you'll be hard-pressed to find."

Kelton began to walk and the trio followed. "These are my quarters," he said stopping before a large tent. "Yours will be here and should be erected within the next twenty minutes. I would like you to play prior to evening mess at 1700 hours. After mess, we will prepare to move out at 2000 hours. We are expected to board a transport train bound for the Somme Valley Region."

"We're here to serve the regiment," Terry said.

"Very good. Now, if you'll excuse me, I have several meetings I must attend, so I'll see you three before mess. It is a pleasure to have met you." The three snapped to attention and saluted as Kelton went off to his meeting at a brisk gait.

A tent was erected in minutes for the pipers. It seemed odd to them to go to the bother of putting it up only to have to take it back down a few hours later, but such are the ways of the military. The accommodations were meager: cots and a small table with a wash basin.

They all washed up, cleaning the grime and dust from their rough trip earlier. Although their cots were calling for a nap, there wasn't much time to tend to the pipes before mess, so Terry and

Doc pulled out their pipes and moved outside to check out their equipment. Dan lay down, however, and was snoring before the others left the tent.

≈

The drones needed some hemping to tighten them up, so Terry ran the thin string through a wad of beeswax to insure the best seal and to protect the hemp from rotting. He then wrapped the loose stocks and tuning pins as necessary to provide the best performance for their pipes. Both men knew the routine well and they quietly went through the necessary steps for proper maintenance of the bagpipes.

The chanter reeds were not in tune so they corked off their drones and tuned up their chanters to match each other. Satisfied with the tuning, Terry moved behind George and tuned his drones and then tuned his own.

They played a couple of tunes to hear how they sounded together and, with the pipes warmed up and in tune, they were ready to perform for the mess.

Colonel Kelton heard the playing and had arrived in front of their tent smiling. "It sounds like our regiment won a fine band, indeed!" he said. "Let me introduce you to my fellow Newfoundlanders."

Dan appeared from his nap holding his drum and the three followed Kelton to the mess area. The men were milling about waiting for the mess call when Kelton called for the attention of his Regiment.

"Men, I know you have all heard of our good fortune in a friendly game of cards," he said. "Now, let me introduce you to our fine pipe and drum band! Privates Terry Manning, George Cohen and Dan McKee."

Terry, always one for reading the moment and a man of excellent timing, called out as if he were ordering a band of one hundred, instead of just three.

"Band Ready! Set One! By the center, quick March!"

Dan buzzed out the rolls, Doc and Terry struck in the drones playing an "E" and began to play the set. Terry was poised in a classic piper pose keeping time by lifting his left leg up and down and touching his toe on the ground to the down beat. It looked like it might have been a ballet move, but it was, in fact, the traditional way a pipe major telegraphs a song's tempo to his band when in a circle.

The reaction was both stunning and expected. The crowd went wild, cheering and yelling as the small band played "Minstrel Boy," "Scotland the Brave," "42nds," and "Maries Wedding." The men seemed to have completely forgotten about dinner and were calling for more entertainment when Col. Kelton stepped in and stopped the music.

"Men, we'll not keep the cooks waiting. I'm sure your pipe band will be available after mess." The good natured style of command that Kelton employed was one reason his men respected him and would follow him into hell if commanded. They noisily clambered over to the mobile kitchen to get their meal. All were in a better mood than they had been twenty minutes earlier.

Kelton smiled at the trio. "Well done, men. We have a new band and you have a new home." His face changed to a serious look "You'll be their inspiration. On the road to war you will be the beat and the tune that will keep the march at a good pace and the men in a good humor. On the battlefield, you will give them the nerve to go over the top and charge into certain death. If the pipes and drums play on, the men push on. You have a pivotal responsibility that can affect the outcome of a battle.

"And after all is said and done and the battle is over, you will play as we lay down those that have fallen," Kelton continued, staring sternly into the eyes of the three men. "You will play to honor their ultimate sacrifice and to provide solace to their comrades who remain to carry on. You will see happy faces and laughter as you entertain them, scared and unsure faces as you pipe them over and hard, tear soaked faces as you pipe their comrades under. Yours is not a task to be taken lightly, for it is an ancient honor that has seen countless wars for untold generations."

The trio stood silently for a moment taken aback by Keltons' words. Terry swallowed a dry gulp and said quietly, "We won't let you or the men down, sir."

Kelton smiled at the men. It was evident that these were good and brave volunteers who would do that which was asked of them. "By the way," he said in a lighter tone. "Even though the 1st Newfoundland Regiment is not a kilted regiment, I have always been fond of the kilt. I believe it adds an air of distinction and frankly, if you were to play in pants, it simply wouldn't look right. Now, let's eat!"

FIFTH CANADIAN GENERAL STATIONARY HOSPITAL AT AMIENS

Sheila Lougheed was changing the bandages on a young soldier in Recovery Ward 51. Ward 51 was one of many quickly constructed buildings that made up the 5th and at about one hundred feet it was twice as long as it was wide. It provided a modest amount of protection from the elements during inclement weather and had ample screened windows to allow cross ventilation in warm weather conditions. There were several free standing coal stoves with their smoke stacks going up through the roof. They could take the chill out of the air and keep the crowded building survivable in winter weather.

Ward 51 was close to the operating rooms, and in cold weather the surgeons and nurses would regularly visit to warm up between operations. Ether was commonly used in the OR as an anesthetic, and because of its explosive nature no stoves or flames of any sort were allowed in the vicinity. Fortunately spring was on its way now and on this day, the stoves were not needed.

The patient Sheila was tending to was a 23 year old man from Wales. His patient charts were hanging on a hook mounted at the foot of his bed and Sheila had made herself thoroughly familiar with the information.

"Douglas Patrick Waren," she read. "Protestant. Multiple lacerations to the legs, numerous burns on lower body."

She unwrapped the soiled bandages and replaced them with new ones. The wounds were improving each day. She took great care to swab the surrounding areas with alcohol and iodine. If the patient's wounds became infected, it would not be because of her poor attention. His condition was not grave and with the care of Sheila and the grace of God, he was expected to recover fully, at least physically.

Waren's wounds were fully due to a German mortar round nicknamed "Minnie," short for Minnenwarfer, the name of the manufacturer. The bomb landed in his trench killing five of his fellow infantrymen and injuring him and two others. The fragments that ripped through his legs had thankfully missed all major arteries and due to the quick actions of a field medic his loss of blood had been kept to a minimum. In fact, he lost far more blood on the operating table with the surgeons digging out the shards of metal than he did on the battlefield.

Young Douglas Patrick was awake and, despite his wounds and the pain from the removal of the dressings, his attention was focused on his attractive young nurse.

Sheila smiled as she worked on his wounds, she knew he was watching her and she marveled at the innate flirtatious nature of young men. It was actually a good sign and indicated that the patient was mentally and physically recuperating well.

As he watched her, Douglas said, "I have a castle in Wales called Caernarvon."

"You don't say," Sheila said casually.

"I do say," he said. "I'd love for you to be my princess and come home with me."

She flashed him a warm, playful smile. "I just accepted a proposal from King George, himself, an hour ago. I can't possibly disappoint his Highness for fear of losing my head."

He let out a loud laugh, "A good choice, he has far more gold than I."

She winked at him and moved on to the next patient. Sheila recalled what her ward doctor had told her one day as he watched her engage the injured men: "A pretty nurse is fine medicine." She knew she had to maintain her upbeat demeanor. She also knew that some men would never fully recover, while others would recover only to be sent out to the battlefield again. Everyday a new crop of wounded would replace those leaving; their bodies torn apart by war and then patched back together again just as those before them.

≈

Sheila had been in France nearly six months now. It didn't seem possible. When the fall semester had ended at Queens University, she had joined the nurse corps. After a short indoctrination, she was sped to the Western Front where her services were sorely needed.

Although she was remarkably outgoing and made friends with ease, she missed her pipers and drummers terribly. Several times a week Sheila would take time out to play her pipes for the patients, doctors, and fellow nurses. Entertainment was a scarce and valued commodity that would serve to take one's mind off of the ugly realities of war. It had a valuable recuperative quality that was totally lost on the head nurse who believed Sheila's playing to be completely unladylike and undignified.

At times the weight of caring for others who were so desperately damaged and whose young futures had been so irrevocably dashed was too much for her to bear. She would be overcome with deep despair. It was a feeling that would have prompted most other people to run away and cry, but Sheila was not one for tears. She would subdue these feelings by playing her pipes and dropping deeply into the pipers' trance. This would blank out everything around her as she totally immersed herself in her music.

≈

There were a total of one thousand beds in the 5th Canadian Stationary Hospital and, thanks to the relentless fighting on the western front, the beds were almost always occupied.

Infection and gangrene were the enemies of the severely injured. The doctors and nurses relied heavily on iodine, alcohol, sulphur, ointments and, most of all, the individual's healthy immune system. Antibiotics had not been discovered yet, of course, but had they been available they would have reduced the number of post battlefield deaths enormously. Ultimately it boiled down to the person's ability to recuperate and a cheerful nurse could only help.

Sheila worked with those that were recovering, but for those that were not expected to survive there was a select ward. It was a sad and horrible place, referred to as "the ward for the hopeless." As is inferred by the name, it was the place where those who had no chance for recovery were taken when nothing more could be done for them.

Most of the wounded in Ward 51 were acutely aware when an orderly came to wheel a patient out to that place. The ward always fell silent and somber as the unlucky man was being moved. God forbid, the patient was conscious because, if he were, he knew that his young life was soon to end. The look of desperation and fear on that patient's face as he was wheeled out would haunt all who witnessed his exit for the rest of their lives.

There were very few that would beat the odds and return from the ward for the hopeless, but, from time to time, it would happen. When one did it would provide a spark of hope to those being wheeled out of the recovery ward. The job of the nurses was to make those who "were being given up on" as comfortable as possible which usually meant morphine.

Morphine was widely and liberally used because, frankly, it worked. It would subdue the worst pain and provide a feeling of euphoria. The downside of the drug was that it would slow down the patient's metabolism and, if given in regular and sufficient amounts, could stop the respiratory system resulting in death. Since this was what was awaiting most of the men that entered that ward, the odds of the patient spontaneously recovering became even slimmer in as much as their natural ability to fight for life was compromised by the negative effects of the drug.

Morphine was commonly used by field medics to ease the agony of those who were wounded beyond the point of saving, a humanitarian practice that would allow the soldier to quietly slip away. Doctors, likewise, would look the other way and use the drug for "humane" purposes in the ward for the hopeless.

If Sheila had a dollar for every morphine shot she had administered, she could comfortably retire.

$$\approx$$

There was one patient with whom Sheila had become quite intrigued, almost infatuated with. He was a mystery and she loved a good mystery. Maybe in his mid-twenties, he was about six foot, quite handsome, and had a strong build. He had been in the 5th Canadian Hospital since they returned from Galipolli about a year earlier. Some of the senior nurses claimed that he was found in a convent near the front. The nuns had taken him in and nursed him along, but were unable to bring him out of the coma in which he persisted. After exhaustive care for many months and endless prayers, they realized that he was beyond their capabilities and alerted a nearby clearing station who promptly took charge of him.

He had been found in a trench and because he was thought dead his tunic and boots had been stolen. It was determine that he was a soldier for the commonwealth but his cold meat tags were gone so his identity remained a mystery.

The injury that had befallen him was a serious head wound and it was a miracle that he had survived at all. It had, however, rendered him completely unconscious in a semi-comatose state. He had stabilized in that persistent state with no improvement so the doctors

were inclined to focus their attention on those who were respond-
ing and all but ignored the mystery patient.

On two separate occasions he had developed a fever that was
thought to be due to infection so they put him in the ward for the
hopeless to die. But, because he was comatose, there was no need
to morph him up so his metabolism was not impeded by the drug.
Miraculously, he spontaneously recovered both times.

Sheila had taken interest in this fighter and spent much of her
free time tending to him. One doctor's observation to Sheila was
that his brain sustained damage but not so severe that he would
never recover. His reflexes and survival instinct gave hope. When
drink was put to his mouth he would swallow, when soft food was
spooned into his mouth he would ingest it and masticate with no
problem.

Sheila made him her project. She even named him "Bully" after
the canned beef issued to the B.E.F. He seemed capable of eating
massive quantities of the substance that most other patients and
soldiers complained about. In fact, his appetite was greatly responsible for his being alive at all.

Several of the concerns that must be addressed in dealing with a
non-ambulatory, bed-ridden patient are muscle atrophy, joint calci-
fication, and tendons tightening. The patient must be moved regularly. Their arms, legs, neck, and back must be moved through as full
a range of motion as is physically possible.

Sheila knew this and would work on Bully several times a day.
The regular movement of the young man also prevented bed sores
which could become quite severe in patients such as Bully. She
would even wheel his bed outside to provide him with some fresh
air and sunshine, often taking the opportunity to play the pipes for
the other patients while Bully was getting his sun and air.

One doctor had warned her about getting too involved with
any patient especially one with such a dismal prognosis. She knew
he was right, but couldn't seem to turn her back on this unknown
young man.

"He's somebody's son," she said in answer to the doctor's warnings.

As she was on break, deep in thought, and pulling and twisting Bully's arms and legs, a thought came to her.

"Perhaps I should have named you Lazarus," she muttered to him. "After all, you came back from the ward for the hopeless twice."

She flexed his wrists and fingers. "No. That would sound stupid. Lazarus. Who would want to be called Lazarus? Bully is better." She moved his head from side to side. She needed this man because he represented a spark of hope where despair, pain, and suffering were the norm. He had to recover. She was too deeply involved.

A doctor tapped her on her shoulder snapping her out of her thoughts. "A train of injured just arrived," he said. "They will be here any minute. We may need extra help in the OR and, most certainly, after they're patched together you'll be very busy."

"Thanks for the warning," she said in an uncustomarily cheerless voice. "Did you inform Sister Kathleen?"

"I was hoping you would take care of that for me," he said in a slightly apologetic tone.

"Thanks," Sheila said sarcastically, as she turned to get a clean apron that would soon be covered with blood. "I'll take care of it," she said over her shoulder.

≈

Most of the senior nurses were sisters, that is, they were nuns. The British matrons, as they were sometimes called, were inducted into the medical corps as majors. The Canadian nurses were lieutenants and, although they were not nuns, they retained the title "sister nurse."

The matrons were wonderful, selfless ladies, devoted to their calling and a pleasure to work with. There were some matrons, however, that were bitter old hags, hell bent on making a miserable situation far more intolerable and leaning heavily on their rank to do so.

Major Sister Kathleen Blighton–or as Sheila and her fellow co-workers called her "Major pain in the ass"–was one of those miserable matrons. Her nastiness and bitterness was so overwhelming that it seemed to manifest itself upon her physically. She was not a pleasant person to behold, thin and ungainly with a large nose and several moles strewn about her face. She had a classic witch face that seemed to be in perfect keeping with her demeanor.

Sister Kathleen would ferret out the weak or mild mannered nurses and hound them relentlessly. She had the mark of a true bully. To her it was more than just some sick game. It was her passion to persecute those under her charge. Sister Kathleen had been at the 5th Canadian Stationary slightly longer than Sheila and, when they met, there had been an instant dislike by both parties.

They were polar opposites, and neither one tried to keep it a secret. Sheila was there to relieve pain and Sister Kathleen was there to inflict it.

Sister Kathleen immediately made her rank known at their first meeting, and began to intimidate and humiliate Sheila and her co-workers. Sheila knew how to handle someone like the sister and calmly complied with all of the orders that were intended to rattle her. That lack of emotion only served to make Sister Kathleen more resolute in her effort to upset Sheila, which in turn made Sheila more steadfast in keeping herself in check.

Sister Kathleen seemed to be unable to jar Sheila's resolve, and things would have continued to escalate had it not been for the keen observations of the chief physician. He had seen the conflict go on too long. It was beginning to disrupt his ward.

"If you two can't work together here, I can send you both up to the front to work in a clearing station for the ambulance corps," he told them one afternoon.

Sister Kathleen, having very little common sense, replied coldly that she should be able to order her nurses in the manner that she deemed appropriate.

The doctor glared at her. "I can have those orders drafted up today and you will be at the front before week's end," he said acidly. "You'll find that there isn't time for this kind of nonsense when you are up to your eyeballs in death and dying."

Sister Kathleen, used to having the final word, struggled to hold back further protests. The doctor stared icily at the pair as he waited for a confirmation that the feud would end.

"Very well, doctor," Sheila said quietly, with her eyes fixed on the floor.

Sister Kathleen's eyes darted from the doctor to Sheila and back to the doctor, whose stare was fixed on her now with greater intensity. The last place she wanted to be was on the Front in harm's way.

"Why, of course, doctor," she finally said. "Now if you'll excuse me, I have nurses that need my direction."

She spun on her heel to leave, pausing only long enough to whisper to Sheila. "You are wasting your time with that hopeless vegetable of yours."

THE ROAD TO SOMME FOR THE 1ST NEWFOUNDLAND

Terry, Dan, and George had assimilated into the 1st Newfoundland Regiment with little difficulty. Their hosts were pleasant, likeable people who were easy to talk to, and they had openly and genuinely accepted the Canadians into their regiment unreservedly.

The Newfoundlanders were ruggedly built Nordic types, with a heritage that might suggest they would ravage, rape, and plunder as their distant ancestors did, but nothing could be further from the truth. They were gallant soldiers and fierce fighters on the field of battle, but on a personal level, they were totally without aggression and the boys found them to be quite charming. They had an open appreciation for the pipes and drums, even though the instruments were not commonly familiar to the average Newfoundlander.

≈

Consisting of eight hundred men, the 1st Newfoundland Regiment was one of four brigades that made up the four thousand strong British 29th Division. A part of the 1st Newfoundland Regiment had been in place on the Somme Front for three months waiting for Haige's Big Push, but now the entire regiment would be called on.

≋

Mess was over and the call to make ready for deployment was given, so the men scurried back to disassemble their tents and pack their equipment for the long train ride.

Most of the men knew the drill and went about their designated tasks. The small pipe band, however, was new to the drill and simply tried not to get in the way of the rest of the 29th Division.

They were to board a train located south of camp. Colonel Kelton asked the band to lead the division on a march to the waiting transportation. Terry gladly accepted the request and they took position in front of the large formation. Kelton looked back down the rows of men and gave an order to form up and dress right. The soldiers shuffled slightly so as to form straight lines using the man furthest to their right as the line's base. The men now stood at the ready in clearly defined straight lines.

With the trio in position, Terry turned back toward the men and yelled the order: "Mark time by the rolls, step off to the street beat."

The order was relayed down the line by officers standing to the right of the formation. Then Terry yelled, "By the right, quick, March!"

Dan began the drum rolls and the formation began to march in place. When Dan started the street beat, four thousand men took their first steps toward the Battle Somme.

≋

The 29th Division marched past the smoking steam engine and stopped about midway down the 25 boxcars that were lined up behind it. It was the first of two trains of equal size. The forward two cars were regular passenger cars intended for the senior officers. The remaining twenty-three cars were standard box cars with a sign affixed to the doors: "30 MEN/15 HORSES."

The men were counted by rows and then assigned a car number. It became clear at once that the thirty-man limit sign was there for show only, and that they intended to cram as many men into the cars as was possible.

Terry was certain that there must have been 80 to 90 per car. "I hope they don't intend to put 15 horses in with us," he quipped.

Dan sat on a bale of hay next to several fellows trying to perch on the same bale. "If they do, I'm walking!" he replied.

The heat of so many men packed into one place created a very uncomfortable environment that was thankfully reversed by the cooling of the evening. The doors were left opened and a breeze produced by the moving train was a welcome relief.

The noise of the spartan freight cars, as they rattled and clanked down the rails, made conversation strained by the requirement to yell to be heard. Because of this, conversation died off and the men sat quietly thinking about family, home, or nothing at all. Many just allowed themselves to be entranced by the hypnotic clanking of the wheels on the rails.

Darkness had fallen over France and the countryside faded to a soft blur of dimly lit farmhouses and villages. The men slept, leaning on each other's shoulders, with their heads rocking back and forth to the swaying of the boxcar. A few men were speaking as quietly as possible, which was considerably louder than normal due to the noise.

Terry looked around the car at his new comrades and marveled at how at ease they seemed. Few appeared to be apprehensive at the thought of the coming battle. He rose and made his way over to the opened door. A small line of men had formed to urinate out the door, which was quite a stunt considering they had to lean out while holding onto the door with one hand and their "Johnson" with the other.

Because of the wind from the moving train, and the inevitability of spray-back, no one sat near the downwind side of the door. Terry hiked his kilt and leaned out to relieve himself. As he hung out the door urinating, his kilt began to flap in the breeze getting too close to the stream and he shifted to try to prevent his kilt from getting soaked. Just then, the boxcar swayed and Terry began to lose his balance. Before he tumbled out of the opening a large hand firmly grabbed the waist belt of his kilt saving him from an embarrassing and possibly dangerous tumble down the tracks.

"We can't be losing our pipe major," Dan smiled. "I'm next, spot me will you?"

It was about two o'clock in the morning, and the only light visible from the boxcar door was that of the occasional floating ember in the smoke trail of the engine. Off in the distance, to the east over the dark countryside, they could see the flashes of some far off thunderstorms.

≈

An hour later, the men were beginning to stir. Terry and Doc were shouting back and forth, trying to have a conversation, but it was increasingly difficult to hear one another's voice. Much harder than it had been several hours ago.

Something was different, but it was difficult to put one's finger on it. It was insidious and had been creeping up on them for the last hour. The rattling and clanking of the train was now being drowned out by a new noise, a dull roar that seemed to come from all sides.

Terry stopped shouting and just looked at Doc with puzzlement. He realized now, it had begun as a low rumble barely audible above the noise of the boxcar. He had almost felt it before it was really heard. A tickle in his chest that he ignored at first, but it was now undeniable.

"It sounds like a motorcar race," Dan yelled. "It's deafening."

One of the Newfoundlanders who had been through Gallipoli yelled over, "That's the Front lad!"

"What? What did you say?" Doc yelled.

"The Front, the artillery!" he shouted. "Those flashes of lightening are, in fact, muzzle flashes from hundreds of canons and that overpowering noise is the reports of those guns."

They went to the door to look out. The sky was still dark, but the horizon over the gently rolling hills was alive with an unending series of strobe-like flashes.

Colonel Kelton, who had been riding with his men in the car, came over. "That's Haig's Big Push!" he shouted. "His plan is to bombard the German lines for about a week, night and day. They say he plans to deliver over a million and a half shells!"

Doc, who was a whiz with mathematics, looked contemplative. "Let's see... Seven times twenty-four is one hundred sixty-eight hours in a week. That divides into fifteen hundred about nine times... move the decimal point three places and you have approximately nine thousand shells per hour. Divide that by sixty, and that's one hundred-fifty per minute, or two point five shells per second. That's a lot of noise."

Dan, Terry and the colonel were staring at George with their mouths hanging slightly open, none of them knowing quite what to say.

"It sure as hell is," Dan finally said.

"Does he always do that?" Kelton asked Terry.

"Fortunately, no," Terry said.

The artillery barrage had been under way for three days now. As the train came to a halt a scant ten miles from the Front, the fresh troops could plainly see that the troops who worked the deployment camp were drawn and tired; the exposure to so much noise for so long had taken its toll.

Dan had been right, the sound of so many guns going off at the same time sounded like a giant engine with no muffler. The guns firing were so large, so frequent, and were fired over such a large area, that no single report could be heard, only a constant roar. The three friends were taken aback by the sound and the enormity of the war machine that was unleashing its lethal power just over the hill. One thing that the men all agreed upon immediately was that they were glad not to be in those German trenches.

The morning sun was just rising in the east, there was an ugly reddish-orange hue to the sky. There was little wind at the time and the air hung heavy with the acrid smell of spent cordite, making the men cough and causing their eyes to water.

In the late 1800's, black powder had been replaced with an almost smokeless charge called pyrocellulose, invented by the Frenchman Paul Vielle. The next year an improved version was introduced by Swede Alfred Nobel called ballistite. The year after that an Englishman and Scot, Sir Frederick Able and Sir James Dewar invented cordite.

Cordite provided more power and was almost smoke free. The smoke produced by black powder was so great that in the Civil War of the United States entire battlefields would be engulfed in an acrid cloud within which the men could actually become lost. Troops on both sides would have to discontinue the battle until the smoke cleared. It was a problem that begged to be solved. Another shortfall of black powder smoke was that it gave away the position of artillery guns, even a sniper could be detected by his guns' puff of smoke.

That being said, when an assembly of artillery fires nine thousand shells per hour, twenty-four hours a day, it produces so much pollution that a dull layer of acrid smog hangs over the area, most noticeably downwind.

The men that were assembling at the base camp of the 29th division were now getting their first taste of the battle Somme.

36TH ULSTER TO THE SOMME

[Transcribed from Ian MacDonald's recording]

One day behind the movement of the 29th Division and the 1st Newfoundland Regiment, Sean, Bill and I were making our way toward the Somme Valley attached to the 36th Ulster Division. Like the 29th Division, the movement of the Ulster Division was an immense and arduous undertaking. So many men and so much equipment had to be moved that often it seemed like pure chaos.

The means by which each part accomplished its job may not have been completely clear. In fact, to me it seemed like a symphony tuning up before a performance. Out of the confusion emerged a remarkable result: intentional Divisional troop movement in a common direction. The sum of the parts, indeed, created a whole.

The 36th Ulster Division was made up of three main regiments: The Royal Inniskilling Fusiliers, The Irish Fusiliers, and the Royal Irish Rifles. Sean, Bill, and I were assigned to the Rifles.

Although we were warmly welcomed into their group, it soon became painfully evident to us that Ireland was suffering from some deep-seated problems of which Canadians—at least we three—were mostly unaware.

It soon became apparent that the 36th–to all outward appearances a strong, tightly knit unit–struggled with real internal tensions. This fine group of men held a deep animosity toward some of their fellow Irishmen. Although the 36th had more Protestants than Catholics, and more Northern than Southern Irish, there was a large enough mix to cause problems within the group.

We were curious about this obvious rift and knowing that Lieutenant McDonnell was a man of sensibilities and reason, we approached him on the subject that afternoon.

"Come to my tent boys and I'll do my best to clear some of the mud from the water," he said.

We followed him into his quarters and were invited to sit as he poured us each a glass of Bushmills Whiskey.

"The story of my country is a sad and tragic one," he began. "My Ireland is an island of passionate people. We're fine fighters, good poets, good drinkers and good workers."

He sipped from his glass. "However, we're also very stubborn and unable to compromise our opinions, and this hampers our progress toward peace and unity. There are zealots on both sides–the Ribbon-men on the Catholic side and Orange-men on the Protestant side. Each organization stirs up the passions of its people to create discord for their own political purposes." He held his glass of Bushmills to the light and peered through it for a moment before continuing.

"The Northern part of Ireland is predominantly protestant and pro-British rule. The southern part of Ireland is predominantly Catholic and favors self-rule. The battle between Protestant and Catholic is not really one of religion but one of politics that is propagated by both religious groups in order to maintain control of their people.

"The British who still rule Ireland feel obligated to maintain their presence and, therefore, protect the Protestants while quelling the Catholic unrest with strong military pressure. It doesn't help that most upper-crust British regard the Irish as nothing more than an unruly, uneducated, drunken lot of ne'er-do-wells."

"But, sir," Bill interrupted, "You're a well-spoken man of obvious education and you have risen to a rank of leadership in the B.E.F."

"That's true," McDonnell said, "but I had to work harder than most of my British counterparts just to reach this rank. And, unfortunately, any promotion in rank will remain confined to that required within the 36th Ulster and not beyond."

The dark amber liquid in my glass burned as I swallowed it. The warm sensation sat for a minute in my stomach as the Lieutenant tried to explain his country's problems.

"The sad truth is that both sides believe that they are right and they are willing to kill and die for their respective beliefs. If you took fifty Protestant and fifty Catholic Irishmen, stripped them naked and put them in a room ordering them not to speak, you wouldn't know one from the other. But, allow them to open their mouths and in ten minutes you'd have two angry gangs of fifty naked fools ready to fight."

We smiled at each other with the ridiculous image, but McDonnell didn't return the smile. This was a subject that obviously tore at his soul.

"I fear my country is its own worst enemy," he said. "The real irony is that after years of fighting for home rule and appealing to the British government for that right, the House of Commons overrode a veto by the House of Lords concerning the Government of Ireland Act. The move by the House of Commons opened the door for Ireland and the prospect for home rule seemed within reach. That was early 1914–the whole subject was shelved because of the outbreak of this damn war."

"You were so close to achieving independence and fate stole it away," Sean said in disbelief.

"Indeed. The Luck of the bloody Irish, eh?" McDonnell quipped. "Despite the set-back, the majority of Irish men put aside the strife of our homeland and answered Britain's call for help."

"That speaks volumes about the character of your people," I said. "I hope someday that all the hatred will be put aside and that your country will be united."

"A united Ireland is now just a dream, and a fading one at that. It gets worse," Owen said knocking back the rest of his glass, his voice lowered into almost a growl. "This year while we were over here fighting for England, some at home couldn't–or wouldn't–wait for a peaceful resolution to our problems. Rather they saw an opportunity in England's involvement in the war. Sinn Fein planned an Easter rebellion starting in Dublin and even accepted guns and ammunition from the Huns for their army. The Germans, of course, were happy to supply the boys knowing that England would now be fighting on two fronts, a distraction the Germans would take full advantage of."

We glanced at each other and nodded. It was a brilliant yet dastardly move.

"On Good Friday last, a German ship came to port in Ireland and off-loaded its deadly and deceptive cargo for our self-proclaimed patriots. The filthy Huns were using the Irish Citizens Army to deliver a blow into England. The I.C.A., in consorting with the Germans disgraced those Irishmen who have died in the war, a slap in the face to those of us that are still here fighting."

Owen poured another whiskey and topped us off. His face was drawn and his brow was furrowed. "The week of Easter was a bloody one for Ireland on two fronts. The British poured twenty thousand men into Dublin. They fired upon our city, and after the rebellion was put to rest, two hundred fifty-four innocent civilians–men, women, and children–had been killed along with one hundred-sixteen British soldiers and sixty-four of the Irish Citizens Army. Now fifty thousand British soldiers occupy my country, and the prospect of home rule has been all but lost. And all this has done is to fan the flames of hate and feed the bellies of the Orange men and the Ribbon men. Do you see what's been happening to my island?" Owen asked.

We all nodded. This was a puzzle to which there seemed to be no answer. I felt sad for these brave men.

"I would like to have a moment alone, if you would be so kind," Owen said.

We left his tent not really knowing what to say. As the three of us walked slowly away, two British officers walked by speaking loudly to each other.

"The bloody Irishmen are an undisciplined lot, wot?" said one.

"Quite so," the other replied.

I wanted to poke one, or maybe both of them in the nose. Then around the corner came three Irish soldiers. They were laughing and poking each other as they approached, obviously chums.

"Well look here. You lads must be our pipes and drums!" one said as the three stopped in front of us and looked us up and down.

"And a fine band, if ever I saw one." another said. The three were members of the Irish Fusiliers who had a distinct green and white feather hackle in their hats to indicate their association.

"Well, I don't know," said the third. "Something's missing. Perhaps this will liven up your glengarry." He took off his hackle and placed it behind my cap badge. The other two did the same to Bill and Sean.

"Now, there's a smart looking trio," he said. "You're honorary Irishmen now and you won't know who'll be shooting at you first, the Brits or the Huns!"

They all broke into roaring laughter and walked away slapping the fellow on the back that made the wisecrack.

"Interesting guys," Bill said, understating the encounter.

GERMAN ARMY AIR SERVICE, "KESTA" #5

Bapaume Aerodrome, June 20, 1916

Aviator Philip Zieger was walking from the hangar toward his aircraft. He lit a Camel cigarette and drew in the smoke. Pausing for a moment he blew a series of perfect smoke rings and smiled at his handiwork. It was quite common for the aviators of the time to be eccentric rascals and American cigarettes were all the rage even though this brand bore the name of his airborne enemy—the Sopwith "Camel."

The heavy morning dew on the grass soaked his boots and leggings but that was of little interest to him at that moment. His attention was on his new aeroplane, the Albatross CV.

What a fine looking bird, he thought as the morning sun crested the eastern horizon behind it.

"You should be called Falcon or Osprey, not Albatross. An Albatross is a clumsy, slow bird!" he said in the cool morning air. "You are a fine bird of prey." He spit out pieces of tobacco from the camel and tossed it into the grass. It hissed as the dew met the hot ember.

The Albatross was a relatively new addition to the German Army Air Service and was far more pleasing to the eye than the previous menace of the Western Front, The Fokker E IV. The Fokker was a monoplane (single wing) and had a maze of wires on top and on bottom of the wing and fuselage to add strength for high "G-load" dogfights. Its long, slender fuselage and small rudder gave it a deceptively non-threatening look. The Fokker was, as were most aircraft of the time, covered with fabric stretched over a wood frame. This combination kept it lightweight but gave it a box kite appearance. It was this aircraft that provided German Aces Max Immelmann and Oswald Boelcke with the bulk of their kills during the early part of the war and it had earned great respect from the allied pilots, who called it the "Fokker Scourge."

The British Sopwith Camel and Pup along with the DH 2 and Neiuport had recaptured the skies over the Western Front for now, but the Albatross was taking it back. There was heavy fighting down south in Verdun and "The Flying Circus"–Immelman, Boelcke and a new ace Von Richthofen had been concentrating their talents on that event for several months. Unfortunately, Immelman had been shot down and killed two months earlier and Kaiser Wilhelm had grounded Boelcke for a while for fear of losing another ace and the demoralizing effect it would have on Germany. This opened the skies for Von Richthofen, who was making a huge name for himself in the process.

Philip Zieger wished he could be down in Verdun to prove himself as well.

"After all it's what I trained for," he said as he pre-flighted his Biplane.

"What?" his gunner asked.

"Nothing," Zieger tersely replied

Zieger, like Manfred Von Richthofen preferred the flight characteristics of this airplane compared to the Fokker. The E IV had an Oberursel, nine cylinder, 110-horsepower rotary engine. This type of powerplant was common in many French, British, and German aircraft because of its simplicity and light weight-to-power ratio.

The rotary engine did, however, have several outstanding drawbacks.

First, the engine was mounted on the aircraft by its drive shaft and the propeller was bolted onto the engine. The entire engine and propeller would spin.

Second, the engine had no carburetor and thus had no control over the power—it was either full power or off, accomplished by means of a "kill switch" mounted on the flight control stick.

Third, the engine was cooled by its spinning, and lubricated by centrifugal force in the process.

To elaborate on these drawbacks, first because the engine was spinning it created a gyroscopic influence on flight characteristics, when you pulled on the control stick to go up, the airplane would lurch to the left. If you pushed down on the stick it would lurch to the right. This made for some very spasmodic dogfighting and presented the pilot with many unwanted inputs during his maneuvers.

Second, because there was not control over the power, the pilot had to work the "kill switch" on and off during a dogfight or on landing. Not that big of a problem during landing, but when you're pulling, banking, looping, and shooting, leaving the power on at the wrong time could over-stress your airplane and structural failure could occur.

Third, because the lubrication of the engine was centrifugal, Castor oil, the best lubricant for that engine, would often spew out and cover the windscreen, fuselage and pilot's face with ample amounts of the smelly, sticky substance.

The Albatross, on the other hand, was amply powered by a Mercedes 220-horsepower, liquid cooled, in-line engine. It had no gyroscopic influence, it was carbureted, and the engine could be controlled from idle to full power by means of a throttle.

The oiling system was fully contained consequently there was no oil to scrub off of your goggles, leather helmet and face.

The Albatross also had a wooden skinned fuselage for added strength, and it was a Biplane, which many believed increased ma- neuverability.

Later in 1916, Manfred Von Richthofen, in a display of either ar- rogance or extreme self-confidence, had his beloved Albatross CI Fighter painted bright red, earning him the nickname of "the Red Baron."

≈

Zieger was not that arrogant and was not ready to challenge the likes of the French Lafayette Escadrille's Raoul Lufbery, England's Al- bert Ball or Canadian ace Billy Bishop just yet. The Albatross, howev- er, was set up as a reconnaissance airplane with a pilot and gunner/ bomber behind him.

Zieger was simply happy to be flying an airplane that would do what a pilot commanded it to do in a dogfight.

This morning, Zieger's mission was to reconnoiter up and down the Somme Valley and report anything of interest. There was no for- mation this morning. He was alone. The fighting down in Verdun had demanded most of the resources of The German Army Air Ser- vice and because the Somme was relatively quiet, there was no need for a full squadron to be present.

Zieger's gunner/bomber was strapped in and tapped Zieger on the shoulder to signal his checks were complete. The ground men were standing by for Zieger's signal for hot magnetos.

Zieger gave a thumbs up and rotated his hand in the air, the "okay" signal for the prop start.

"Mags on!" yelled the propman.

"On!" responded Zieger.

The propman grabbed the large wooden propeller and swung his leg high in the air. As his leg came down he used the momentum, like a baseball pitcher, to pull the prop down and move away from it all in one smooth movement. The engine coughed, but then died.

"Mags Off!" the propman yelled as he moved in for another attempt. Zieger pushed the primer twice to add some fuel directly into the engine in an attempt to coax her to life. This time she started easily with a small puff of smoke unlike the billows of smoke created by a rotary engine.

The pilot looked over the right side of the nose to see his guideman with two flags beckoning him to come forward. There were wing walkers running alongside holding the wing tips steady as Zieger began to taxi clear of the other aircraft and hangers. They held onto the wings until he was lined up for his take off roll into the wind.

From a nearby small tower, the controller gave the "all clear for take-off" signal with his paddles, and Zieger pushed the throttle smoothly to full open. The Albatross lumbered forward picking up speed, quickly leaving the wing walkers behind. There was now sufficient aerodynamic control from the ailerons so the wings could be kept level by Zieger's stick movement.

The tail came off the ground as the airplane accelerated and he began to work the rudder pedals back and forth to maintain directional control. She bounced once, then again; a little gentle back pressure on the stick and they were airborne gracefully banking to the right as pilot and airplane became as one.

This was Zieger's favorite moment as he and his machine achieved what had been believed unachievable just fifteen years before. Manned flight.

≈

Philip had performed this reconnaissance loop may times before and saw no reason to believe this would be any less uneventful than all the others had been. But, as he started his slow right turn at around three thousand feet to head north, he noted some increased activity about two miles ahead and to the east. He knew that there was an encampment there but it appeared to have doubled in size from two days earlier.

It was a beautiful smooth morning and he gracefully banked his Albatross into a thirty-degree left turn for a closer look. Craning his neck from left to right he scanned the horizon in search of enemy aircraft, he throttled back, and began a slow descent.

As he approached the encampment, Philip was stunned by what he saw. The main road that was just behind the rolling hilltop was jammed with troops and equipment as far as the eye could see. Miles and miles of what looked like lorries pulling artillery and carrying thousands of troops to the Front. This was a massive troop buildup.

Zieger's heart quickened as he knew British plane spotters would soon be pointing out his intrusion to the anti-aircraft batteries and they would be trying their best to prevent him from returning with this valuable information. He made several quick mental estimates about troop size and artillery types; there were a great number of large guns, sixty-pounders he guessed.

Over the roar of the Mercedes and the hiss of the slipstream a familiar sound caught his attention. Zieger banked abruptly to the east, as he knew he was now a target. Thud! That confirmed it. The thud was coming from the ground and he knew what was coming next. A large explosion of flak pounded the sky off to his left and, luckily for him, about a thousand feet too low. This was the first of many explosions that would be coming.

The volley of thuds that followed was so numerous that Philip knew he was in trouble. The sky exploded all around the Albatross rocking and jarring the airplane. Thick black puffs of smoke that spewed shards of metal were hammering the sky everywhere. Tracer bullets from anti-aircraft guns streamed up in arching waves like a line of white Christmas lights from the ground.

A series of holes stitched across the left wing leaving several large rips in the fabric, but somehow miraculously missing the wooden structure itself. Philip descended as quickly as possible and changed direction abruptly in hopes of avoiding the gunfire and flack that was being generously directed at him.

Pop, pop, pop–the sound of anti-aircraft rounds impacting the wooden covered fuselage of the Albatross causing the skin to splinter and severing the rudder cable in the process. Philip felt the rudder pedals swing freely and immediately realized he had lost the use of that flight control. As the airplane continued to descend Zieger moved his ailerons to check their control, the wings rolled left then right but the tail yawed back and forth due to the lack of rudder capability. Then he checked his elevator by pulling back on his stick. The nose began to rise as requested. That was good news! He could live without rudder control.

He glanced back at his gunner to signal him to keep his eyes open for enemy aircraft but saw that the gunner had been hit by one of the rounds that had severed his rudder cable. The man was either dead or unconscious. Either way, Zieger was now without defense. He was descending rapidly through a thousand feet and going for the ground, the lower, the better. Flack was no longer a threat at this altitude and the lower he got, the harder it was for the anti-aircraft gunners.

Zieger was keenly aware of his vulnerability to other aircraft and scanned the sky to his six o'clock position, but there was still no sign of enemy planes. As he pulled back on his stick to level off at around a hundred feet, the Albatross began to shake violently.

He glanced at his wings and noticed several guide wires on the left wing were trailing in the slipstream. The upper wing had a noticeable twist in it which was causing a buffeting effect and shaking the airplane. Zieger slowed his airspeed and the buffeting subsided. He was passing over British trenches now and was low enough where he knew that the only danger he faced was that of ground fire and that was slight, at best. As he sped over No Man's Land, he momentarily glanced at the barbed wire entanglements that went on for miles and thought how fortunate he was not to be a foot soldier.

Suddenly there was a horrific scream that flew past his wounded aircraft and exploded in the German trenches causing a cloud of dirt and debris to engulf the Albatross. It was a British artillery round. The explosion's shock wave shook the airplane causing it to groan and creak, yet the sturdy aircraft stubbornly continued its homeward trek.

Philip was now aware of a warm fluid covering the upper portion of his legs, he immediately worried that an oil line had been hit and looked down to inspect the damage. He knew instantly that it wasn't oil at all—it was blood. He'd been hit in his side and he was losing blood rapidly.

Philip pressed his right hand into the wound and the blood loss subsided to a trickle. He had to land soon. With a severely damaged aircraft barely staying aloft, one hand on his side to slow the blood loss and the other hand on the stick to maintain control, he had far too much going on to even be aware of the pain.

The wounded Albatross had by now passed well over German lines, and with the comfort of the aircraft engine running strongly, the sweat that had been pouring down Ziegers' face had started to decrease. In fact, it began to evaporate in the slipstream as he moved farther away from danger. He was feeling better about his prospects of survival.

Several platoons of German soldiers below were cheering and waving as the broken airplane and wounded pilot flew past. Seeing the tattered airplane defiantly staying aloft after the terrific pounding it had taken was truly inspirational to these mud-soaked trench rats, but Zieger didn't notice. He was focused on keeping the machine airborne and returning to the field.

He now had a new problem. A gray mist was forming in his peripheral vision and a constant high-pitched ring was beginning to drown out the barking exhaust of his Mercedes engine. The loss of blood was taking its toll on him, he could feel the cool grip of unconsciousness beginning to wrap its arms around him. The mud and desolation of the artillery battered No Man's Land had given way to green fields and farmhouses. He knew the field was near, but was having trouble orienting himself.

Then, miraculously, he saw the Maltese Cross Flag waving at the end of a long field. He banked the Albatross gently around in a wide semicircle in order to line up for his final approach. It looked like a light wind, maybe five knots, down the runway according to the orange windsock. He was almost home.

≈

Gunther Erhert was drinking a coffee and smoking a cigarette he had just rolled as he sat on the fender of the airfield ambulance. It was a quiet morning, a cloudless sky with a warm sun, not much going on. The only flight out had left forty minutes ago and was not due back for another hour. Just a routine reconnaissance flight, all the action was down south.

As he exhaled a large plume of smoke, the distant sound of an aircraft engine caught his ear. He held his breath to get a better listen. It was a distinctive sound and his well-trained ear recognized the Albatross engine's characteristic purr as opposed to the harsh growl of a Sopwith or a Neuport.

He looked at his wristwatch. It was too soon for Captain Zieger to return–unless something was wrong. He slid off the fender of the ambulance on which he had been comfortably perched and walked a few steps away from the buildings and vehicles for a clear view of the western horizon. His long shadow fell across the lush green grass as he scanned the western sky searching for the aircraft responsible for this morning's interruption.

There it was, low, west by northwest, barely visible. Erhert cupped his hand over his eyes. Even though the sun was to his back it seemed to enhance his vision somewhat. No trailing smoke. He picked up his pace toward the tower stand where his binoculars were and shouted out to the ground crew.

"Achtung, mein herren!"

The crew set down the cards they were playing and the letters they were writing and trotted out to see what had caught the controller's attention. Gunter had, by now, climbed the wooden tower stand and grabbed the binoculars. He was turning the eyepieces to get a better focus on this incoming aircraft.

"Die Albatross! Kapitän Zieger!" he yelled with the cigarette dangling from his mouth.

As the airplane came closer and slowly banked to the left, Gunther got a clear view of its twisted profile. He grabbed the cigarette from his mouth and threw it to the ground below, he then pressed the binoculars harder against his eyes. How is this aircraft still aloft, he wondered.

"Crash team, crash team!" he yelled, while simultaneously grabbing and cranking the handle of the crash siren. It let out with a deafening howl and the airfield came to life. Tent flaps flew opened and trucks clattered to life. The base doctor was picked up and spirited to a mid-field position by a BMW sidecar motorcycle with a large red cross over a white background painted on it.

It was important that the doctor be among the first to the crash scene in order to tend to the aviators who were considered to be the knights of modern day.

As the field made ready for the impending crash; the once beautiful and graceful Albatross shuddered and banked right as Zieger lined the airplane up from base leg to final approach. It was now clear to Controller Erhert that the Albatross was worse off than he had originally thought and Zieger would have no idea of the imminent danger he was about to encounter. Because of the lower wing restricting the Pilot's view he would have no idea that he had only one landing wheel remaining.

Erhert grabbed the red flag and waved it frantically hoping that the Captain would abort the landing and fly by the tower for hand signals.

≈

Zieger reduced power on the crippled bird and the airframe vibration lessened. He cautiously glanced at his airspeed indicator to ensure he didn't slow too much. To experience a stall in this condition and at this low an altitude would be disastrous.

The normal final approach speed of the Albatross was eighty knots and sixty knots over the fence for landing, but he didn't dare go below ninety knots in his present un-airworthy condition. Barely hanging on to consciousness, he fought to maintain control over the airplane. There was no time for fear. This was simply survival now. He looked down the field and noticed the red flag being waved from the tower. Zieger knew what the Controller wanted him to do, but there were only moments of consciousness left. This was a one-time deal, no second chances.

Just a little over forty minutes had passed since his dawn departure and the sun was still fairly low in the southeastern sky. At about two-hundred feet, as the Albatross continued its slow, deliberate descent toward the grass landing strip, Zieger slipped into unconsciousness. The airspeed began to bleed off as he let go of the control stick and the airplane began to shake violently in a prestall buffet.

Zieger was startled awake by the shaking and grabbed the stick lowering the nose in an effort to recover his deteriorating airspeed. He had to hang on just a little longer. The Albatross was now flying at a far greater speed than he would ever consider for a normal landing, but he knew that he could allow it to bleed off in his flare.

There is a condition known as ground effect which allows an airplane to fly at a much slower than normal airspeed when it is just feet off the ground. It is important to slow the aircraft to as slow a speed as is possible for two reasons. First, if you are at or below stall speed, the aircraft won't bounce back off the runway. Second, the airplane had no brakes, only a tail skid to slow its ground roll.

As the tattered Albatross neared the landing point, Zieger began his gentle back pressure on the stick. Then, even in his dazed condition, he suddenly realized the shadow in front of him in the grass was wrong. He now knew what the controller was warning him about. The plane's right tire cast a long shadow, but the left was missing.

Although he instinctively tried to hold the airplane off for a moment, he knew there was no alternative–he had to land anyway. Zieger let go of his side and grabbed the stick with his blood soaked hand while he eased back on the throttle with his left. Holding the ailerons so as to keep the left wing high, he instinctively pushed on the rudder to counteract the tendency of the airplane to turn, but it was completely inoperative. He had to act fast.

The right wheel touched the grass and began to pull the airplane more to the right. He lowered the airplane onto the strip and felt her lurch momentarily as it skidded lightly across the wet grass. She continued straight down the runway for several moments until the speed bled off and the ailerons could no longer hold the weight off the left side of the airplane. The bare left axle began to plow into the grass, digging a long furrow into the runway and leaving a trail of dust and soil.

The Albatross spun hard to the left as the remaining pieces of the left gear contacted the ground and broke away. The left lower wing then hit the runway, which caused the counter clockwise twist to increase in intensity. The centrifugal force of the violent maneuver threw the weight of the aircraft hard against the right wheel and it quickly snapped off leaving the Albatross on its belly.

As a result of the right wheel digging in and snapping off, the spinning wreckage was jolted hard to the right, which slowed down Zieger's corkscrew ride. The propeller also came apart as it contacted the ground, causing great clouds of dirt to spray in all directions. The prop quickly disintegrated leaving only the bullet shaped nose cone and two splintered stubs of wood. The strength of the large wings kept the airplane from cartwheeling and it seemed the landing was going to be survivable after all. The wreckage slid to a stop some 500 feet from touchdown, an unrecognizable tangle of wood, fabric and wires; all was silent for a moment.

Gunther Erhart dropped the red flag to his side, as there was no point in waving it now. He watched as the Albatross, which had been the newest airplane in the aerodrome fifty minutes ago, touched down and became a spinning piece of junk in mere seconds. He slid down the ladder and hit the ground running, stopping only to ignite a red smoke flare as a danger signal for any other inbound aircraft that might be considering landing.

Two sturdy ground crew members had grabbed a large red fire bottle on wheels from its position by the tower and were pulling it at a trot in the direction of the wrecked airplane. With the dust cloud still hanging in the air, Gunther, the fire team, the doctor in his sidecar and the ambulance arrived upon the scene.

No fire–that was critical–but there was smoke and where there's smoke, time is of the essence. The fire crew blew the CO_2 fire bottle off at the hot engine and areas of potential fire. It trumpeted out a howl and engulfed the area in a cool fog. Another ground crew member cut Zieger's safety belt off and began to drag the injured pilot clear of danger. He then attended to the gunner bomber, but it was too late for him.

≈

The doctor with his black bag of medical tools and supplies barely waited for the ground crew to get out of his way. He knew right away that there had already been massive blood loss and it was imperative that he stop it from continuing.

He ripped open the pilot's blood soaked uniform shirt and began to clean the area with alcohol, causing Zieger to bellow with pain. The doctor ordered the assisting medic to administer morphine, but the semiconscious Zieger held up his hand and tried to speak.

Nothing that he said made sense. The doctor sternly nodded at the medic to proceed. As the medic was about to inject the morphine, Zieger's bloody hand grabbed his wrist in a viselike hold. With his other hand he grabbed the doctor's white coat by the lapel and pulled him close to his pale face with remarkable strength.

"Massive troop buildup, tens of thousands, all sectors...artillery... hundreds of big guns... pass information on to command...."

Both the doctor and the medic were stunned by Zieger's strength and impressed by his sense of duty in insisting the information be passed on even before they tried to save him. The doctor looked up at Gunther and orderd him to get the information to command immediately.

Gunther tagged the motorcycle driver, and the two sped off to the communications officer shed. As they left, Zieger loosened his grip on both the doctor and the medic and passed into unconsciousness.

German command acted swiftly on the information and began preparing for what would become one of the major offensives of the war.

Aid station on the Yser Canal

The Sunbeam ambulance that carried Dan Mckee to The 5th Canadian Stationary Hospital.

The brave men of the 36th Ulster

Ziegers' Albatros CV

After the crash

The carnage of trench warfare

The infamous Minnie trench mortar

HMS Olympic in dazzle paint

Piper and comrades on the Somme

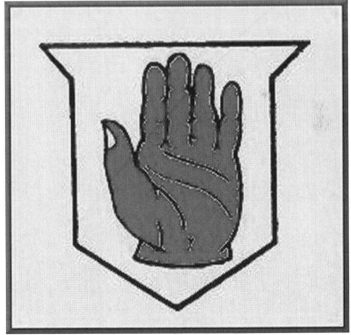

The divisonal badge of the 36th Ulster

Soldier sleeping in the trenches

Stretcher bearers under horrific conditions

Badge of the 1ˢᵗ newfoundland

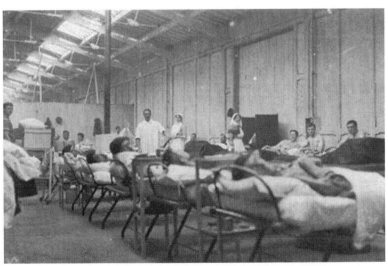

Typical building of the 5ᵗʰ Canadian Stationary Hospital

PART SIX
IN PREPARATION

5th Canadian Hospital, Amiens

The buildup of troops in the Somme Valley was now common knowledge among the staff at the 5th Canadian Stationary Hospital. After all, it made sense to alert your Hospital units of the potential for a large influx of wounded. Preparations were made to deal with the high volume that was anticipated. Enormous amounts of supplies were being requisitioned at an extraordinary rate. Sheila was having a casual conversation with a fellow nurse as they both surveyed the long line of supply wagons and lorries unloading their cargo. They had both been around long enough to know that preemptive supply distributions always came before an offensive, but this one was by far the biggest they had seen.

"I wonder how big a push this really is going to be?" Sheila's friend asked.

"I heard that Field Marshall Haig wants to push the Germans right back to Berlin. And judging by the number of supply wagons, this is the biggest yet," Sheila said.

"Maybe that will be enough to put a stop to this thing and we can all go home again," her friend said. "It would be a grand thing if that were to happen."

Sheila nodded, but didn't want to pin her hopes up on the chance of that happening.

≈

It was a lovely warm day and many convalescing injured men were outside enjoying the weather and smoking in the newly designated courtyard not far from where the ladies were talking.

There was a strict rule against smoking inside the hospital due to the widespread use of oxygen and ether, both of which were highly combustible. The problem was that most of the men smoked. This actually provided an incentive for a patient to recuperate enough to walk, wheel, or be wheeled out to the smoking area.

There was also the added benefit of social interaction with fellow injured patients. It seemed to help with the men's attitudes and Sheila correctly believed that a major portion of the healing process came from the mind. She had fought hard for the formation of an official smoking area, against the ardent objections of her nemesis, Kathleen Blighton.

Sister Kathleen believed that smoking was a sin against God's temple, but curiously overlooked the sin of destruction of God's temple by means of shrapnel or bullets.

The smoking area was a bone of contention between Sheila and the Sister until the issue was brought before the chief surgeon, Dr. Robert Churchill only two days before. Dr. Churchill was a pipe smoker himself, but he did not let that influence his input on the matter. He was a wise and observant man by nature and could clearly see that the psychological benefits derived by this social interaction outweighed the health risk of the habit.

Churchill called a meeting of the nursing staff to listen to input from both sides before he announced his decision on the subject.

Now, it should be noted that Dr. Churchill had a very dry and warped sense of humor, and it should also be noted that he appreciated the dedication and service of both of these nurses. However, he disliked Sister Kathleen's officious demeanor and, therefore, had a predisposition toward Sheila's argument.

There seemed to be a naughty schoolboy side to the doctor that had remained from childhood. He would often make a point using sarcasm presented with a remarkable degree of feigned innocence. With his reading glasses perched halfway down his nose and a clipboard in his lap he called the meeting to order.

"It has been brought to my attention that an area for our convalescing patients to congregate and smoke outside the confines of the ward may be beneficial. It has also been brought to my attention that this idea could have negative health implications. We are here to examine the issue and to come to a decision."

The doctor looked down at his clipboard and then back a both Sheila and Sister Kathleen. "The fact is that smoking is a habit that is common among the men that existed prior to their visit to the 5th. While I personally believe that smoking is an objectionable habit that carries with it potential long term negative health implications—"

Sister Kathleen smiled and sat up straighter in her seat in anticipation of Dr. Churchill nixing the idea.

"It is not, however, the objective or obligation of the hospital or its staff to cure smoking," he continued. "Rather it is our goal to cure the patient, smoke or not. There are arguably positive benefits to the idea which must also be considered."

Sister Kathleen deflated momentarily, then rose to the defense. "Doctor, allowing the patients to damage themselves further with a filthy habit is contrary to the objectives of—"

Churchill glared over his glasses pointing his pen at the Sister. "Stop!" he ordered. "You have amply presented your case to me in the past. This is a verbalization of my thoughts and will be followed by my decision. There will be no further interruptions."

Sister Kathleen's mouth went taut and her lips pressed together so tightly they seemed to disappear.

Dr. Churchill raised one eyebrow, and an almost undetectable devilish smile came to his mouth while he looked down to hide any sign of it. The warped and naughty side was beginning to surface. He looked up and continued in a serious tone, "As I was saying, there are some positive benefits that must be considered. For example, I believe that an area for smoking may improve the incidence of healthy intercourse between patients which can only improve their mental states and, therefore, enhancing their eventual recovery."

All the nurses in the room looked at each other regarding the doctor's curious choice of words. Sister Kathleen shifted uncomfortably in her seat. This was just the beginning of Churchill's innuendos.

"It is not my suggestion that a large erection is necessary to promote such social behavior. On the contrary, a simple open air court will do," he said.

Several nurses were well aware of Churchill's antics and blurted out in coughing spasms in an effort to stifle laughing. Sheila tried desperately to force down a smile and stared down at the floor trying to keep her amusement hidden.

Churchill continued in a mock serious manner, ignoring the guffaws of the crowd. "I believe that this type of intercourse will be a welcome stimulation for the patients and, of course, as the patient becomes more stimulated, they eventually come..." Churchill paused and drank some water "closer to achieving a recovery."

Sister Kathleen's mouth was fully opened, aghast in shock and disbelief. Many nurses were holding their mouths with both hands trying not to laugh out loud. Churchill looked off in the distance keeping his deadpan expression.

"It is hard...very hard to predict the total value of this idea, but I know that with the help of a cooperative yet firm staff, this type of intercourse in this newly designated area will be easily achievable."

Sister Kathleen's dumbstruck expression had now changed to a red faced scowl of total disapproval. She had heard enough. She jumped to her feet. "Doctor, I would have a word with you, alone!" she commended.

"Of course," Dr. Churchill said with a look of surprise. They walked out of the room into an adjoining area.

≈

When they were alone Sister Kathleen spun around and pointed an accusing finger. "Doctor, I have every intention of reporting you to your superiors regarding that disgusting speech you just delivered."

"I have no idea what you are talking about," Churchill said.

"You know very well what I'm talking about," the sister snapped.

Churchill's face went uncustomarily hard and his voice became low and stern. "As chief of medicine here, I don't take well to being reprimanded or threatened by a nurse, especially one with a filthy mind."

She gasped. "I have nothing of the kind."

"Quiet!" he barked. "You will report to my office at 0800 hours tomorrow at which time I will have your transfer papers ready."

Sister Kathleen was momentarily stunned by the doctor's harsh response. Her tone completely changed. "Doctor, surely, you can't mean what you are saying. I am the head nurse, we are short staffed, and we are about to be swamped with a massive number of casualties."

Churchill's steely stare was unchanged. "Rest assured," he said evenly, "this decision has been a long time in coming and is final."

With that, Churchill turned and walked away leaving the dumb-founded nurse standing alone in the room.

In the adjoining room the nursing staff sat as quietly as they could, all straining to eavesdrop on the confrontation. They were all equally stunned at this remarkable turn of events. Sheila was awash with mixed emotions. Part of her was almost giddy at the prospect of Sister Kathleen's departure, and another part felt sorry for her, not wanting to wish ill on anyone. She somberly left the room leaving the nattering staff behind.

≈

Two days later, standing with her friend, Sheila quietly excused herself and walked down the hallway alone. There was still plenty of time before her scheduled rounds, so she went to tend to her project, Bully, the comatose patient. He continued persistently in his semi-vegetative state and, although, his weight and overall health was good, his stubborn condition caused Sheila to begin to doubt whether he would ever recover.

She changed the linen on his bed, gave him a sponge bath and then began his physical therapy, which consisted of her moving his arms, legs, and neck in a full range of motion. She spoke to him softly as she tried to counter the tightening of his tendons.

"Your favorite fan has left the hospital—that's right Sister Kathleen. I know you're disappointed. It's brave of you to hold back your feelings, but you can feel free to let it out, it's just the two of us here."

As she moved his shoulders from side to side he let out with an uncustomary groan. She stopped and looked at his face for a sign. Nothing.

"Well, I had mixed feelings too," she continued. This was really therapy for both of them. Sheila would speak to Bully of things that she would share with no one else, he would silently listen, no judgments or objections. There was a strange one-sided bond that was forming. Perhaps it was her maternal instinct. After all, he was helpless and without her attention, he would not survive. He needed her and she needed him. Doctor Churchill had seen this strange relationship develop before and had gently warned her to be cautious of the possibility of personal involvement, but she dismissed the notion. She now reflected on his advice and realized he may have been right.

This emotional turmoil was dampening her normally upbeat demeanor so she decided it was time to give Bully some fresh air and time for her to play her pipes. She wheeled his bed out into the courtyard and retrieved her pipes. Entertaining the men always lifted her spirits and, of course, the men loved it. She tuned her pipes in less than a minute as the men began to gather around always eager for entertainment. A beautiful Scottish lullaby was her first choice followed by a snappy rendition of "The Black Bear."

The men cheered her on as she slid into a spirited jig and then a measured strathspey. Sheila knew that to perform the bagpipes for an audience was like serving a rich dessert after a meal. Smaller portions are easier to digest and are more satisfying. So, she concluded her musical session with the old Queen's University fight song and then snapped her pipes under her arm the way her old instructor Victor Matthews had taught her.

As she walked away from the clapping men toward Bully's bed and the cheering subsided she heard the faint singing of the Queen's fight song.

"Ka Ya, Ka Ya, Ka Ya" was softly being sung over and over. She looked around to see who knew the Queens song, but no one was near. Her heart suddenly pounded as she realized that the soft singing was coming from Bully. Sheila almost dropped her pipes as she raced the remaining steps to his side. Could it be possible? Could he be singing? Could he be conscious? As she leaned in close and watched his mouth, his eyes remained closed, but his mouth was moving and he was singing "The Oil Thigh," the nickname of Queen's fight song. A flood of emotion came over her as her eyes welled up and she began to happily sob at the realization that she had finally reached him.

OUR HOME ON THE SOMME, THE 36TH ULSTER

[Transcribed from Ian MacDonald's recording]

O ur billets for the 36th Ulster were spread throughout a small village just five miles from the Front. The artillery assault was, we were told, started three days earlier and had been continuing night and day. The noise was constant but after a while we all became used to it. The division occupied every available house, hotel, barn and church for its lodging. I must say that the people were remarkably hospitable about our intrusion. I doubt I would have been as gracious.

Sean, Bill and I stayed with five other young Irishmen in a small, well-built brick barn on the east side of the village. The barn was relatively comfortable and was one of the cleanest barns I had ever seen. The smell of animals was faint, far less than one would expect. It was, however, enough to bring back some warm memories of my family's farm on Wolfe Island.

I marveled at the old man and his wife–Dobsavage was their last name–who ran this small farm. Here they were so close to the Front and the bombing, being intruded upon by a foreign army, and they stubbornly remained on their farm carrying out their chores as if nothing were out of the ordinary. The small weathered looking farmer who had several teeth missing and his even smaller craggy wife, who had an abundance of facial hair, were so kind as to feed us eggs, toast and the best coffee we had ever tasted every morning. I do believe that we were eating far better than our officers who were put up at the towns Hotel. In turn, for their kindness, we all would help the old couple moving heavy rocks, rebuilding fences and mending weak portions of their small farmhouse roof.

The couple was especially interested in the bagpipes when Sean, Bill, and I would practice. The first time we played, they stopped their routine chores and shuffled over, curious as to the unusual noise. They both sat down on the nearest available object and lit up cigarettes giving us their full attention.

The farmer would lean over and pat his wife's knee, point to one of us and chatter in French. She would nod and smile. It seemed as if they were enjoying our concert because they always put down their cigarettes and clapped enthusiastically at the end of a set. When we practiced, thereafter, we would tune inside their house because of the interference of the constant artillery noise outside. The drones are quieter than the chanter and it was almost impossible to tune with the racket blasting outdoors.

"We're five miles from the front and it's hard to hear. Can you imagine how loud it is at the Front?" Sean asked.

"We'll find out soon enough," Bill said.

Two cows, one old horse, five or six Muscovy ducks and several chickens were the other occupants of our billet. The ducks and chickens were constantly under foot, in fact, several of the ducks seemed peculiarly fond of our boots. These birds also had a bad habit of laying their eggs in the most random places, so a careful check of our straw beds before lying down was prudent.

Bill learned this the hard way one evening when, exhausted from a hard day of helping on the farm, he dropped onto his bed, then jumped back up when he heard the cracks and felt the wetness of several broken eggs. We all had a good laugh over the event–all except Bill that is. He erupted into an uncustomary volley of profanity that sent us into fits of coughing laughter. Because of the free-style egg laying habits of these birds, our first chore of the day was an egg hunt. We used straw baskets just like an Easter egg hunt to collect these treasures. The upside of this daily chore was that Madame Dobsavage, our hostess, would make us omelets along with Bully Beef that tasted surprisingly good. I marveled at how only the French could take something as plain as canned beef and transform it into something delicious, a proverbial silk purse from a sow's ear.

Lieutenant Owen McDonnell joined us one morning and was so impressed with breakfast that he became a regular morning visitor. Sean asked the Lieutenant if we could expect to have the rest of the officers joining us for breakfast tomorrow.

"Not on your life!" McDonnell said smiling. "We'll just keep this our little secret."

≈

The waiting is the most difficult part for a soldier prior to battle. Fortunately for us, we were kept busy around the Dobsavage farm so we had little time to become stressed over the impending fight.

A small group of fellows who apparently had been separated from their unit joined us one night. They were old salts, hardcore killers who were on their way to re-up with their regiment "The London Scottish."

These men had been on the Western Front for over a year and were truly hardened veterans of the trenches. At night, after supper, we coaxed them into telling us stories of their experiences. One by the name of Pinkerton had been in the Battle Lille and recounted the tragic losses sustained by the Blackwatch, which was, of course, my grandfather's regiment.

The London Scottish was among the regiments waiting in the trenches for the word to advance, but those in command were having mixed thoughts about when to start the charge. "We were in the second wave, ready to go; the delay was driving us all mad. After hours of standing ready in the muck of the front trenches and just minutes before we were supposed to charge, we received the order to stand down."

We were all riveted to what Pinkerton was saying as he paused to take a drink of some rum that we had commandeered.

"The word didn't get to the forward trenches in time. The Blackwatch Regiment was to be the first over the top. They were prepared, ready, and able. When the time came to finally start the attack, they charged up and over, unaware of the order to stand down. Into the fire of the deadly barking maxim 08 machine guns they ran, and we could only watch in horror," Pinkerton recalled.

"One hundred yards of No Man's Land to cross before they reached the German trenches. One hundred yards, without a walking artillery blanket being laid down as cover. We in the Scottish were screaming for them to return, but the battle noises drowned out our pleas. They charged ahead into the onslaught. At the fifty yard point they had lost half of the five hundred men in the regiment. But they continued, never looking back, and as they made it to the German's 1st trench there were only about a hundred men remaining.

"We in the Scottish began to charge to help our comrades, but were ordered to stand down by our officers. They threatened us at gunpoint to obey their orders. We could do nothing but watch the carnage," Pinkerton said, his voice cracking and his eyes welling. "Thirty men from the Blackwatch were battling hand to hand when they realized there would be no backup support. They threw off their packs and webbing and sprinted back across No Man's Land. These men had shown unspeakable bravery and gallantry in this unaided charge and how did the Huns show respect? They mowed them down—shot these unarmed brave men in their backs without mercy."

Pinkerton let go with an uncontrollable sob, but quickly regained his composure. "The entire regiment had been wiped out in a matter of minutes."

We all sat silently, stunned and horrified by this account.

"That night we formed a large, all volunteer, recovery party, of which I was a member. We retrieved all but fifty of these fallen heroes and made sure that they received the proper burial that they deserved," Pinkerton said with a heavy sigh. "Our pipers played them under to 'Flowers of the Forest.' I can tell you this: After that night, the London Scottish and the Blackwatch have taken not one German prisoner."

Pinkerton's fellow Scottish grinned with sardonic smiles but Pinkerton had a cold cruel gaze as he spoke.

Bill Lewis looked at me and shook his head. "Five hundred men lost because of a blunder in communications and indecisive leadership."

"A frighteningly horrible waste," I agreed.

Sean and several of the 36th Ulster lads were talking about the account and it seemed to have motivated them with a desire to go into the battlefield so that they could return some of the kindness that was metered out to The Blackwatch.

Pinkerton overheard some of their conversation and felt that he should impart some battlefield wisdom to these novices.

"Lads, the worst parts of a battle are the waiting before and the roll call after," he said. "During the battle itself you think of nothing, you react as you were trained to do and you fight, not for God or country, but for your comrades that are dropping around you."

Pinkerton asked if anyone could spare a fag and several men quickly produced cigarettes for him. One of the Irishmen asked Pinkerton where he and his group had come from.

"We five men have just finished training for sniper and are now going to Verdun to practice our newly learned skill." He smiled and took a drag on his smoke. The stories were clearly over and the men were breaking up into small groups and discussing Pinkerton's recounting of his experiences.

This was a fine time to break out the pipes and drum and change the somber mood of the evening. Pinkerton and his men were delighted with our practice. They were good Scotsmen and the pipes were in their blood. Sean chose to keep it light and snappy with lots of jigs and reels and the men were soon upbeat and lively. We laughed, drank our rations of rum, smoked and spoke of anything other than the war.

Pinkerton beginning to feel the rum said in a loud brogue, "Only real Scotsmen can appreciate such fine pipe'n, you're wasting your talent on these Irishmen."

If not for his playful smile, some of the boys would have taken exception to such a remark. Lieutenant McDonnell, always quick on his feet, replied, "We Irish gave the pipes to you Scots hundreds of years ago as a joke and you still haven't figured it out yet!"

All the Ulstermen burst into raucous laughter. Even Pinkerton and his men couldn't hold back their laughter and joined in.

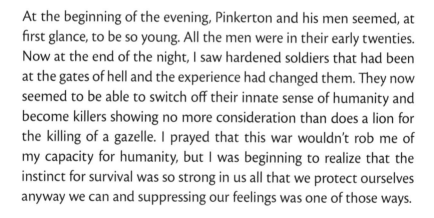

At the beginning of the evening, Pinkerton and his men seemed, at first glance, to be so young. All the men were in their early twenties. Now at the end of the night, I saw hardened soldiers that had been at the gates of hell and the experience had changed them. They now seemed to be able to switch off their innate sense of humanity and become killers showing no more consideration than does a lion for the killing of a gazelle. I prayed that this war wouldn't rob me of my capacity for humanity, but I was beginning to realize that the instinct for survival was so strong in us all that we protect ourselves anyway we can and suppressing our feelings was one of those ways.

"MY LODGINGS IN THE COLD, COLD GROUND"

Deadly Moles – June 25, 1916

Bert Carol was a master at his trade. He truly was worth his weight in gold. Sir John Norton-Griffiths was keenly aware of the value of men like Bert, which is why he was in the process of recruiting as many men with these unique talents as was possible. Prior to the war, Bert had provided his family with a respectable income, although his field was now in decline.

By today's standards, he would be considered upper middle class, however, the upper class still looked down on him because of his profession. Bert, being good-natured, would toss it off. He knew that because of him they were warm and dry, but they were just too dull witted to realize it.

Most of the houses in the British Isles were protected from the rain and sleet by slate roofs and were kept warm on those cold, damp nights with coal, both mined in Welsh mines by men like Bert. Before he was recruited, Bert was a foreman for Ebbw Vale Steel, Iron and Coal Company. He had followed the footsteps of his father in the mining profession at the early age of sixteen and was recognized quickly as a natural miner and leader. He rapidly developed both technical and practical talent which, along with his good nature and leadership qualities, allowed him to advance to lead and then to foreman, a position well above that of his father.

His father was immensely proud of Bert's achievement and would regularly brag about his boy, whom he called "the boss." Both men were well respected by miners and management alike and were often teased good naturedly as a sign of affection.

≈

If asked to do so, Bert and his team of tunnelers could efficiently and quickly build a mine or tunnel from here to there with remarkable accuracy. And now, that is exactly what Sir John Norton- Griffiths was asking of him. Norton-Griffiths wanted it to be a tunnel of deadly accuracy, not just remarkable accuracy.

Bert and many men like him were being employed by the B.E.F. to dig mines–land mines, that is. These were not the land mines of today, consisting of small yet powerful explosives, buried not too deep below the ground surface. The kind of land mine that Bert specialized in were actual tunnels dug under the British trenches and continuing under no-man's land, and ending under German positions of interest. At the end of the tunnel, a large vault would be dug in which tons of explosives would be placed for detonation.

In late 1914, several months after the start of the war, the German forces dug and detonated ten land mines on the Western front in hopes of breaking up the stalemate produced by trench warfare. The desire was to break a hole in the allied resistance. The result was devastating and wiped out the better part of a British colonial Indian regiment. It did not, however, breach the front as was desired, although it did prove to be a formidable and valuable weapon.

Norton-Griffiths was, at that time, a representative of the House of Parliament, and a former mining engineer. He took immediate interest in the incident and seeing the value of the weapon, began lobbying for the formation of a Royal Engineer Corps with the specific task of engineering and building land mines. Both houses of

Parliament quickly approved the proposal, and the Royal Engineers corps came into existence.

Promoted to the rank of major, Norton-Griffiths was put in charge of the project and quickly began recruiting men from the fertile Welsh, Scottish, and Australian mining industries which were suffering the recent loss of their second biggest customer, Germany.

Simply to demonstrate the value of these mining engineers one need look no further than their pay stubs. The engineers were collecting six shillings a day. The "Sappers," who were included in the Royal Engineers, received two shilling, six pence, and the average "Tommy" got just one shilling.

≈

Bert was among the most experienced and respected of the engineers, which was the reason his command placed him in charge of the Hawthorn Ridge Mine. This was to be one of the three big mines that were to be detonated along with eleven smaller mines prior to the attack. Bert had been present when the plans were being discussed and his feeling was that many of the mines were simply being used as the icing on the cake. It seemed to him they were to be nothing more than exclamation points at the end of the artillery sentence.

His tunnel, however, was planned to blow up the Hawthorn Ridge Redoubt, a large and very strategic German fortification that had been responsible for the deaths of a great number of allied soldiers.

The Redoubt was occupied by the German 119th, a battle-hardened division that was the object of Bert's efforts along with the redoubt structure itself. The work had to be stepped up due to the time constraints imposed by Haige and his Big Push plan. There was just a week left before the ground assault and the B.E.F. artillery barrage had begun in earnest.

Bert knew the earth-pounding artillery onslaught increased the chances of a tunnel collapse, so he took special care to brace his tunnel beyond that which was required by a normal "hole".

He also remained at least fifty feet below the surface where there was a layer of hardpan. Unlike the softer, moist earth of the Flanders section farther north, the rolling hills of the Picardy region had abundant chalk beneath the topsoil, which proved to be a much sturdier material for tunnel walls and thus increased the safety of the project.

An added bonus was less silting and better footing. Chalk did make for a hard dig, but most of his men were coal and iron pickers, so the white material was no great effort. At fifty to sixty feet, even a Brit 60-pounder wouldn't rattle the timbers, but under the British trenches, the Germans would occasionally lob Big Bertha's pill, and Bert was unsure of how his tunnel would fare. The task of engineering a tunnel of more than four hundred yards with the objective of pinpointing a location—while maintaining a precise depth—was a marvel.

Bert had his surveyors check the direction and level every one hundred feet of progress. He dug the first 100 yards at sixty feet, the total rise was ten feet overall, to put the vault at fifty feet below the redoubt.

Bert had helped develop a system to expedite the removal of the earth from the Hawthorn Ridge tunnel. Every one hundred yards, his engineers elevated the floor two-and-a-half feet to compensate for the rise in floor elevation. The ore car held about four yards of earth and would roll easily along the gentle decline from the dig to the end of its rail, where it would tip up and dump its load into the next cart waiting two-and-a-half feet below it.

This relay system cut the removal time to a fraction of what it would have been had one cart been used to travel the entire length of the tunnel, and reduced the manpower needed for the movement of debris.

≈

With the advent of every new weapon comes the necessity for counter measures and the land mine was no exception. The British had developed listening devices to detect the sounds of mining below the surface. One was called a Geo phone, an Australian had invented another he called "The Wombat," and of course, the Germans had their own mining detection inventions.

To counter the counter measure and reduce the possibility of detection, rubber wheels had been installed on the ore carts to muffle the noise caused by steel wheels clanking over steel rails. The earth was relatively rock free so the shovel and pick ax made minimal noise. When a rock was hit, all digging would stop, in fact, all movement would stop, everyone would wait ten minutes to prevent detection and triangulation by those listening up top or in nearby enemy tunnels. The rock would gently be pried out of its resting place and placed in a dug out in the tunnel wall. Every effort was made to avoid transporting rocks because of the noise created when being transferred from one steel cart to another.

Bert had been ordered to build a vault capable of housing twenty tons of explosives. He quickly set out to calculate what would be required to house such a charge and was stunned by his findings. Each crate of explosives weighed one hundred pounds and was three feet long, two feet wide, and one foot high. Twenty tons was equal to four hundred boxes, and would require a vault eight feet high, thirty feet wide, and forty feet long-- an enormous room. This room allowed for the stacking of crates two feet above the floor to prevent water damage due to constant seepage and left room around the stacks for proper bracing and movement.

One of the major problems in any mine is lack of breathable air, so a large bellows was operated at the mouth of the tunnel that pumped a constant supply of fresh air through a pipe to the furthest point of the mine. The fresh air would then travel from farthest point back to the mouth pushing the foul air back out of the opening.

The miners had small cages set up every fifty feet or so with canaries in them. A light was placed next to the cage to illuminate the small bird, and if the bird fell from its perch, the men would take immediate note suspecting either gas or lack of oxygen.

Bert had designed the mine to have a gradual grade at the mouth rather than a vertical drop like many other engineers preferred. The slope made the removal of dirt faster and easier employing a mule to pull the cart up the incline. The progress on his tunnel was right on schedule and, in fact, with the artillery bombardment commencing, the bombing allowed his diggers to pretty much disregard the caution they had been exercising concerning noise. No one was going to detect their digging with an artillery barrage going on around them.

≈

The vault was near ready and had passed Bert's initial inspection and approval on the morning of 26 June. He was making the hike back alone and whistling "My Lodgings in the Cold, Cold Ground" a Scottish funeral favorite. Walking up the shallow incline at the end of the tunnel, the muffled and muted noises of cannon fire was becoming louder with each step. He had made the trek along the entire length of the tunnel many times and despite the cool air underground he had beads of sweat forming across his brow. His headlamp cast a dim beam of light illuminating the well-worn dirt path that paralleled the rails for the coal carts. Several hundred feet ahead the midday sun was providing an ever increasing amount of light that over powered the dim head lamp, but caused a glare that actually made seeing the path more difficult.

Bert put his left hand out and ran it along the rough tunnel wall to keep a steady bearing and to avoid vertigo, a trick miners learned to rely on in poorly lit areas. Up ahead, Bert could make out two figures near the entrance of the mine. The silhouetted figures seemed to be arguing over something but the brilliant sunlight made it impossible to make out who they were.

The timbers and earth shook as the Germans delivered the first shell in a return barrage. Loose dirt fell from the cross beams, but the mine held fast. The men ahead stopped talking for a moment, the taller of the two looked around nervously, the other shorter man, remained unflinchingly fixed on the tall one. The tall man started to lecture again and his voice was becoming more audible as Bert drew closer. From behind him, the clip, clop of a mule pulling a cart up the rail was catching up, accompanied by the sound of the gentle coaxing of the mule driver.

"See here, ol' boy," the tall man said. "I am going to have to take something substantial to my superiors about this matter and I am going to hold you personally responsible if I don't get any resolution soon."

Bert could just begin to make out the figure of one of his lead engineers, Mel Bohlig. The taller man an officer, was pointing his finger at Mel and doing all the talking. Bert stepped up his gait, someone was chewing on one of his men and he was not about to tolerate it. Bohlig was a broad powerful man who could have snapped the spindly British officer like a toothpick but, like most of Bert's team, he was quiet and unemotional with an overall good nature.

"Sir, the gentleman you want to talk to is coming up the ramp, perhaps you should address him for your resolution," Bohlig said with a steady voice.

"Very well then," the pompous officer said turning toward Bert. "With whom am I speaking?" he demanded walking toward Bert with a purposeful strut.

The short Welshman who normally had an even temper could feel his face flush as the officer approached. Bert ignored the question and instead growled his own. "Who are you?"

"Lieutenant Hollings. And I repeat–to whom am I speaking?" Bert's muscles on the sides of his jaw were beginning to knot up as he clenched his teeth.

"Chief Engineer Bert Carol," he said. "What is it you want?"

"What is your rank, Carol?" Hollings asked condescendingly.

"What is it you want?" Bert repeated through clenched teeth, his jaw set and head stretched forward.

Hollings, for the first time, backed down a bit. "Well then, I need some progress information on this mine for my superiors. This other chap couldn't have been less helpful."

Bohlig moved uncomfortably close to Hollings causing him to take a step toward the tunnel wall. Hollings nervously looked at Bohlig, then back at Bert.

"See here! My superiors ... your commanders have sent me here to check on your progress," he stammered. "This mine is vital to our assault and must be finished on schedule."

An artillery round pounded the trenches nearby sending a shower of dirt down on all three men. Hollings covered his head and instinctively crouched looking nervously at the thick timbers holding up the mine. Both miners stood over him ignoring the mine's protest to the shelling. Hollings slowly stood up dusting off his formerly clean tunic.

"Look here! My job is to see that all is being done that can be done."

The mule cart and driver had made it up the ramp and paused next to the three men. The mule driver, an old miner, tied off the reins and set the hand brake. He came over and stood next to Bert sensing that something was amiss. He looked at his fellow miners and then fixed a hard stare at Hollings letting go with a spew of chewing tobacco.

The Lieutenant began to perspire, seeing that he was outnumbered by men who couldn't care less for rank and standing.

"I don't need any monkey business here! I simply need to report that all is being done..." His voice cracked and faded away into a mumble.

Bert leaned in toward the man, his substantial eyebrows fixed in a deep frown. "Until I see this tunnel's dirt caked under your and your superior's fingernails and until I see bleeding blisters on your and their hands," Bert said slowly and evenly, "all that can be done is not being done. Until that moment arrives, don't bother me or my men again. This tunnel will be completed on schedule with no thanks to you or your superiors."

Hollings moved around Bohlig, who had been standing motionless and expressionless throughout the entire encounter, and moved up the tunnel looking back and saying "You are borderline insubordinate".

The mule driver looked at Bert and Mel. "I'm glad he left, there's only need for one ass in this mine and that would be Bessie here." He gave the mule an affectionate slap on its rump.

They all broke into loud laughter. Seconds later a whizz-bang hit directly over the entrance causing a partial collapse of the mine sending the three miners running to try to shore up the fallen timbers. Outside miners ran into the dust cloud belching out of the mouth of the tunnel with picks and shovels not knowing the danger below. They only knew that there had been a collapse and that men were down there, fellow miners.

RECONNAISSANCE OF THE SOMME

The artillery had been constant night and day for almost a week and the word had gone out that it was soon coming to an end. There wasn't much piping going on by Terry or Doc. No point. It was impossible to hear. Terry Manning was sitting on his cot with cotton stuffed in both ears. He had read his letters from home so many times that he could recite them by heart. So, while he and Doc (George) were tending to their pipes – rehemping the tuning pins for the drones, the chanter, and the blow pipe, Dan Mckee was drumming on a German helmet he had won in a card game. All were just nervously waiting for the word. The knots in their stomachs were tightening as the zero hour, which had not yet been announced, drew inevitably closer. The tension within the division was as thick as no man's land mud. The normally calm and even keeled Newfoundlanders were agitated and nervous, it didn't help that a British Commander had come in to oversee the regiment.

Colonel Harold Winsted came from what would have been considered a blue blood family, so regardless of his ability he had been given a command. He was a gangly, Ichabod Crane sort of fellow who was insensitive to his own inabilities. He rather believed that he was a shining example of superior command ability and would bark out pointless orders in an effort to convince himself of this.

Colonel Kelton, who the men trusted and looked up to, would follow Winsted around and try to temper the poor command of this
inept fellow. Kelton often stood in the background giving the men
an understanding nod and they would in turn follow the orders of
Winsted no matter how ridiculous and nonsensical they were.

The men had been well trained and were battle ready. The Regiment had seen action in the Gallipoli campaign in Turkey and many
were battle tested, they didn't need to be needlessly ordered about
to bolster the ego of an incompetent buffoon. So, Kelton suggested
to Winsted that he pick several men to form a reconnaissance party
to survey the forward trenches and reconnoiter the area, as the
British bombardment was supposed to have destroyed the massive
barbwire entanglements laid down by the Germans.

It was well known that the Germans had set up strong defenses
by means of a 3 trench system. The 1st trench was heavily fortified
with strong barbed wire entanglements, the 2nd and 3rd were several
hundred meters apart and were the forward defense points heavily protected by machine guns. The intended effect of much of the
bombardment was to destroy the entanglements and open a clear
path to the German trenches and troops. Colonel Kelton was concerned that the entanglements may have survived and thus the suggestion. Colonel Winsted poo-pooed the idea but reluctantly gave
in when Kelton himself volunteered. With Kelton gone, Winsted
would have free rein without his constant interference. The decision
was made and Colonel Kelton had only to pick volunteers for this
dangerous mission. He went to Terry, Doc and Dan and explained
the situation.

"No pressure, strictly volunteer. It's for tonight and the word has
come down from the top that the morning after tomorrow is Zero
hour - 07:30."

The trio looked at each other wondering what to say, a double
header had just been dropped into their laps. Dan spoke first.

"Count me in, anything beats sitting around here waiting and
going deaf."

The other two agreed and Kelton proceeded to lay out the plan for the evening.

"I have dark clothing for us to wear to help conceal us, so we'll don that around 2300 hours and depart at 0000 hours. We will blacken our faces with coal oil smudge from the lamps. We will be traveling light, no packs, Enfields, or canteens, only waist belts and holstered pistols. We must avoid German detection and return with our information, so, no killing Germans unless completely unavoidable. Artillery fire has been instructed to move south of our intended path which will be past the danger tree and right up to the 1st trench off Beaumont Hamel. Beaumont Hamel is the objective of the 29th Division on the morning of July 1st, a day and a half away." He stopped and waited for the inevitable questions.

Terry asked. "Did you just tell us the battle begins on July 1st?"

Dan asked. "Can we eat before we leave and will we be back in time for breakfast?"

"Yes, to both questions." Kelton continued. "The Germans will be sending up stare flares, so when one goes up, you drop down and lay very still. We will stay together, so it is imperative that no one is detected, if one is seen, we are all dead! The danger tree is, as you know, the ragged tree stump that marks where German machine gun fire is the most intense and concentrated. The distance we must travel this evening will be approximately 1,000 meters one way over very rough, shell battered terrain, so the going will be very slow. We will only have 5 hours before dawn, so we must keep a steady pace to the cover the total 2000 meters before we're daylight targets."

He looked at the three men and asked.

"Are you still up for it?"

"Yes" all three agreed.

"Then get some sleep now because you won't be getting any tonight."

The three men turned in and got several hours of fitful sleep before they were awakened by Kelton at 2200 hours. The cook had prepared a special meal for the team and they ate well in Kelton's tent. At 2300 hours they smudged their faces and donned their dark apparel and set off for the trench system. Kelton was intimately familiar with their trenches. Unlike many of the commanding officers, Kelton believed that one should lead by example so he would often join the men in the trenches. The quartet moved along St. John's road trench which led to the front trenches. The bombs were still dropping unendingly, but none of that mattered to them. They were oriented to the mission and had faith in each other's ability to pull this off. The evening had cooled off nicely to about 58 degrees, still sweat was forming on all the men. They made their way past the last Sentry and listening post.

"Look for us around 0500, don't shoot us" Kelton said with a wisecrack smile.

The Sentry replied back.

"God go with you, Sir, I'll not shoot my own brave lads. Good Luck."

Kelton had kept up a good pace through the trenches, but now they had to go over the top and the going would become slow and arduous. The three men crouched down and followed the Colonel as he bobbed and serpentine across no man's land. The flash from shelling exposed them briefly, but it was the star shells that could end the mission and, of course, their lives. The four hit the dirt as a star shell hissed high into the black night. Terry glanced at Doc and Dan, both to his right, as the broken and pocked landscape was illuminated with an unnatural light. Their eyes met as they lay prostrate, all hoping that the Germans could not see them as well as they could see each other. The sweat glistened on the men's blackened faces as the star shell arched and began to diminish in intensity. As the last sparkles of phosphorus burned out, Kelton quickly resumed his crouching run toward the German front lines with the men close behind. Suddenly, Kelton disappeared into the blackness. The men stopped their run and moved forward at a cautious pace. They came to the edge of a shell crater commonly referred to as a crump hole and heard the muted cursing of Colonel Kelton.

"You ok Colonel?" Dan whispered.

"Other than being covered with this butt stink mud, I believe I'm ok! Help me out of this crap hole, will you, please!"

The bottom of the crater was full of about 4 feet of mud. It could have been worse had it been early spring. Many men in full gear had drowned in mud filled shell holes. The sides were still very steep and slick, so the men made a human ladder with Dan holding Terry's heels and Terry holding Doc's heels. Kelton climbed out cursing under his breath.

"I couldn't see a friggen thing. Good thing you lads weren't right tight behind me!"

He looked up and then left and right trying to regain his bearings and determine the direction of the German lines then began trotting in a crouched run again. The men followed from a cautious distance. For about two hours, the four slowly weaved their way across no man's land hitting the deck for the frequent star shells. Terry learned that once the star shell was shot off and you hit the deck, that it was best to keep your eyes closed tightly to avoid the temporary night blindness that followed. The others were quick to follow this sensible method of maintaining modestly good night vision and hopefully avoid another visit into a mud filled hole. Another star shell hissed skyward and the four dove for cover. Kelton dove into what the thought was a slight depression, but once again, he rolled down a steep embankment. This time he was not met by mud, but by the sharp stings of barbed wire. This was the outer German trenches heavily fortified with wire. He lay still so as not to further entangle himself and surveyed the situation. As the star shell arched high, the trench lit up with the ghostly light and to his horror he saw that the barbwire entanglements were intact in both directions as far as the eye could see. All those shells had missed their marks and the 1st line of German defense was still very much so intact. As the star shell fizzled out, the others scurried down the trench embankment to help their leader out of the wire.

"This friggen wire is untouched! How could they have missed it so completely?"

No one answered as they were equally stunned by this revelation. As the men finally snipped the last of the wire off of Kelton, he seemed to have escaped the encounter, as before, with just a few light cuts and bruises.

"We have to get this information back to headquarters! If they try to move on Beaumont Hamel, they'll be slaughtered!"

The men agreed, this section of the German 1st line of defense was unscathed, to attack here would be suicide. Suddenly over the background noise of war, the foursome heard German voices accompanied with some clanging and rattling of equipment. They froze and slowly sank into the rough landscape trying to remain invisible. A German work party of about seven men were noisily walking on the opposite side of the 50 foot wide entanglement inspecting and repairing any damage. They seemed to be quite bold in the lack of stealth, obviously believing that while in the trench they would be safe. Using their shovels as walking sticks gave a clang with each step. Their conversation was loud so as to be heard over the sound of artillery. No need for caution, no one would be mad enough to be out here! Anyway, they won't attack until the artillery fire subsides.

"Not much to do out here, the entanglements are in fine shape". One German said.

"Das ist gut." was the reply.

The party moved slowly past the four men and continued their slow stroll down the German side of the trench until they were no longer seen or heard.

Kelton scrambled up the slope of the trench followed closely by Terry, Dan and Doc. The four began their long and dangerous trip back with this important information.

Kelton yelled back.

"At the very least, one of us has to get this information to the Command! Too many lives are at stake, understood?"

"Understood" was the collective response as the men continued to run, crouched over ready to hit the deck.

A star shell flew high into the sky! On the way to the German lines, their faces were toward the German guns and they could easily see the star shell being fired as it left a tracer before it burst into its brilliant light. On the way back to British lines, however, their backs were to the guns and they couldn't see the telltale tracer. The shell burst into bright light and the four were plainly visible. They dove for the ground, but were followed by the familiar rattle of the German Maxim machine gun fire. The ground exploded around them as they scrambled to get into a shell hole as two more star shells arched into the sky. The front was now alive like an angry hornet's nest. The British Vickers machine guns barked out their response to the German Maxim's rattle. Stuck in the middle of this wild crossfire was the four man reconnaissance team, heads down and hoping for a lull in the action. Terry noticed first, Kelton, who had been cut and bruised was clutching his side and seemed to be in some agony.

"Doc!" Terry yelled. "Kelton's been hit!"

George Cohen scrambled over to Kelton and said "Let me see what you've got!"

Kelton released his blood soaked hands and Doc pulled his shirt up. In the dim light of the distant artillery flashes, Doc could see the wound. A bullet hole in his front right side, too low to hit a lung and too far to the right to catch the liver. George rolled him over to inspect his back. A clean exit wound which seemed to have missed the kidney, the blood was red not black.

"You're lucky" George said out loud, more to himself than to Kelton.

The Colonel glared up at George "lucky would have been not getting shot!"

Doc responded "I'll need to get some pressure wraps on this wound to slow down the loss of blood."

Terry and Dan removed their leg puttees and shirts as Doc packed and wrapped Kelton's side wounds.

"Would you guys stop frigging around with me and get that information back to command, I'll be fine.

Terry said "Doc and I'll go, Dan, you stay with the Colonel, get him out when able."

It was agreed upon and between the moments when one star shell hissed out, another was fired, the two leapt from shell hole to shell hole forging slowly, but steadily toward the British lines. They were past the danger tree and knew that the German fire would lessen, but there were still the snipers or the stray lucky machine gunshot, this was too important to get careless now! They continued hopping from crater to crater until finally they slid down the embankment of the British front trench.

The two lay there for a few moments. They had made it and it took a few minutes to realize it.

"We have to get this information to the Command and give the artillery the approximate position of Dan and the Colonel".

They bumped into the sentry that they had spoken to on their way out. It seemed like so long ago.

"Where are the others?" he inquired.

"About 200 yards out, just the other side of the danger tree. Colonel Kelton has been hit, one of our men is with him."

"I'll say a prayer". He responded as Terry and Doc trotted away.

The artillery Commander was given the approximate position of the two trapped men and began working on a shell pattern to provide some relief and possibly an opportunity for escape.

Major Henry Winsted was weighing up the information that had been passed on by Terry and Doc and seemed reluctant to accept their assessment of the German 1st line trench.

"I'm quite certain that that cannot possibly be a correct observation. We have been bombarding that area for a week with the finest British cluster bombs which dispense of barbwire with relative ease."

"None-the-less the wire entanglement is fully intact." Terry insisted.

"It was dark and the ink is still wet on you chaps. I suspect your inexperience and apprehension are clouding your recollection of the entanglement." Winsted continued.

"Sir, Colonel Kelton said himself that it would be a wholesale slaughter if we advance on that trench in its current condition! I implore you! Please consider what we are telling you." Terry insisted.

Winsted paused several moments with one aristocratic eyebrow perched high and simply replied "Quite, well then you're dismissed."

1ST NEWFOUNDLAND REGIMENT

"Greater love hath no man than this, that a man lay down his life for his friends." – John 15:13

Leslie Greenhow was a conscientious objector. Born in England in 1895, Greenhow's family left Great Britain in 1910 and moved to Windsor, Ontario, Canada when he was fifteen years old. Four years later, when the Great War broke out, there was an expectation that all British men between the ages of 18 and 20 would answer Britain's call. This presented a real dilemma for Leslie who, as a devout Anglican, firmly believed in the Lord's commandment *"Thou shalt not kill" but*, still held a strong loyalty toward his country of birth. Several of his friends at church had refused to join the armed forces and had been harassed and chastised by their peers, some even receiving letters with a white feather, a sign of cowardice and an unspeakable insult.

Leslie was no coward, so he joined the British Armed Forces as a conscientious objector requesting a non-combatant position. The British Armed Forces were happy to oblige and awarded Greenhow with a position as a stretcher bearer. They weren't doing him any favors by this assignment. The simple fact was that the degree of danger involved in the job was greater than that associated with a standard foot soldier. The likeliness of your being mowed down by machine gun fire or being picked off by a sniper was excellent because a bearer needed to stand erect and walk slowly carrying the stretcher along the crater rims. You became an easy target for the enemy. An infantryman could run serpentine and dive into crump holes to avoid being shot.

Now, two years later, Leslie had been in countless battlefields, retrieving hundreds of wounded B.E.F., French and even the occasional German soldier. Red or yellow, black or white, he'd say. He had been on the Somme for two months and had already been out into No Man's Land several times to retrieve the wounded.

Now the cat was out of the bag and everyone knew of Haige's plan for the "big push." This meant countless wounded were going to depend upon his services.

Greenhow often recited the 23rd Psalm as he walked through the muddy uneven real estate of No Man's Land. *"Yea, though I walk through the valley of the shadow of death, I will fear no evil, for thou art with me."* Having a deep firm faith allowed him to venture into the most horrific raging battle fields with a calm that was admired and respected by his colleagues.

Because Leslie had been in and out of so many vicious fights with not so much as a scratch, many of his fellow bearers believed he was protected by the grace of God. It was not unusual for there to be a scramble to be on his stretcher team.

Leslie knew that when God wanted to take him, he would take him. He was confident in his belief that heaven awaited him after this life. "What greater love hath a man than he lay down his life for another?" he often quoted. He knew that if he were to be killed while retrieving his wounded fellow man he would be blessed for his sacrifice in heaven.

≈

This day he sat on a rock jutting from a berm, a short distance from the St. John's supply trench. This position put him several hundred yards away from No Man's Land. He sat casually smoking a pipe. It was a bad habit, but certainly less vulgar than that of cigarette smoking. He drew a heavy toke on the ornate pipe and let out with a cloud of smoke. Smoking was frowned upon by most Christians, but pipe smoking seemed to be more easily tolerated by believers on the Front.

Occasionally his guilt would get the better of him and he would wonder what his mother would say should she ever find out.

"Your body is a temple unto the Lord," he could hear her scold. He tried not to think about it as he took another puff.

≈

The shelling by the B.E.F. had moved further to the east in an attempt to pulverize the German's pill boxes and bunkers, and from Leslie's perch the panorama of the Front toward Beaumont Hamel was fully visible. Word was that a reconnaissance party had gone out last night and come back minus a couple of men who had fallen victim to German fire. The missing men were Pvt. McKee and Colonel Kelton. Leslie was mentally prepared for the orders that he knew would eventually be issued.

The reconnaissance party knew where the two men were. They were trapped – wounded or dead – in the worst possible position in a shell hole near the danger tree, the point at which you were in the sights of at least five German machine gunners.

"Tough spot," Leslie whispered as he surveyed the landscape. The continuous rattle of the Maxim 08s told him that the men were not yet satisfactorily dead in the German's minds. That meant there was hope. The Germans were expending an inordinate amount of energy on these two men. The "thunk" of a Minnie lobbed a shell high into the air and it came down near the danger tree with an explosion.

The Minnie was the nickname for the German trench mortar, the Minenwerfer. It was a portable cannon that could fire a small, but deadly shell at between forty-five and seventy degrees trajectory, dropping the shell almost straight down onto the enemy. Perfect for trench warfare, it inflicted maximum damage when it landed on its mark. The Germans were now trying to fire the Minnie into the shell hole to finish off McKee and Kelton.

"Things are not looking up for you lads," Greenhow mumbled trying to spot the men. As he sat quietly praying for the men trapped in the crossfire, he was startled by a massive volley of eighteen-pounders several hundred yards behind him. These guns were a favorite of the B.E.F. being portable field cannons of medium range, and usually horse drawn. These weapons, along with an expert team, were capable of delivering twenty to thirty rounds per minute, but lacked the accuracy of the French 75s.

≈

Greenhow jumped to his feet as the ground between the danger tree and the German front lines exploded into a huge wall of earth and debris. Something caught his eye as the cloud of dirt fanned out.

Through the dusty veil, he could make out a large figure lumbering ungainly forward. The uneven terrain made it tough going but the figure pressed on with the Maxims firing wildly from the other side in hopes of a lucky strike. As the figure got closer Leslie could clearly see that it was not one man, but two – one being carried on the back of the other.

He took his pipe out of his mouth and craned his neck to get a better look at this remarkable drama unfolding. People often seem to stand and crane their necks or stop smoking when watching some life and death drama. Perhaps it's a reaction that suggests that you want to do something to help but there isn't really anything you can do. Just the act of standing is at least something.

A fellow stretcher bearer came running over to him excitedly. "Leslie do you see what's going on out there?" he yelled. "Have you been watching?"

"Yes, those men are in serious trouble," Leslie replied.

"What do you think? Should we contact our superiors to see whether we should help?"

Greenhow was never one for military chain of command. He felt that if a bearer waited for an order to get the wounded, there would be no wounded, only dead bodies. Leslie emptied the tobacco out of the bowl of his pipe by tapping it gently on the heel of his boot, wrapped it in a handkerchief and put it snugly in his tunic pocket. He had made his own decision.

"Let's get our field packs and stretcher."

The two men grabbed their gear. Leslie carried the canvas stretcher, while the other man held the pack of first aid supplies.

Leslie and his colleague had charged fearlessly out into melees far worse than this, but this time was different. They had never seen such a concentration of firepower directed so intensely on just two men. The team members raced through the trench system, yelling to clear the way as they made their way toward No Man's Land.

≈

Dan McKee had seized the opportunity as soon as the barrage began and hoisted the wounded Kelton up onto his back. He climbed out of the crump hole and began to make his escape as quickly as he could. But the going was painfully slow with Kelton's dead weight and the muddy, pocked earth between him and safety. Dan knew that the diversion and debris screen couldn't last forever, so he began to trot in a half-run, which caused Kelton to groan from the pain of being jostled around.

"Sorry about the rough ride Colonel, we haven't the time to look for the smooth paths," Dan called over his shoulder.

The ground around them was exploding with little pops as the Maxim 08s swept the cloudy wall behind Dan. The big man continued his jolting progress past the danger tree. Bullets whizzed past him like angry bees, but he was more hopeful with each step.

Then he felt two burning stings on his right thigh. McKee stumbled, but did not fall, as the searing pain from the two 7.7mm bullets was transmitted up his leg and to his brain. It was intense at first, but quickly became numb as the nerves in his leg went into shock.

"You Okay?" Dan asked Colonel Kelton, as he steadied himself.

"Couldn't be better," Kelton cracked, as he faded in and out of consciousness.

Dan smiled through the pain and tried to keep going. His right leg was not doing what he wanted it to do. He had to compensate by hopping with his left leg and dragging his right, trying to use it to steady himself. Sweat poured from Dan's matted hair and his breathing became labored as he struggled with his injured colleague. If he had been alone he could have kept up a steady pace, but with the weight of Kelton and a bad leg, the journey was becoming impossible.

≈

Greenhow was trotting through the forward trenches and did something even a neophyte to the trenches would never do: he popped his head above the parapet to see if the two men were still alive.

He saw that Dan was staggering and that there was a crimson flow running down his right leg. He was impressed by the big man's perseverance, but knew that it was just a matter of time before he went down under their combined weight. The good news was that they were beyond the danger tree and every inch they moved closer improved their chances for survival.

Greenhow and his partner had raced through the zig-zag maze leading to the advanced trenches and scurried up the gentle grade over the top into No Man's Land, running straight toward McKee some twenty yards away. The two covered the distance at a sprint and reached the wounded men just as Dan collapsed and rolled into a shallow shell hole. The rescuers slid down the walls of the same crump hole and intercepted the wounded men with remarkable speed.

McKee looked up in total amazement as he realized that he and Kelton were not alone.

"What the hell?" he said, dumbfounded.

"Don't swear," Greenhow said and stretched out his hand. "Leslie Greenhow is the name. We're here to help."

"I could use some and am I ever glad to see you," Dan said. They shook hands as if meeting at a social function.

"Let's see about that leg," Leslie said, getting to work. "How's your friend?"

"He's lost a lot of blood. We stopped him up as well as we could, but that was some time ago," Dan said.

Greenhow applied a tourniquet to Dan's leg and dressed the wounds temporarily while his partner inspected Kelton.

"This looks like an expert applied this pressure wrap!" Greenhow's partner said.

"One of our party was a med student before he joined up." Dan said.

"Nice job," Greenhow said, nodding. "Now, let's get you out of here. Can you walk?"

"I'll keep up," Dan grunted. "Don't worry."

The two bearers grabbed the semi-conscious Kelton and slung him neatly onto the stretcher.

"Ready?" Greenhow yelled taking up the aft and the most dangerous position on the stretcher. "Let's go home, shall we?"

They lifted Kelton smoothly up and began to walk up the rim of the shell hole. Dan hobbled along grimacing with the pain, but true to form, kept up with the stretcher team. Artillery shells continued to explode nearby and the machine gun bullets relentlessly whizzed past them in search of a target.

"Only fifteen yards to go," Leslie said as they ran, stumbling around the rim of a large shell crater.

≈

Gunther Bayer was struggling with his Minenwerfer, along with his fellow artillery men, through the forward trenches. With four ten-pound bombs strapped to each man's waist belt and the 250 pound trench mortar on a two wheeled trolley, it took two strong men to make the weapon even modestly portable over the rough trench floor.

"Is this thing getting heavier or am I just getting old?" he asked his comrade with a smile.

"Yes," was the reply.

"Ha!" Gunther laughed. The men had covered about two hundred yards of trench and their legs and arms were beginning to burn as one pushed and one pulled.

"Break," Gunther said, and the two men stopped and put down the small cannon. Both men put their hands on their lower backs just above their rumps and stretched backward trying to loosen their taut muscles.

"Dummkopfs!" Gunther barked.

"Who? Our side or theirs?" his partner joked.

"Both!" he shot back. Both men roared with laughter this time. Their orders had arrived less than one hour ago stating that they were to go to the most forward trench and deliver their bombs so as to reach a target between the danger tree and the British trenches. They were given an approximate grid position, but no further information.

Gunther took his trench periscope, a three-foot tube with an angled mirror on the bottom and another on the top which allowed one to safely peer over the trenches, and took a look toward his target. All he saw was a wall of dust, dirt, and debris being created by the barrage.

What could his commander possibly be thinking about? It couldn't be a major assault or they would be sending up troops and using their own artillery. This made no sense.

"Fifty more yards," Gunther said. "Then we lighten our load and drag this little beast home." The men took their positions and continued their arduous trek.

Gunther had been on the Somme for several months, he knew the trenches like the back of his hand and they hadn't changed position the whole time of his deployment.

Nothing has changed but the men keep dying, he thought. They finally arrived at the spot that he knew would give him the best position for firing his gun. They removed the weapon, anchored it with spikes to the dirt, and pointed her in the direction of the target. The distance would be around three hundred yards to the 1st British trench, so he set the Minenwerfer's trajectory angle at forty three degrees. That would give the small shell nearly two hundred eighty yards of throw, give or take ten yards for possible differing conditions. He would then increase the trajectory by two degrees each round and walk the explosions back toward them.

His partner took the periscope and looked over the parapet. "Nothing but a cloud. What is it we are shooting at?"

"A grid box," Gunther shouted over the noise. His partner grabbed one of his bombs and held it ready at the mouth of the mortar awaiting the command.

"Fire!" Gunther yelled.

His comrade let go of the bomb and turned away from the gun, covering his ears, as did Gunther. The load slid down the barrel and hit the firing pin igniting the charge that would propel it toward the enemy.

Thunk! The shell was sent high over No Man's Land to its final destination. They loaded the next round.

≈

Just ten yards to go now, Leslie could see the parapet of the most forward trench plainly. With each step closer came an ever increasing feeling of safety. He knew he could go no faster than the man at the lead and Leslie knew him to be one of the most capable men he had ever worked with. The muddy, rough terrain made for painfully slow going nonetheless.

Through the explosions of the eighteen-pounders and the rattle of the Maxims came a familiar sound – and not a good one. Thunk! It was the distinct sound of a Minnie. He hated that sound.

Leslie had been doing his job long enough to know that to run for cover was pointless. It was better to simply continue what you were doing and try to complete the save. He recited the 23rd Psalm again to himself.

The lead had also heard the Minnie and picked up his pace as fast as he dared. Leslie felt the tug of the increased step and followed suit. The shell exploded about ten yards ahead of them sending a shower of dirt over all four men but miraculously they were not hit.

Thunk! Another round was on the way but it appeared that they had made it. The lead man stepped carefully over the edge of the wall of the trench when the ground behind Leslie exploded, heaving another shower of dirt over them and knocking Dan McKee over the edge to the trench bottom.

The force of the explosion threw Leslie forward down to his knees but he got up and carried Kelton over the edge and into the safety of the trench. At the bottom of the trench the lead began to set the stretcher down as he felt the rear also being gently set down.

He turned to see Leslie drop to his knees and fall forward with a low groan.

"Get off of me!" Kelton howled as Greenhow landed on him. He had no way of knowing that the back of Greenhow's uniform was tattered and scorched and covered with blood.

"No! Leslie No!" the lead cried out, and scrambled around Kelton to assist his fallen friend. Dan hoisted himself up off the trench floor and limped over to help the leadman with this fallen hero. They rolled Leslie off of Kelton, but Greenhow's partner turned away, knowing by the extent of the injuries the man was dead.

Somehow Leslie Greenhow had summoned enough determination to carry Kelton down the trench, despite the fact that by all rights he was dead at the trenches edge.

Dan was left cradling Greenhow's lifeless body as his partner groaned.

Colonel Kelton suddenly realized what was happening, he leaned up on his side and looked into the face of the man who had just saved his life. Stunned, he looked at Dan, and his eyes welled up. He gave his life for me," he said.

McKee held Greenhow in his exhausted arms as if he were a small child and began to sob.

To Minnie
(dedicated to the P.B.I.)
In days gone by some aeons ago
That name my youthful pulses stirred,
I thrilled when'er she whispered low
Ran to her when her voice I heard.
-:0:-
Ah Minnie! How our feelings change,
For now I hear your voice with dread
And hasten to get out of range
Ere you me on the landscape spread.
Wippers Times/ Somme Times

36TH ULSTER

We were three miles south of the staging position for the 29th Division where Terry, Dan and Doc were a part of the 1st Newfoundland Division. Sean, Bill and I were pretty much fed up with the endless racket caused by the unending artillery barrage. Two days of heavy rain and inclement weather had persisted, which made it totally impossible for the forward observers to access the progress of the bombing. Also, no one had the slightest clue that the Germans had built such remarkably strong bunkers, or that the entanglements of the first trench had escaped the intention of our bombardment. All we knew was that our ears had become obvious casualties of the Somme offensive.

Because of the foul weather head command had delayed the ground assault by two days to 1 July. We had two more days of deafening waiting to look forward to. The rain had eased up some and the forecast was for more favorable weather over the next few days, which suited us just fine. Standard issue tents provided minimal protection against the rain unless a liberal oiling had preceded the downpour. Fortunately, we had slathered up our abode just days earlier. Nevertheless, we could not avoid the wet sloppy conditions completely which added to our misery.

Sean and I had just finished seasoning our bagpipe bags. This is a process that is required with leather bags maybe twice a year to keep them soft and airtight. One must remove all the drones and the chanter and cork off the holes going into the bag. A sticky, smelly, oily substance called seasoning is poured into the bag which is then corked and blown up like a beach ball. You work the seasoning into the bag by rolling the bag around, and the sticky sealant plugs the seams while replenishing the oils the leather loses by being bathed constantly in moisture and saliva. Then it is left to sit for several hours before being played.

Not having much else to do, Sean produced a newspaper and began to read it on his cot. Within five minutes he was laughing hysterically over some article he had been reading.

Bill and I looked at each other, annoyed at being left out of the joke.

"Hey, Giggles, what's that you're reading?" Bill asked.

Sean stopped laughing and, wiping his eyes, said, "It's this paper I found in the latrine. It's called The Wipers Times and it's all tongue-in-cheek, very funny stuff."

Just then Lieutenant Owen McDonnell poked his head into the tent. We all hopped up to attention, Sean dropping the paper onto his cot.

"At ease, men. How's my band today?" He saw the paper on the cot. "Oh, so that's the reason for all the laughing – the latest Wipers!"

"What's with this paper?" I asked. "We've never heard of it."

"Well, about two years ago a couple of limey wisecrackers who were in the infantry in the 1st Battle of Ypres were going through the demolished town of Ypres, which, being cheeky buggers, they pronounced Wipers. They came upon a printing shop that was not totally destroyed," McDonnell said. "So they put together the first issue of this irreverent rag. They take pot shots at everyone and everything – nothing seems off limits. Even the name 'Wipers Times' has a double meaning, since it can also be ripped into strips and used as bum fodder in the latrine."

Bill and I smiled at the idea that there were such creative trench rats providing entertainment for the troops out there.

"Bum fodder for the bomb fodder!" Bill quipped.

Owen laughed. "Very good, perhaps you should write for them. They do accept articles and poems from almost anyone as long as they're poking fun at someone or something."

Sean picked up the paper and leafed through it. "Here's a series called 'Herlock Shomes,'" he said.

"One of my favorites," McDonnell said with a smile. "They were on the case of 'Napoo Rum' and I believe they were close to cracking it."

He saw our puzzled expressions. "Napoo is trench slang, a mispronunciation of the French phrase 'il n'y a plus,' or 'there is no more.' The B.E.F. tried to shut down the paper, because of negative remarks made by the editors. The men went into near revolt and the muckety-mucks backed off – but then they tried to take over the paper! Of course, the editors would have no part of that. So, the brass turns a blind eye to the paper and tolerates it because it seems to make the men laugh in the midst of this brutal conflict."

Sean coughed out a laugh.

"Let me read this article to you," he said. "It's titled 'The Lecture.'"

"If at any time you happen to be at all depressed – though of course this is extremely unlikely out here where there is so much to interest and delight one – find out whether there is a lecture on anywhere, given by the G.S.O. first or second of a Division about to be relieved, to the officers of the relieving Division, and go to it at once. It will make you realize that war is worthwhile.

"Roughly speaking, the show will be as follows: The room is packed with an expectant but nervous conglomeration of officers, of whom certainly not more than the first two rows will hear a word of the glad

tidings. That doesn't matter, however, there is a screen and a magic lantern which you may be deluded into thinking is going to show you a reasonable clear picture of the trenches – don't be had by it – it's only a trap.

"Well, eventually a Staff Officer mounts the platform, and you gather from his opening remarks that he has been deputed to give the lecture, that he is not much of a hand at the job, and that you must forgive him. This is greeted with sympathetic noises – the audience apparently attempting to ingratiate themselves into his good offices thereby, and hoping that, if they are successful in this, he'll let 'em down with a minimum of forgetfulness.

The Staff Officer is not moved in the least. He proceeds as follows: 'As a matter of fact I haven't been up to the front line for – er – some time (the audience appear incredible) but when I was last up, a " " had fallen in, and of course most of the communication trenches had been – er – crumped in.'

"The audience seem to appreciate the fact that there are still a few trenches extant. 'I will now show you some photographs of the craters.' The operator having woken up, the lantern is lit, and a beautiful bright light, accompanied by a very realistic imitation of the odours encountered at Hooge is given. Unfortunately the lighting effects are poor, but anyway you have a quiet ten minutes in which to give your pal instructions what to do with your corpse.

"Eventually a picture is shown, which may remind you of your late Uncle Bill, who used to suffer severely from warts. As the lecturer invariably holds his pointer at least one foot from the screen, you will naturally look at the wart indicated by the shadow, but that always adds to the amusement, and you can run a book as to which smudge is the crater.

The grand finale is always worth paying attention to. 'The enemy shoot at you from three and a half sides, some officers make it three and three quarters, though personally I incline to the latter view.' The Staff Officer then tells you that he doesn't think he has anything more to say, and though everyone seems grieved to hear it, he subsides into a chair next to the G.O.C.

The best part of the lecture is, of course, that it leaves you with a magnificent thirst. P.B.I. (Poor bloody infantry)"

≋

Sean finished and we all had a good laugh.

"Boys," McDonnell said finally. "I'm afraid we'll have to be serious for a moment." We all settled down and gave him our full attention.

"As you know, our orders have been issued and I know that there are rumors galore about them, so I would like to dispel or confirm these rumors and clarify our objectives for the morning of the morrow next."

We had all moved to sitting positions on the edge of our cots, leaning forward with our elbows on our knees intently waiting for the Lieutenant's input. For the first time since leaving Canada, I felt a shot of adrenaline cause my heart to pound hard giving me a light headed feeling. I didn't think I was afraid, but the realization that the battle was now so close gave me pause.

I looked at Sean. He seemed to be serious – no sign of fear – then Bill, he was cool as a cucumber sandwich. He winked at me and gave me a reassuring but very slight smile then turned his attention back to Lieutenant McDonnell.

"At 07:30 our artillery bombardment will cease and a number of land mines will be detonated. The number of which is classified, but suffice it to say it shall be impressive. After the dust settles, fifteen minutes to be precise, we will commence the attack."

"Won't the fifteen-minute delay give time to the enemy to prepare for our attack?" Bill interrupted.

The Lieutenant looked at Bill with a curious expression of impressed appreciation. "Very astute of you Mr. Lewis. This subject was a bone of contention during the planning stages of our attack. Some of our commanders wanted no delay, and others wanted lengthy delay, so, a compromise was met and it was decided that fifteen minutes would be the wait."

Bill nodded understanding, while McDonnell continued. "Several well-marked paths will have been cut through our own barbed wire defenses, which will lead to No Man's Land. Multiple lines of the 9th Irish Fusiliers will be at the ready and will be preceded by a team of wire cutters and Grenadiers."

Lt. McDonnell continued to call them Grenadiers, even though, as I said before, the BEF preferred them to be called Bombers. It was Owen's little dig.

"Our eventual objective is to capture and hold the Beaucourt Rail Station, but to accomplish that we must fight past the Schwaben Redoubt, a heavily fortified position manned by the battletested German 10th Bavarian Division. To add to our difficulty, we are uncertain of the condition of the German entanglement. There is a rumor that a scouting party found it untouched, but that is being down played by Command, hence the cutters will be in position prior to 07:30.

"We will plan on having a great many men across the Ancre River and as close to the Enemy as we dare, the run up the hill toward the Schwaben Redoubt is a long one, especially under fire."

McDonnell paused, scanning our faces to underscore the gravity of the task ahead.

"Our Divisional Commander, Major General Nugent, is a good fellow and has, in my observation, not underestimated the enemy and their ability to withstand our pummeling barrage," he continued. "He has given the word to be in position, be ready, and when the time comes attack fully in running waves accompanied by Lewis guns and backed up by Vickers in case the tide should turn."

The Lewis Gun was a highly portable, lightweight machine gun capable of five hundred to six hundred rounds per minute. The Vickers was a heavier gun similar to the German Maxim requiring a team of three or four to set it up and operate it efficiently. It, however, had longer range and had far more destructive capabilities. At between four hundred-fifty and six hundred rounds per minute, it could decimate advancing Germans at several hundred yards.

"We, of course, will be preceded by one final artillery barrage to keep the Germans, hopefully, in their trenches," McDonnell concluded. "Then it will be up to us."

"Where do we fit in sir?" Sean asked.

"I realize that you three can't do your job at a charge, you will be expected to march forward slow and steady. The sound of your pipes and drums will carry our lads forward inspiring them to do things that no men should ever be asked to do. As long as they hear the pipes, they will keep going so don't let them down. The weapons that you possess have carried untold generations of Celts into countless battles for centuries. They have a strong and ancient affect that reaches down into a man's long forgotten past and awakens his warrior spirit."

We were quietly taken back by the lieutenant's speech and his almost poetic comments about our instruments of war.

"As the whistle is blown to advance," McDonnell continued. "You gents will begin playing and follow the troops up and over the top and into hell to piss on the devil. By the way, I have it on very good authority that the German's despise the pipes and refer to you as The Ladies from Hell, so give them their money's worth."

He smiled a friendly, honest smile. "See you in the trenches when you're kilted and dressed to kill."

McDonnell turned to leave and we all stood up to attention. "As you were," he said quietly.

"Quite a speech, eh?" Sean said.

"Kind of scary," I replied.

Bill grabbed The Wipers Times from Sean's cot and anxiously flipped through its pages.

"I need a laugh," he said.

PART SEVEN

THE REVELATION

NOT A BLIGHTY

Dan McKee had been seriously wounded on his return from the reconnaissance mission. After being patched up, somewhat, at the Advanced Field Station, his next stop was the evacuation depot for transport to a hospital. McKee, despite being shot twice and suffering from extensive blood loss, objected strenuously to the doctor's orders of being sent from the Front insisting that the wounds looked worse than they were. Orders are orders, however, so he resigned himself to the road trip.

He was waiting for the medics to load the ambulance that he had been assigned to and saw, to his relief, that Colonel Kelton was one of the passengers to join him on his ride. Kelton was unconscious and heavily sedated, but the doc said his recovery should be complete, although it would take at least six months.

One medic, in a talkative mood, said to Dan, "Well, old boy, looks like you may have your blighty."

Dan looked puzzled. "Blighty? What's a blighty?"

"You know. Your ticket back to England" the medic replied.

Blighty was trench slang for a wound serious enough to require time to recover back in Great Britain.

"Not if I can help it," Dan said. "I've got a message I'd like to hand deliver to the bums who shot me and dropped a Minnie on my friends."

The medic smiled at McKee's fortitude. "Good Show! You're a good man. Best of luck to you," he said, and went off to fetch more wounded to load.

Dan was one of the few who could sit for the ride and had perched himself up near the front of the box near the driver.

A man poked his head into the rear door just before they were about to close the gate and looked over at McKee. "Do you remember me?" he asked.

"Of course," Dan replied. "You were one of the stretcher bearers, the one who carried Colonel Kelton."

"I hope you don't mind... and I'm glad I caught you," the man said hesitantly. "You see, I have a favor to ask of you."

"What can I do for you, my friend?" Dan said reassuringly.

"Well, you see, my friend – Leslie Greenhow – was the man who died in your arms."

"I shall never forget," Dan said solemnly.

"I have a small box of his belongings that I collected from our tent. A bible, some letters, several photographs, you see – and I have written a letter to his parents as well – and I would be most appreciative if you could see that his things and the letter are delivered when you get to the Hospital." He seemed worried about his intrusion. "The letter and box are properly addressed and have adequate postage..."

"It would be my honor. The man was a selfless hero." Dan said, interrupting the man's long sentence, as a lump formed in his throat.

Eyes cast down, the man said, "Thank you. Thank you very much. He was a fine gentleman." He turned and began to walk away, but stopped as if he'd forgotten something and returned to the door.

"One more favor if you would," he said. "You see, Leslie was from a very religious family and they would never understand, you see... He smoked a pipe and I saw no reason to let them know about his habit. I kept the pipe, but I have no use for it, so perhaps you would like it. It's quite beautiful." The man produced a magnificent white carved bone pipe.

"Holy smoke! That is a real work of art," Dan said, accepting the gift. "I will cherish it always and repeat the story of your friend's heroism often when people admire this beautiful piece of art." Dan choked on his words and began to lose his composure.

"Thank you so very much," the man said. His eyes were welling up and he turned away, not wanting Dan to see his emotions. He took a deep breath and let out a heavy sigh, then walked slowly away, not looking back.

Dan sat on the hard wooden bench looking at his beautiful gift. A driver cranked the engine of the ambulance to life and slid behind the wheel. He released the emergency brake handle and with a minimum of grinding, put the transmission into first gear. With a jerk, they were off.

Dan's dour mood was quickly jolted out of him by the rough ride of the truck on the unimproved road. The truck's tires were almost solid rubber, and that, along with the buckboard spring suspension and no shock absorption made for a bone-jarring ride. The motor ambulance was a new Rover Sunbeam Autocar, which looked very much like a Model T Ford truck, except an ambulance box had been placed on its back. It had an open driver's compartment, no windscreen or doors. There was an opening between the driver and the box to allow him access to the back. The box was set up to carry up to four stretchers, and as many as eight walking wounded along with one attendant.

Every bump caused a shot of searing pain to run up Dan's already throbbing leg. He shifted position trying to favor it. He knew that the morphine was wearing off.

He studied his new pipe. It was carved intricately around the bowl and stem, not like scrimshaw, but deeper, more distinct cuts forming a pastoral scene of jumping deer and woodland animals.

The stem was about five inches long with a slight curve, and the bowl was about the size of an egg, which provided adequate area for tobacco. The stem had yellowed slightly from use, which gave it even more character, and Leslie Greenhow's name was carved on it in small letters. The ambulance hopped over a rut and Dan let out a holler from the ever-increasing pain and pushed his arms down to take the pressure off of his leg.

"Sorry 'bout that mate" the driver glanced over his shoulder at Dan. "Believe it or not, just two months ago you would have been clomping along in one of the old Mark 3 horse-drawn ambulances. Rough ride they are – wooden wheels and all. Slow too, never much faster than three to four miles per hour. This here is the real deal. Nothin' too good for our wounded boys."

The driver caught sight of Dan's new pipe. "Hello, now what 'ave we 'ere?" he asked. "That's some fine stoker you 'ave there mate."

"A present from someone I knew. You a pipe smoker?" Dan asked.

"Indeed I am," the driver said flashing a sparsely toothed smile.

"I'm not really a smoker," Dan said, "but since I've inherited this beauty, perhaps I should give it a try."

"Listen, mate," the driver said, "I've got a treat for you. Reach into the left breast pocket of me tunic and you'll find a pouch of tobacco and a box of blue tips." He leaned over so Dan could reach his tunic. "I'd join you, but I can't drive wif two hands and smoke a pipe at the same time."

Dan reached into his pocket and found the leather pouch and the small cardboard box of blue tip matches.

"Now what?" Dan asked.

"Take out a pinch of tobacco and fill the bowl, then tap 'er down wif your thumb, not too tightly now."

Dan opened the pouch releasing the aromatic sweetness of the moist tobacco and did as instructed. "Smells like candy – good enough to eat," Dan commented.

"Me own blend. I soak the tobacco in cherry juice and rum for a week, then dry 'er out for smoking. Me Grandpop taught me that back in Queensland."

"Aussie, eh?" Dan asked as he tamped the tobacco into the bowl.

"Right on, Canuck, eh?" the driver responded, with a extra emphasis on the "eh." They both laughed.

"Well, I think we're ready to give her a test run," Dan announced.

"Well then, give er a toke or two and be on wif it. Do the old boy a favor, will ya mate, and be good enough to blow some smoke my way," the driver asked.

"It'll be the least I can do." Dan struck a blue tip along the wooden posts that make up the box frame of the ambulance. The flame from the match was drawn into the bowl and then belched back out as Dan puffed the pipe to life. The result was an ever-increasing cloud of the sweetest aromatic smoke that Dan had ever smelled.

He blew a large plume of smoke across the face of the driver who in turn drew the smoke deeply into his lungs. The beautiful aroma emanating from Dan's new pipe replaced the ever-present smell of spent artillery shells and death.

"That's a smell I could get used to," Dan said.

"The smoke transports me away from all this," the driver said, looking off into the distance. Both men became momentarily lost in the brief distraction from reality. The moment was too pleasant to interrupt with casual conversation. For a spell, they were afforded an escape from the madness and they both wanted to keep it pure.

≈

Several minutes had passed in silence when the steering wheel of the ambulance was abruptly jerked out of the hands of the driver sending it veering sharply to the left, almost up on two wheels. The driver grabbed the wheel and yanked it to the right correcting the swerve and putting it back on the correct side of the road.

"Sweet friggin', bloody, bugger all!" he shouted while he fought to regain control of the vehicle. "Pardon me foul language mate," he said, as Dan hung onto the frame of the ambulance box, grimacing in pain from being tossed about. "Me wife says I have a short fuse and a foul mouth."

"This is a war pal," Dan said through clenched teeth. "You're allowed to use bad language – besides your wife isn't here."

"Ha! Right you are mate!" The driver saw that Dan was in pain. He knew the morphine's effectiveness, which usually lasted about two hours, was beginning to wear off on Dan and the rest of the passengers in the back.

"About one more hour to the hospital, mate, and the road improves from 'ere on in." Dan nodded a grateful thanks and remained quiet on the bench trying to stifle the pain.

The road did improve as the driver had promised, and the ambulance was able to pick up speed, increasing from ten to almost twenty miles per hour. Forty-five minutes later, they had joined a long line of ambulances – both motorized and horse drawn – that were awaiting their turn into the triage area of the 5th Canadian Stationary Hospital.

FINDING LAZARUS

The sorting area of the 5th Canadian Stationary Hospital was normally abuzz with activity, but nowhere near as much of a madhouse as it would soon become. Doctors, nurses, and orderlies performed triage, methodically attending to each patient in order to determine the severity of the wounds and separating those who required immediate care.

This was another link in the chain of retrieval set up by the Royal Army Medical Corp. The system was actually very well thought out and organized. Like a family tree, the outer branches were regimental aid posts, a forward position that would be attended by field medical officers, orderlies and several stretcher-bearers. The aid posts were located in the advanced trenches. They were often dugouts covered by corrugated steel and sandbags to protect its inhabitants from debris.

Regularly four aid posts were attached to one advanced dressing station and they would bring the wounded there to replace field dressings and better attend to their wounds. Because the trenches were narrow, the stretcher-bearers often employed a wheeled stretcher. It was simply a rigid stretcher with two large wheels located in the middle. The wheels had pneumatic tires that aided in transport over muddy terrain.

The advanced dressing station was located at a more comfortable distance from No Man's Land, but was still in the outer edges of the trench system. That meant it had to be a deep, well-built dugout – sometimes as deep as thirty feet – or even the basement of an abandoned farmhouse. They were also located close to a supply trench or road to allow the wounded to be taken rapidly away by ambulance.

The ambulances leaving the advanced dressing stations reported to the main dressing station, where the wounded would be cleaned, warmed, and fed. Those needing further medical attention would either be treated or sent to the next link in the chain, the stationary or railhead hospital. These hospitals were called stationary, but could be quickly packed up and moved to another location so as to better serve the requirements of the front. These hospitals were the first link in a new chain referred to as the evacuation zone and could send great numbers of wounded by ambulance train to connect to hospital barges, and then to hospital ships and back to Britain.

≈

This was the path of the wounded and those lucky enough to have earned their blighty. And this is how Dan McKee found himself climbing out of the back end of the Sunbeam into the activity of the 5th Canadian Stationary Hospital casualty clearing area.

Two orderlies had taken Kelton away on a wheeled stretcher and another had come over with a wheelchair that Dan refused to use. He was very stiff from the rough ride and thought it might help to try and stretch a little before he let the system take him hostage. He hobbled around the ambulance several times leaning against it with his arm and keeping as much weight off of his wounded leg as possible.

≈

The driver had left to relieve himself so Dan had several minutes to try to get his kinks out. The buzzing in his ears remained although the noise of the artillery was distant. He muttered to himself, complaining about the inconvenience of his pain.

On his third circuit around the Sunbeam, Dan began to feel light-headed. The loss of blood – and now the exercise – was causing dizziness.

Then, a loud female voice screeched above the busy sounds of the clearing area. "Holy Crap! McKee!"

Dan was startled and, without thinking, spun around on his bad leg almost collapsing from the pain of his quick movement.

Running at him was a nurse, at full speed. Sheila Lougheed hit Dan at a full run, which would not have been a problem had Dan not been wounded. Unable to catch her – or stop her – and already off balance from his quick turn, Dan went down and they both hit the ground with a thud. The pain shot through McKee's body like a lightning bolt, he let go with a low growl through clenched teeth trying not to pass out.

"Oh! Oh! Oh! Dan, I'm so sorry! Oh, God! Are you alright?" she pleaded.

"I feel like a million bucks," Dan said through his pain. "I just got beat up by a woman."

Sheila's expression quickly went from concern to hilarity at her friend's joke, and she laughed loudly. She quickly realized that Dan was hurt.

"Oh my God! What's wrong with you? What happened?" She saw the dressing on his right thigh, the blood showing through the bandages. "You're injured – your leg!"

"Sheila, stop! Take a breath!" Dan commanded as he attempted to get up to a standing position.

She froze, eyes wide, and remained silent. Dan's gruff, pain-riddled face was slowly replaced by the warm McKee smile as he regained his footing.

"I love you," he said. "Now I believe I'll take that wheelchair be-fore I pass out."

Sheila grinned, gave him a warm hug and went to get a wheel-chair. Within minutes she returned with an orderly and a chair, the big man would have been a struggle for her to wheel alone.

≈

"I'll take you to the best doctor I know," she said. "He's unusual and speaks with a difficult accent, but he is the best. We'll catch up after you're taken care of."

Dan felt much better now about allowing the system to take him knowing that he had a guardian angel on the inside. They moved into a large semi-permanent building in which there were a number of doctors, all inspecting and assessing patients in small areas divid-ed by drawn curtains. Sheila led the orderly into one cubicle where a doctor had just finished with a wounded man.

The doctor was a tall man, in his early forties, and about the same size and build as Dan. He had dark hair, a baby face, and a very laid back demeanor. He looked tired and seemed to have some stiff-ness in his back, a result of his college football days. With warm eyes and a closed-mouth, crooked smile the doctor greeted them.

"How y'all doin?" he asked. "Kin ya hop up on the table or do y'all need help?"

Dan glanced at Sheila, who whispered, "I told you, didn't I?"

"I can make it up," Dan said as he stretched out on the examina-tion table. "It looks like a couple of clean bullet wounds."

The doctor ignored Dan's statement and cut the bandages off the wounds. "Ahm Doctor Bill Bradley," he said as he inspected the wounds and prodded with a surgical prod. "And what's your name doctor?"

Dan was momentarily taken aback but quickly recovered. "Well, I wasn't trying to tell you your job, Doc. I was just making small talk."

"Ah don't do small talk," Bradley said in his heavy southern accent as he flushed the wounds with saline solution. Dan stiffened from the hot pain produced by salt water on an open wound. "Here's what y'all are lookin' at. Your statement 'bout a clean-through wound wasn't completely correct. Did ya fall down into the mud after y'all were shot?"

Dan nodded, still fascinated by this man's unusual accent.

"Ya see, the soil in these here parts is cultivated by horse and cow dung and has been for hundreds of years. That along with rotting bits and pieces of your fellow soldiers, rats, vermin and sewage makes for some remarkable infections. First, y'all need a dose of tetanus antitoxin so ya don't end up twisted up like my grandpa in the Civil War. Then, I'm gonna start y'all on a new program developed by a French surgeon, Doctor Carrel. Ya see one of the real problems created by that bad soil in y'alls deep wound is somethin called "Gas gangrene." Doctor Carrel's procedure reduces the incidence of gangrene and, therefore, the possibility of losing y'alls leg by 'bout forty percent." He paused a moment allowing the information to sink in.

The thought of losing a leg was not one that Dan relished. "When do we start?" he asked.

"We sorta just did," Bradley said. "I'll have to open your wound a little more to remove any dead flesh and muscle, but the procedure is quite simple. We bathe or irrigate the wounds with saline solution several times a day and keep a close eye out for infection. The procedure does extend the healing process some, but the pluses outweigh the minuses. Oh, and as you've already discovered the irrigation can be quite painful. Now you ready to proceed?"

"Do what you need to do and leave the pain to me," Dan quickly shot back.

"Very well, then. Sheila, give the patient some morphine and a leather strap to bite on."

Several minutes of gut-wrenching pain from the cutting was followed by still more intense pain from the saline bath, but Dan bit down and powered through with little more than a muffled growl.

Both men instinctively appreciated each other's directness and obvious inner strength. In different circumstances they would have become great friends, but under the present conditions socializing was kept to a minimum.

"He'll be square dancin' in no time," Bradley told Sheila, who watched the procedure intensely. "Now find this man a good bed with a view. This table has a waitin' line."

Both men smiled and nodded. "Be seein' y'all," Bradley said.

"I'll buy you a beer when this is all over." Dan said.

"Hope I don't die of thirst first!" Bradley quipped. As Dan was wheeled away, another badly wounded soldier quickly took his place.

≈

After the procedure, Dan was drained. The cumulative effect of the long night in No Man's Land, the wounds, the transportation process, and now the pain of the procedure had taken its toll. As he stood to get out of the wheel chair and into the bed, he passed out in a heap.

Sheila and two orderlies got him off the floor and into his bed where he slept for the next fourteen hours.

≈

At 0500 hours, Dan was awakened by some noise in the ward. He looked around in the predawn darkness, puzzled as to his whereabouts.

The haze was slowly lifting and he realized where he was, the throbbing of his leg also became noticeable. He moved his hand down to feel under the sheets. "Still there," he said softly with a sigh of relief. He had heard enough stories about men feeling phantom pain in a limb that had been taken off, the tingle in a foot or itch of an arm that was no longer there. He was clearly glad to find the leg still attached.

A gentle voice came out of the darkness. "I'm still here, too." From a wicker chair three feet away, Sheila had been keeping watch over her friend. "You've been asleep for a long time," she said. "You must need to go to the bathroom. I'll call an orderly."

"You're a mind reader," Dan said. Several minutes later after an uncomfortable struggle with a bed pan Dan felt better indeed.

"Hungry?" Sheila asked.

"I'm so hungry, I could eat Bully Beef!" Dan said with a broad smile. Sheila suddenly was reminded that she needed to check on Bully. She had been preoccupied since Dan arrived and now made a mental note to do so.

"We can actually do better than that. How you feeling?" she asked.

"Like a million bucks. What time is it, anyway?" It always seems to be one of the first questions a person asks after an operation or after a long sleep.

"Six in the morning. I'll get you some food and tea," Sheila said, and disappeared through a doorway.

The light from the morning sun was now chasing away the shadows and the cool air of the night was being replaced by comfortable warmth. There was an increase in activity throughout the ward when Sheila returned with Dan's breakfast.

"You're lucky, six months ago you would have lost that leg." She said while plumping up the pillows behind Dan's head.

"Yeah, the Doc told me. Nice guy, the real deal," he said with a mouthful of scrambled eggs.

"When you're finished, we'll go outside for some air. It always smells bad in these wards."

"Smells better than No Man's Land," Dan replied somberly.

≈

After breakfast and a changing of bandages, Dan could feel his strength returning. With the help of an orderly, he got into a wheelchair and Sheila pushed him out into the courtyard. Because his leg had to be elevated, Dan's wheelchair had a lift that kept his leg sticking straight out. This long protruding leg was a magnet for everything and caused both Dan and Sheila to shout to on-comers, "Watch the leg!"

They moved into a sunny spot of the courtyard and chatted for a while until something seemed to catch Dan's attention. He leaned forward in his wheelchair squinting his eyes and looking past Sheila with a puzzled look. Behind Sheila, a man across the courtyard was walking using two canes.

Dan's puzzled look became a grin. "Hey! You friggin' farmer," he shouted. Sheila spun around to see who Dan was hollering at.

With a stunned look, she turned back to Dan. "Do you know him, Dan?"

"I should, eh. I've played rugby with him about a hundred times. If that's not Ian Macdonald's older brother Alan, I'll eat my hat."

GUELPH VETERAN'S HOME, PRESENT DAY

"Mr. Macdonald? Mr. Macdonald," I said quietly to the old man. It was no use, he had nodded off after going on for hours about the war and his amazing experience. His accounts of his past were so clear and detailed that there was no doubt in my mind that these events had been a true recollection of history and not some fictitious story made up by a lonely old man.

Even Mike, who at first seemed more interested in the soap opera playing on the TV in the next room, was drawn in and captivated by the old gentleman's stories.

"Do you think he's okay?" Mike asked.

I sat back in my chair, put down my pen and notebook in which I had scribbled pages of notes and took a deep breath. "I'm exhausted just listening to his experiences, he's reliving them. I'm sure he's okay. He just needed a nap."

I continued to look at this ancient piece of living history with a degree of respect that I wouldn't have believed I possessed. Even though I sorely wanted to awaken him and beg him to continue, I knew that the right thing to do was to let him sleep. What a time for him to nod off and what a remarkable story.

My curiosity was pegged out. So many questions were swirling in my head. Was that really his brother? What happened to all his friends? Had they made it through the battle Somme?"

I had written down as much information as I could and backed it up with three hours of digital recording. But I really needed to do some research and find out more about the Somme offensive.

"Let's head home Mike, I need to Google some stuff," I said.

"Yeah, I'm right there with you," he replied. "I don't remember anything about World War I."

It was about two o'clock and I decided to drop about three hours of research into my project and then return for more of Mr. Macdonald's recollections. I was completely stoked about this project now. History had always been kind of boring to me before, but now that I could put a face to it, now that it had a personal reality, it became poignant and meaningful.

Since Mr. Macdonald had fallen asleep I decided to use the time wisely and find out more about the battle Somme. In an odd way it almost seemed like cheating. You know – reading the ending of the book before you're there, but the fire was burning and it needed more fuel.

It only took a few minutes to boot up and Google the 36th Ulster, Battle Somme. Just typing in that search string returned more than forty thousand results, so I had to focus my search. I started to visit the top sites and read up on the subject. Most all of them agreed that the success of the 36th Ulster Division was the only success of the first day in that horrid battle.

One letter I found written by a Colonel Blacker to a comrade after the first day of the Somme illustrated how even the most successful battalion took massive losses!

"Dear Fitzgerald It is with a heavy heart I take up my pen to tell of the doings and losses of the Battalion on July 1. After being five days in the trenches during the preliminary bombardment, we came out for two days rest, then went on at midnight on June 30, and took up our positions ready for the assault, which was for 7:30 am, July 1.

The Battalion was on a four company front, each company being in a platoon front, thus being in four waves: two leading waves in (the) front trench line, 3rd wave in (the) communication trench, 4th wave in (the) 2nd line trenches. Order of companies from right to left: A, B, C, D. These dispositions were completed about 3 a.m. We suffered 50 casualties while waiting. The opposing lines were about 400 yards apart, with a ravine some 70 yards wide with steep banks about 20 feet high, about half way. The order was for the leading wave to get within 150 yards from German lines by 7:30 am to be ready to assault the instant our barrage lifted at 7:30 am. To do this the leading waves went over the parapet at 7:10 am, 2nd waves at 7:15 am, 3rd at 7:20 am and the last waves at 7:30 am. Ansor, Atkinson, Johnston C, and Brew were in command respectively and 11 other platoon officers, that was all that were allowed in the actual assault: and about 600 men. Of these Johnston was killed. Atkinson, Townsend, Hollywood, Montgomery, Seggie, Stewart are missing, believed killed. Brew, Gibson, Jackson, Shillington, Andrews, Smith, Barcroft, Capt Ensor are wounded and 516 other ranks are casualties.

The first wave got away without suffering badly, the 2nd wave had many casualties, and the 3rd and 4th waves were mown down by machine gun fire, frontal and enfilade, before they reached the ravine. After the machine gun fire the Germans put a barrage between us and the ravine and few of C and D companies got to the German front line, but a number of A and B companies got through the German line and reached their objectives at Beaucourt Station, past the German 3rd line. Of these none have returned. Owing to the failures of Battalions on our left, they were cut off. The gallant and splendid leading of the officers and the steady advance of men even after their officers were down, was magnificent, and makes me proud indeed to have been associated with such heroes. For four nights after, parties went out and searched for the wounded and brought in several (Ensor and three others on the 4th night), and then we were moved back 12 miles and the Border Regiment continued the search and rescued many of which we owe them deep gratitude. Cather was killed *bringing in wounded in daylight, and Menaul slightly wounded. Alas, many of our best have gone and we only marched back 281 strong, including transport. The Battalion in the hour of trial was splendid as I knew it would be, but I am heartbroken. The gallant friends and comrades we shall see no more. So few have come back unwounded it is hard to get any information as to individuals. Of the 48 Lewis Gunners, only 7 are left.*

In 'A' Company, Sgts More, Whitsitt, Hegan, Kirkwood, McCourt are wounded and Sgt Wilson is missing believed killed. In 'B' Company, Sgt porter is killed and Sgts Caulfield, Keith, Barr, Courtney, Johnston wounded. In 'C' Company, Sgts Hobbs and Byans are killed and Sgts Brown, Love missing. In 'D' Company, Sgts Mullen, Gordon, Thornberry killed, Sgts Hare, Balmer, Sewell, Hughes wounded and Sgt Bunting missing. McClurg, the Primate's chauffeur wounded. We want Lewis gunners badly, the Signallers escaped well, we still have over 30 available. Your draft of 53 came last night and I saw them today, very well turned out and good lot.

What can you do further? I fear little - nearly all our bombing teams are gone. We are right back now, not more than 30 miles from Boulogne and are hoping to get drafts and trying to refit and sort things out. Fortunately, the four Company Sgt Majors and four Company Quarter Master Sgts were not allowed over the parapet so the Company Staff is intact. Cather's loss is a severe one, he was quite wonderful as an Adjutant, but his glorious death and his name has gone in for a posthumous Victoria Cross. He brought in one wounded man from about 150 yards from German wire in daylight! And was killed going out to a wounded man who feebly waved to him on his calling out to see if there were any more near.

There has [sic] been a lot of extravagant words written and published in the Press, which is a great pity. The Division behaved magnificently and the point does not want labouring. Please be careful that this epistle does not get into the Press. I am still dazed at the blow and the prospect in front of us all, but we must not be downcast; and must remember the glorious example of the gallant band

who so nobly upheld the honour of the Battalion, and who have died
so gloriously, leaving their example to live after them, and to inspire
those who are left.

Of the nine Victoria Crosses awarded on that day, six were earned by men of the 36th Ulster.

≈

I then Google searched the 1st Newfoundland Division to see how Mr. Macdonald's friends made out. The results were not good. This division sustained losses that could only be described as unimaginable.

According to the website "Newfoundland and Labrador Heritage," approximately eight hundred men made up the Division. At 09:15 their commander made a monumentally fatal judgment call and ordered his men to leave St. John's supply trench and cross open land to join the battle. Within fifteen minutes the Division was wiped out. Only sixty-eight men made it back for roll call. It seemed inconceivable that so many men perished in such a short time. How many family lineages came to a halt, how many fathers, mothers, wives, and children mourned after that senseless and ill-conceived charge?

Both Mike and I had to stop reading for a while. The incredible losses of one day in a war that lasted four years were staggering. We went downstairs for a beer. Sensing our somber mood, my mom asked if everything was all right.

"Yeah," I said. "We've been reading up on the battle Somme. We had no idea it had been so horrible."

"I guess that generation never felt it necessary to share the horrors of that war. They simply carried it with them to their graves," she said.

"That's what makes this so incredible," I said. "We are getting the story from someone who lived through it, it's almost like a sacred moment."

My mom smiled understandingly. "It really is a window to the past that is closing quickly," she said. I looked at her and a chill came over me. What if Mr. Macdonald was to die today? The story would go untold. We had to get back to the home.

I put down my unfinished beer. "Let's go Mike, see you later Mum," I said and we headed out. "This guy has seen the depths of hell, how could he have carried those memories with him his whole life and remained even remotely normal?" I asked Mike.

"I don't know. How long do you figure has it been since we left Mr. Macdonald sleeping?"

"About three hours, so I hope he got rested up and feels like continuing."

Soon we had arrived at the veteran's home. I parked my sweet old Datsun and we went in.

"Is Mr. Macdonald awake?" I asked the receptionist.

She smiled. "I believe he's been asking for you. He's in his room, number 147. His door should be ajar."

As we approached the room, a voice came through the cracked door. "Well, where have you lads been? Come in, come in. I thought I had bored you both to death with my stories and they had carted you away to the morgue." He chuckled at his own joke.

"Oh, no sir, in fact, we'd love to hear more if you're up to it," Mike jumped in.

Mr. Macdonald smiled and winked. "If you listen, I'll talk. Now, where was I?" His asking, I think, was more of a test than a real question.

"You had just told us about Dan McKee seeing someone he thought was your brother at the hospital," I said.

"Oh, yes" he said with a sly smile.

5TH CANADIAN STATIONARY HOSPITAL

S heila looked at Dan, and then back at Bully with a look of disbelief.

"He came in over a year ago with a head injury. A bullet pierced his helmet and lodged in his brain. A convent, unable to help him any further, had passed him along to a clearing station outside Ypres who sent him to us," she explained. "We had the only surgeon in France capable of operating on such a wound. After the operation, he remained semi-comatose until about a month ago. He became my pet project and I gave him the nickname Bully because the only thing he seemed to be interested in eating was bully beef."

Dan couldn't believe the story after thinking that his friend was dead for so long. "How could he get so easily lost in the system?" he asked.

"No cold meat tags," she said. That's what we call dog tags. "Ypres was a busy place at the time, he was left for dead and with no identification he became a lost soul. The clearing stations had no time to research a John Doe, especially one whose prognosis was so bleak. He was just another unknown wounded soldier."

Dan shook his head. "Does he not know who he is?"

"No clue" Sheila said. "I have to get this information into the office so they can notify his family. They must have given up all hope.

Dan, you are sure about this, aren't you? I don't want to notify the Macdonald family unless you're absolutely sure." She looked at Dan searchingly.

"There's no doubt in my mind, that's Alan," he responded turning his wheelchair toward Bully. "Hey Al, come over here," he called to his old friend.

It was unmistakable to Bully, the large fellow in the wheelchair was talking to him. He began to hobble over using his canes for support.

"I thought you said he had a head wound," Dan asked Sheila. "What's with the canes?"

"After a year of immobility, his muscles have atrophied. He almost has to learn to walk all over again," she said.

Alan approached this big man with obvious caution. "Do we know each other?" he asked sheepishly.

"Friggin' A we do! You and I have been ice fishing about a hundred times and you were the guy I'd have to look out for in the rugger scrum, you friggin' farmer!" Dan said, smiling warmly.

There was something about this big fellow –- his voice, his smile, the "friggin' farmer" crack – it all seemed to be somehow familiar, but the picture was unclear.

"Your little brother is sure going to be excited to have his brother, Al, back," Dan continued.

"My little brother?" Alan asked, unsure.

"Yea, Ian the bagpiper, you know," Dan said.

Alan stared down at the ground looking at nothing. He shook his head and tried to rattle some of the beans into place, but to no avail. His eyes then came up to Dan's with an expression of frustration and fear.

"I don't know...I can't remember," his voice broke.

Dan could see that his old friend from Wolfe Island had no recollection of his past. "Don't worry, pal, I'll work with you," he said. "I have a lot of time on my hands and we can use it to catch up. "Deal?"

Alan licked his lips, a nervous gesture, and gave Dan an appreciative, but weak smile. "Deal."

≈

The morning sun was now warming the courtyard as the two old
friends were getting reacquainted. Sheila excused herself and went
to report Alan Macdonald's rebirth to her superiors. Then, without
warning, the building shook and they all felt a wave of compression
followed by the sensation of the air being sucked away.

The leaves on the trees shook as if a huge blast of wind had just
blown by. Then came the huge sound of explosion. It was monstrous,
beyond anything they had experienced at the hospital.

"Oh, my God!" Sheila screamed, running back to Dan and Alan.
"Are they shelling us?"

Dan suddenly realized what it might be. "What day is it?" He
asked.

"Monday."

"Monday what?" Dan demanded.

"The first of July," Sheila said nervously. "Why?"

He looked at his wristwatch. "Oh, Lord, it's begun," he said in a
solemn voice.

"What? What's begun?" Sheila asked, regaining her composure.

"It's the Big Push. Those were the land mines," Dan said.

A series of explosions followed in rapid succession, none so powerful as the first, but massive nonetheless. The first was the Haw-
thorne Ridge mine, which was later reported being heard all the way
in London.

"It looks like we'll be seeing some increase in wounded," Sheila
commented.

"I'm afraid you'll be seeing a lot more than just an increase,"
Dan said. "I was wounded coming back from a night reconnaissance
mission and I can tell you that the German entanglement trench is
completely untouched. Those boys will be charging into a shoot-

ing gallery where they will be the targets and those Maxim machine guns make killing easy."

Dan's comment stunned both Sheila and Alan.

"But, I thought the artillery bombardment was supposed to destroy the barbed wire and drive the Germans out of their trenches," Sheila said, realizing the failure of the British guns and what was to come next.

Dan shook his head.

"Oh, God no, they'll be slaughtered!" she said.

Alan, who had no knowledge of the Somme offensive, was somewhat lost. "Who – the Germans? They'll be slaughtered?"

"No, our kids," Sheila said, sympathetic to his confusion.

Alan grabbed Dan's robe by the shoulders. "My brother – is he among those boys going to their deaths?" he asked desperately.

"Yes, Alan, I'm afraid Ian is among them," Dan answered solemnly, not daring to look into Alan's eyes.

Alan sank down onto a nearby bench and cradled his face between his hands. "He may die never knowing that his brother is still alive and I may never see his face, a face I still can't even picture. I hate this war."

PART EIGHT

THE TIME HAS COME

"Ocean Villas" 1st Newfoundland Division

George and Terry were concerned about their friend Dan. He had been taken away before they had a chance to see him, and they had to rely on reports and information from strangers as to his whereabouts and condition.

The Division had moved even closer to the front and they were looking for a place to billet for several nights. The beautiful rolling hills and unending fields of the Picardie region of France had been transformed into a bleak and broken countryside. The choices for places to stay were limited to half destroyed farmhouses, barns, or tents. The boys were leaning toward barns.

One of the Newfoundlanders told them to head up the St. Johns road about half a mile where they could stay at the "Ocean Villas."

George looked at Terry. "That's ridiculous we're nowhere near the ocean." Several of the Newfs burst out laughing. They explained that when the Tommies first showed up in the little town of

Auchonvillers they couldn't properly pronounce the name so they instead called it Ocean Villas, and the name stuck among the P.B.I.

"Let's go take a look," Terry said. The two lads went in search of their lodging.

≈

As they entered the badly damaged village they noticed a farm with several barns still standing. The barns were brick and slate and all but one seemed in good condition. The largest was demolished and seemed to have had the main house attached. A pile of rubble was all that was left of the once beautiful home.

Oddly, there seemed to be an unusual amount of activity around the pile of debris. Men were coming and going through trenches carved into the earth, lined with sand bags and covered over with a corrugated metal top. The boys were drawn by the mystery and went in for a closer look.

"What's all the fuss about?" Terry asked one fellow as he came out of the shallow trench.

"Advanced dressing Station," the man replied as he rushed by.

The two pipers entered one of the trenches and followed it into a bunker. It was lit by several bare light bulbs hanging from the ceiling that did a nice job of illuminating the room. The bunker was brick and had a curved or arched ceiling that gave about seven feet of headroom at the apex. It had two chambers. The first, which the boys entered, had several wounded men on bunk beds along the far left wall. Some of the men were unconscious but, others were awake and busily scratching their names into the brick wall. They stopped momentarily to see who had come in and then returned to their tasks. This was too well built to have been simply a bunker and in fact it turned out to be the basement of the demolished farm house.

To the right was a door into the second room in which several doctors had just finished working on a wounded man. They looked tired as they wiped the blood from their hands.

One of the doctors noticed the boys. "Bringing more in boys or are you just here to watch?" the taller of the two doctors asked.

George moved closer and almost tripped over a pile of bloody rags as he thrust out his hand. "George Cohen, third year med, Mcgill." The doctor raised his eyebrows and he smiled.

"We have a fellow professional, Kranston," he said to his colleague.

Kranston was a short, broad man with very dark hair and one large eyebrow. "Humph, I'll be outside having a smoke," he said as he brushed past George and Terry, never making eye contact.

"My apologies for my partner's lack of social graces," the doctor said. "We've been on post for over two weeks and now things are starting to pick up so he would appear to have lost his sense of humor. I am Doctor Nichols, Mark Nichols. Welcome to our humble post Ocean Villa."

Terry joined in on the introductions but was not doing well with the combined smell of the blood soaked floor, old buckets of God knows what and ether, not to mention the odor of filthy men.

"I believe I'll join your friend outside for some air," he said and quickly exited the basement.

"Does your friend always have that odd yellow-green color?" Doctor Nichols asked jokingly.

"I think he may have been nauseated by the sight of blood and the stale smell down here," George said seriously, failing to recognize Nichols' biting humor.

Nichols looked at George for a moment and said, "Yes, I was kidding my young friend. So, to what do we owe this visit?"

"Well, we were told that this area is a good place to find a billet and we were drawn in by the activity. Just plain curiousity I guess."

"Good show. We happen to be housed in the adjacent barn and there is plenty of room. You and your friend are welcome to billet there if you like," Nichols said. "What division are you two with?"

"We're 86th division, 1st Newfoundland regiment," George explained. "We're bagpipers."

"Good people, the Newfies. Very strong, and thoroughly honest. And a piper you say? I hope you'll play for us later, I love the pipes," the Doctor said. "But why aren't we taking advantage of your medical talents?"

"Military intelligence," George said.

Nichols laughed loudly. "Quite so – the oxymoron. You do have a sense of humor after all. Perhaps I can rectify the military's over sight, I am not without influence."

George smiled at the offer. "I still have an obligation and a responsibility to The 1st now, but I would love to explore the idea further with you at a later date if that suits you."

"Very admirable," Nichols responded.

That night the four men talked about the war, politics and family, all over several scotches. The brusque Kranston turned out to be a very friendly and likeable fellow after a couple of drinks and he, too, was a great fan of the pipes.

Terry spent most of the evening entertaining Kranston while George and Nichols talked medicine. Doctor Nichols was so impressed with George that he would later make good on his offer to have the piper moved to the Medical Corps, but not in time.

36TH ULSTER DIVISION

109th Brigade, 9th, 10th, & 11th Royal Iniskilling Fusiliers, 14th Irish Rifles "G" Company

I hadn't slept at all. I just lay there all night waiting for the sound of the bugle and looking at my wristwatch from time to time. In the darkness, I could hear the rhythmic breathing of Sean and Bill. How could they sleep? I cupped my right hand over the dial to make it easier to read the illuminated hands – 0200 hours. One more hour to go before we had to get up and move out.

A bugle startled me – I must have finally nodded off. Bill and Sean hopped up and struck a match to light the oil lamp. They were up too quickly to have been asleep.

"Up we go sleeping beauty," Bill called to me.

"You must be a pretty cool customer to have been so soundly asleep," Sean said. I just smiled and yawned. The yellow flame from the lamp's wick cast a dim light, but we fumbled around the tent getting dressed as best we could.

We had taken to putting our kilts under our bedding and then sleeping on them. It helped to press our pleats and keep them sharp. It normally took ten to fifteen minutes to dress properly. Kilt, hose, puttees, hobnail boots under shirt and tunic all took time.

The bugle blew again for assembly, so Sean and I tuned our pipes quickly and popped on our glengarry bonnets.

"How do I look?" Sean asked with a smile.

"Like the girl of my friggin' dreams, come true," Bill joked as we exited the tent.

"Maybe Fritz *will* think I'm a girl and not shoot me." Sean continued to joke.

"If Fritz thinks you're a women and *doesn't* shoot you, he has terrible taste in women," Bill laughed.

The tents were staying put this time. The intention was that we would only spend three days in the trenches and then be relieved, so the tents stayed. Assembly was held in a large area at the center of the camp. There were lamps everywhere to light the area.

At the east end of the assembly area was a platform with some electric lights shining on it. A sea of men had come together and, as a whistle blew, we all turned our attention toward the platform.

Owen McDonnell stood on the platform with a whistle in one hand and a blowhorn in the other. After several moments, the throng fell silent, the cool night air blew lightly across us giving me a chill. Lt. McDonnell lifted the blow horn to his mouth and began to speak, broadcasting across the mass of men.

"Men, my fellow Irishmen, today we have the unenviable task of meeting our enemy on the field of battle," he began.

I could hear the breathing of the men around me. I thought I could almost hear their hearts pounding.

"I will not try to make you believe that this day will show you the glories of war," McDonnell continued. "To the contrary, you will see the enemy kill your comrades and you will avenge their deaths by killing the enemy. This is not about glory. It is about duty. Duty to Ireland, duty to Great Britain and the King, and duty to each other. We did not start this awful war, but we are given only one of two choices by our foes. Surrender to them or beat them. We will not surrender, rather we will vanquish them, we will drive them back to their homeland and we will make them regret their evil assault on our allies. We will leave them powerless and broken to ponder their mad aggression and grieve over their dead..."

The crowd was still quiet and hanging on the powerful message that had been delivered.

"I would like to have Father Patrick Maguire bless us and pray for us now." McDonnell stepped aside and a tall lean man took the bullhorn. He was in uniform except for the very visible white collar signifying his position as a priest. "Let us all bow our heads my sons of Ireland." He began with a soothing Irish lilt to his voice.

"Our Holy Father, hear thee I pray the prayer of thy children who call upon thee in their time of danger and difficulty. Forgive me, I pray thee, for all my sins which I so often committed against thee in thought, word, and deed. Make me ready to endure hardness as a good soldier of Jesus Christ. Fill me with thy holy spirit that I may know thee more clearly, love thee more dearly, and follow thee more nearly."

I thought of the hymn that we used to sing at church back on Wolfe Island from which he borrowed the line.

"Strengthen me and uphold me in all difficulties and dangers, keep me faithful unto death, patient in suffering, calm in thy service and confident in the assurance that thou Lord wilt direct all things to the glory of thy name and the welfare of thy church and country. Bless the King, whom we serve, and all the royal family," he said, his tone sounding more obligatory than heartfelt. "O Lord, grant me the grace that no word or act of mine may be spoken or done rashly, hastily, or with anger toward those who differ from me."

Bill Lewis, out of the side of his mouth with his head down said "I thought they wanted us to kill these guys." I shushed him.

The priest continued. "Bless all my comrades in the Ulster Volunteer force and make me forgiving and gentle, obedient to my leaders, and faithful to my beliefs. And in thine own good time bring peace to Ireland. For Jesus Christ's sake. Amen."

A rumble of Amen passed through the newly religious gathering. It seems that the prospect of imminent death brings many men to the Lord. I poked Bill in the ribs for his sacrilegious wisecracking.

"Ouch!" he said, looking at me apologetically. "Look, my only hope is that God is really, really forgiving."

I shook my head. The man was incorrigible. Father Maguire looked up to the crowd and yelled into the blow horn. "I would have liked to see this large a crowd last Sunday ." He lowered the horn to show that he was smiling. The gathering laughed at this joke more out of nerves perhaps than genuine comedic value. "Boys, fight hard, take care of each other, and come back safely! Walk with the Lord today and everyday. Dismissed!"

A cut and dry military ending to his prayer! Not very inspirational, I thought. I looked around at the men near me. They were strangers who, in the poor light, had a ghostly look about them. Their faces were drawn, and their expressions looked like what I would imagine a man would have on the morning of his execution. An expression of resolution to one's fate. A chill ran up my spine.

My dour thoughts were broken by Lieutenant McDonnell. "I've been looking for you boys," he said. "Are you ready to lead our troops over the top?"

"As ready as we ever will be," Sean said confidently.

"I may piss myself," I said half-jokingly.

McDonnell turned to me with warm, fatherly eyes. "Son, I've seen better men than you piss themselves prior to a battle, but when the fighting began, not a one faltered."

My face flushed. "I was kidding," I said defensively, but he ignored my excuse. "Not a one," he repeated, looking at me.

"Now then," he continued in a business-like manner. "You three will be up in the advancement trench with me. As you will remember, we will have a team of cutters and bombers out in No Man's Land lying in wait, backed up by Lewis gunners. They will be over one hundred yards advanced of our position, but will be moving slowly so it won't take long for our rifles and fusiliers to reach them. I will lead the charge along with you men. But, because you must march and we will be charging, we will outdistance you quickly. Not to worry though. The subsequent waves of men will come at one hundred pace intervals so you'll have plenty of men to inspire as you march headlong."

He paused to see if we understood. We nodded. Sean told him that we had selected the tunes and rehearsed them well. We'd be playing "Minstrel Boy," "Men of the West," and "Gary Owen."

"They're lively tunes," McDonnell said. "They'll do just fine. I know you men will make me proud."

≈

With the coordination of the officers, the mass of men began to transform into an orderly army ready for battle. I looked at the lighted hands on my wristwatch. It was 03:40.

The mile march was quiet and took less than forty minutes. The trenches were cold and muddy, but with so many men jammed into them in full battle dress, the cold morning air was replaced by the heat, smell and sweat of thousands of anxious men.

We had stayed by Lieutenant McDonnell's side, and at 04:30 we were in the most advanced trench of the B.E.F. There was nowhere else to safely traverse under the cover of the trench.

McDonnell lit up a cigarette and offered us one, but we declined. The eastern sky was starting to show signs of light as the moments passed. I saw the stars in the cloudless night fade until only the brightest remained. The curtain was being lifted on the theater of death and we had a front row seat.

The endless work of the sappers was done hours before, shoring up the trenches and repairing the duckboards. I could now see the men, standing three abreast. They stretched off through the trench systems leading up to the assault trench where they lined up in rows of forty, ready to run up the shallow bank into No Man's Land.

The 14th Royal Irish Rifles stood ready to rush into the unknown. It was 05:30. Our artillery had slacked off and things were relatively quiet when the still morning air was ripped to pieces by a massive German artillery response to our own.

I believe, in anticipation of our attack, the Germans were attempting to block our advance. Those of our men that had been ordered out into No Man's land were now exposed to this hellish maelstrom with nowhere to go for refuge. Crump holes were their only escape from the attack. We had more than fifty casualties brought back before 06:30. Each injured man carried past those waiting for the whistle was an omen of things to come.

The German attack ended abruptly at 06:30, and for a few moments all was quiet again except for the ringing in our ears.

My expression must have given away my reluctance in wanting to walk out into that hell. It just didn't seem like the prudent thing to do.

Bill reached over and put his hand on my arm. "We have a job to do," he said. "We'll just do it." He made it sound so simple.

Then, the horizon behind us lit up as the British Royal Artillery delivered our response to the German bombardment. For a solid half-hour, the German trenches were pummeled and we were cloaked in smoke from the big guns. There was a slight westerly breeze. Good news for us as far as German gas attacks went, but not good news as our smokeless gunpowder from the artillery was not altogether smokeless.

At 07:10 all was quiet again except for the cries of the injured and, of course, that ringing. Like two exhausted boxers, both the German and British artilleries took a short break.

The men around us were fidgeting and restless. Lieutenant McDonnell was like a rock, square jaw set and looking up at the edge of the trench, focused. It was quite quiet now, the men keeping their Enfields up at a forty-five degree angle out of the mud, when suddenly – and quite clearly – a young man directly behind us let out with a royal fart.

We all turned to see who had popped off Gabriel's horn so magnificently. Even Lieutenant McDonnell's trance was broken by the sound and he turned to look. A young, ginger haired, freckle-faced lad turned beet red.

"Pardon me, sir," he said sheepishly.

"Not at all," McDonnell said, with one eyebrow raised and a slight smile. "That was, in fact, quite a brave move my boy, maybe even bold." The front line broke out in spontaneous laughter, it was just the relief we all needed. The laughter was infectious and spread quickly as the incident was passed on.

But the laughing was silenced as the ground shook again as if convulsing. Dirt fell from the soft trench walls and many stumbled to catch their footing as the earth trembled. Our vision blurred like an out-of-focus picture and then the ground rose up to our northeast about two kilometers away. It seemed as if it were giving birth to the devil himself.

This mountainous boil exploded hundreds of feet into the air carrying acres of land and thousands of tons of dirt with it. Hundreds of unsuspecting German soldiers were instantly killed when the Hawthorn Ridge mine blew ten minutes ahead of schedule. The shockwave blew past us like a tsunami of wind followed by the most enormous sound I had ever heard. It was not a sharp sound like that of a cannon or bomb, but it was low and deep and grew to a point where it shook your body from within. Like rolling thunder, it passed over us and left the area.

"Jesus help us!" Bill blurted out. I just looked at my friends, wide-eyed and frightened.

McDonnell glanced at his watch and shook his head. "Fools," he cursed, as he returned his gaze toward the parapet. "Steady! Lads, Steady! There's more to come!" he yelled.

Indeed at 07:30 a series of mines exploded to the north and south of us. The massive Lochnagar mine was closest to us and had a similar effect, although its impact was diminished by the mass of other mines exploding simultaneously.

McDonnell called to Sean. "Pipes up!" he shouted.

Sean looked at him with surprise. "I thought we were to wait fifteen minutes?"

Owen looked at Sean with a sly grin. "I believe it has been fifteen minutes after the first mine!" The whistle went to his mouth and his arm went straight up. With a long blow on the whistle, his arm came down. Similar whistles blew all down the front line and the men charged up the trench and over the top.

Bill held his sticks up. Sean shouted out over the chaos. "By the right! Quick, march!"

We blew up and marched up the grade playing "The Minstrel Boy" into No Man's Land. Men ran past us yelling and screaming like banshees toward the pre-cut paths through British barbed wire and on to the German lines. The maxims started to bark out their deadly spew and Irishmen began to fall in droves, but an amazing number pressed forward toward the enemy.

My head was spinning as the long awaited moment was upon us. I fought to concentrate on my tune, but with the confusion of the battle going on around me, it became almost impossible. I had to try to shut it out, focus my attention on the ground six to eight feet ahead of me. I struggled to block out my surroundings. I had to step around a fallen rifleman, his unseeing eyes staring up at me. I looked away trying to hold onto my Piper's trance.

Shells were now coming from the German guns adding to the confusion, but I didn't really notice. I was becoming detached. I knew that I was as good as dead and it didn't matter now. The only thing that mattered was my duty – my bag-piping. "I didn't piss my-self," I thought.

THE 1ST NEWFOUNDLAND REGIMENT, 07:20 HOURS

"Lions led by donkeys"

The 29th Division was made up of the 86th, 87th and 88th brigades. The 29th was positioned about three kilometers north of the 36th Ulster Division and had the unenviable task of attacking the gauntlet protecting Beaumont-Hamel. To advance through the area of triangulation of firepower known as the danger tree was suicide, but to be given the orders to push five thousand meters to Beaumont-Hamel seemed madness. Nonetheless, this was the objective of the 29th division on day one of the Somme.

The 86th and 87th brigades were to be in position for the initial advance and the 88th brigade, made up of the Essex and the 1st Newfoundland Regiments, were to reinforce their efforts. At 07:20, the Hawthorn Ridge mine exploded and because the 29th was less than two kilometers away, the effects of the blast were even more intense. The 86th and 87th were shoulder to shoulder in the trenches awaiting the whistle and weathered the shock of the blast relatively well except for several partial trench collapses which were quickly repaired by the sappers of the Royal Engineering Unit.

The 88th, however, stood ready in the St. John's supply trench. A large, more open trench several hundred meters to the back of the most forward lines. As the blast of the mine rolled past, it knocked many men down, including both Terry and George.

"Holy, Crap!" George said as he scrambled to his feet.

"Check your pipes," Terry said as he gathered his senses and stood up. Fortunately, their pipes were made of tough African black-wood and came through the encounter unscathed.

Terry looked at his watch. "What gives?" he asked out loud.

The same perplexed expression was plainly visible on the face of Major Henry Winsted, the Commander of the 1st Newfies. Ten long minutes later, the entire valley erupted into explosions and gunfire. The Germans were ready and had obviously survived the week long pounding almost unimpeded.

Major Winsted was a nervous man by nature and was pacing back and forth in the St. John's trench, looking at his watch and then toward the Front. Winsted, a tall, willowy man with a sallow complexion, came from a well-to-do British family. Having attended the finest military schools and then being rapidly promoted through the ranks, he thought that being given command of such a small regiment of colonials could only be considered an insult and he resented the whole situation. What's more, instead of the glory of being the 1st to charge over the beaten German Army, he and these outsiders were to mop up!

"It's a disgrace!" he yelled in frustration.

He had a proclivity for impeccable uniforms and could always be seen with a riding crop, which he used to wave around while giving orders, otherwise it was tucked tightly under his right arm. Today, however, the crop was absent. "The battlefield is no place for such bobbles unless you are cavalry," his commander told him, and being a good soldier, he had left it behind this morning. In a move he had performed many times with his crop, he slapped his right leg with his imaginary whip.

"Damn it, why are they not moving?" he blurted out. He kept looking at the entry trench, which was blocked by the Essex. They hadn't budged in 20 minutes. "What the devil!" he yelled.

His sallow face turning an odd shade of reddish yellow – not quite orange. He strode over to a passing private and barked an order. "Private! You there! Go and find out some information as to what is the difficulty!"

"Yes sir, straight away sir," the private responded while snapping a crisp salute.

This was supposed to be a walk in the park through German ruins with the enemy either throwing up their hands or dead, he thought. "Bloody idiots! Could they not have foreseen this?"

The private soon returned to the pacing Major. "Sir, I was told that the trenches are jammed with wounded men being brought back from the advanced attack. It would seem things are not going well," he reported.

"Fools!" Winsted howled, waving his imaginary crop around. "That will be all private – dismissed!"

"Yes sir, thank you, sir," the private said as he spun around and ran off to continue his original task. Both Terry and George had been watching intently as Winsted lost the composure he never really had.

"Our leader seems to be somewhat anxious," George said.

"Maybe unhinged," Terry replied. "I hope he doesn't do something stupid."

"Me either, this is very unsettling."

Both knew the condition of the German entanglement trench from their reconnaissance mission and it was clear to them why the troops were being held up.

Winsted glanced over at both men, they had provided him with information two days ago regarding the barbed wire and he had dismissed it. Could they have been correct in their observations?

He quickly looked away when their eyes met and slapped his leg again with his nonexistent crop. The fight was obviously under way in good order. From the St. John's you could see the exploding earth rising up above the parapet, hear the whiz bangs and the rattling of the Maxim 08s being answered by the snarl of the Vickers guns. Even the battle screams of the men charging and dying were audible.

≈

The men of the B.E.F. were being mowed down at an unimaginable rate. A blunder of epic proportions was unfolding and no one
seemed to be interested in stopping it – except perhaps those dying.

More than an hour had passed and the men of the 88th had
only moved about four meters. The Essex still stood at the entrance
of the trenches while the 1st Newfoundland stood at the ready.

"This is preposterous!" Winsted snarled, looking at the trench
wall toward the battlefield. From the German lines inexplicably
came a series of flares, shot high over the battlefield. It may have
been a signal to artillery or to ground the troops, we will never know.
Perhaps it was a mistake, the real reason is not of great consequence.
The outcome, however, is.

≈

Several teams of horses came racing up the St. John's at a full gallop.
Behind each team of six horses was a driver and three thirteen pound
field artillery guns secured in tandem. They were part of the Royal horse
artillery and their mission was to move artillery rapidly in the field of
battle so as to maximize the effectiveness of the field cannon.

The drivers hollered and yelled as they drove through the trench,
there were men and equipment everywhere and they had to clear the
way. To add to the danger of having six, twelve hundred pound beasts
charging at more than thirty miles an hour, the last cannon in each team
would whip back and forth wildly, often flipping over in the process.

The cannons were designed to be towed right side up or upside down with equal ease and without damaging the weapon. Of
course, anyone within fifteen feet either side of the whipsaw was in
real danger of being killed so proper respect was shown by all.

The three teams flew wildly past Major Winsted slinging mud
in all directions with no regard for rank or status. Consequently,
he was showered with a considerable amount of dirt and mud
spattering his meticulously neat uniform with brown blotches.

In an unexpected display of self-control, he brushed the large clumps of dirt off of his tunic and trousers, turning his gaze back toward the Front.

Terry and George witnessed the entire event.

"I think he took that rather well," George said.

"Indeed my dear Doctor," Terry replied in a false British accent. "Smashingly well".

≈

The flares that were arching across the eastern sky eventually caught the Major's eye and he stiffened at the sight.

"Flares? They are too close to have been sent up by the enemy, so they must be ours. What does it mean?" He continued to watch the torches fizzle across the horizon. Could this be a signal? Perhaps a breakthrough – or the possibility that aid is needed?

He desperately searched his memory, could he have missed something during briefing the day earlier? His eyes darted back and forth for another officer with whom he could consult, but there were none in sight. He spun around looking for anyone to confirm the meaning of the flares, but there was no one to consult.

The flares could only mean one thing. After all, one wouldn't use a flare normally in the battlefield. It had to be a signal to advance! He looked at the trench, which leads to the system, still jammed with Essex unable to advance. Of course, it has to be a request to advance.

But this could be his moment for military glory. If he could lead these Colonials straight to the front and save the day, he would go down in military history! As there were no other officers to be found Winsted had to make the command decision.

"Form up," he said in an almost inaudible voice. He cleared his throat. "Form up!" he hollered this time.

The men around him turned in disbelief. Terry and George rushed over to him. "What are you saying, sir?" Terry asked in shock.

"I want my men to assemble in wave formation," he said. There was a sense of desperation in his voice. He was near hysteria, knowing the enormity of giving such an order.

"Sir, with all due respect, the Essex haven't budged in an hour," George said calmly, hoping to settle this overly anxious officer down.

"I intend to have the regiment exit the St. John's eastern wall and march up to the enemy lines," Winsted barked.

"That's suicide," Terry spat.

"Careful piper! That's insubordination! I shall report you after the battle!" Winsted said shrilly.

"Beg your pardon sir, but there is no cover – it's open field. We'll be sitting ducks for their gunners," Terry pleaded.

"I have received a signal that requires my regiment to act, and act we shall! Form up now, men! In waves, to maintain fifty paces spacing! That is an order!"

The men, being good and well trained soldiers formed up in eight lines of one hundred. The pipers couldn't believe what they were seeing. This fool was about to break the cardinal rule of trench warfare and he was going to commit the entire regiment to this madness. It was inconceivable, but it was happening nonetheless.

"Pipers ready!" Winsted commanded, waving his imaginary crop as he spoke. "Men ready! Follow me – on to victory!" He scrambled up the side of the St. John's trench with the 1st Newfoundland Regiment on his heels.

George and Terry started playing "Scotland the Brave," and attempted to climb at the same time, but with limited success. Once over the top, the men formed orderly lines fifty paces apart and marched toward the front lines across open land. Remarkably, there was no resistance, the regiment moved forward at a steady pace and not a man had fallen. They just kept moving with their emboldened leader holding his invisible crop high in the air.

THE GERMAN 119TH RESERVE REGIMENT

Three hundred meters away from the St. John's trench, the German 119th Reserve Regiment was well dug in. After a week of living in bunkers, it felt good to get out, even if it was to do battle. They had withstood the best pounding the British could muster and now had a renewed sense of determination in their fighting.

Hartwig Bier was the lead in one of the machine gun nests that covered the forward position between the Front and Beaumont Hamel. He was senior man in his sector, with five nests spread out over four hundred meters of Front. Each nest was equipped with two Maxim 08 guns, and they all seemed to be performing well.

Bier had his men paying particular attention to the cooling of the guns. The water levels had to be meticulously maintained to prevent the possibility of overheating. He had never asked so much of these fine machines and knew he was pushing them to the limit.

Each gun had a team of four men: the gunner, the feeder, a cooler, and a shoveler. At five hundred rounds per minute, times two guns per nest, one could quickly become buried in the spent 7.9 milimeter casings if not for the shovelers. In typical German fashion, everything was well thought out, the guns were placed at thirty-degree angles to one another, and the nests were positioned to maximized their advantage with relation to topography. The Germans had created a wall of death and the point of triangulation was around the area known as the danger tree.

Bier's teams were blanketing the British advance trenches with fire and completely stopping the British from making any headway toward their lines. The system was working extraordinarily well.

One of his men slapped him on his back. Hartwig turned to see what he wanted. The noise levels in these nests were so high that verbal conversation was not possible. And, as a protective measure the men had cotton stuffed in their ears but, the noise was still loud enough to be painful, so they had to communicate through hand gestures. His team member pointed at his eyes and then pointed out toward the front where there was open sloping terrain. Biers looked in the direction his man was pointing and shook his head in disbelief.

"Was ist los?" – what's going on – Biers asked disbelieving, mouthing words that couldn't be heard.

They could see what appeared to be a regiment marching in formation down the gentle slope. Perhaps as many as eight hundred men, Biers estimated. He looked left and then right scanning the battle area and assessing the situation. It could be some kind of diversion to draw attention away from the real attack. It made no sense.

He looked at the fellow who had brought it to his attention, they exchanged puzzled looks and shrugged their shoulders. He leaned forward to get a better look and noticed the kilted pipers in the front. He scowled. Hartwig hated the instrument and the god-awful noise it produced. "I shall shoot you two first," he said.

He turned to alert the other gunners in his nest. He had a job to do and it involved killing British, so he needed to focus his men on this new threat. He turned his gun toward the nest to his left and spat out a short burst at the earth in front of it. Dirt and mud flew up in front of the gunners and they looked to their right to see what the matter was.

As the other soldier had done, now Hartwig pointed first to his eyes, then to the advancing 1st Newfoundland Regiment. The gunner shot back a questioning look. Hartwig held up one finger, he then pointed at the sitting ducks and repeated the gesture pointing at the British front lines. One gun was to train on the regiment and one on the British forward lines.

The gunner relayed the message to the next nest, and a total of five Maxims prepared to unload a brutal amount of firepower on the Newfoundland men. That amounted to twenty five hundred rounds per minute that were readying to decimate the brave young soldiers of the 1st Newfoundland Regiment – wholesale slaughter.

≈

As the men marched down the slope toward the battlefield, they moved at double-time, and soon four rows had passed George and Terry who had to keep a more modest pace.

The lack of resistance was about to abruptly change. The sounds of the battlefield were now changing. A gun gives off a different sound when it is aimed and fired at you. It's inexplicable, but very recognizable.

The unending rattle of the German machine guns took on that different pitch and the 1st row of men began to fall. A gray haze of bullets formed in the air, spraying everything in the vicinity of the men. It sounded like heavy raindrops hitting the ground in a downpour and the second row went down. The men marched past their fallen comrades and leaned into the onslaught as if it were merely a driving rain. The third row went down.

≈

Hartwig Bier looked out above the crosshairs of his Maxim. "Dummkopfs!" he shouted over the deafening sound of his guns. He was frustrated, as he watched hundreds of men dying under his nest's relentless fire. "Why don't you turn and run or look for cover? Are your lives so worthless?" He shook his head. Why were they making him slaughter them this way?

≈

Terry and Doc could no longer advance. The bodies strewn about made it near impossible to march over them. Yet, the well-trained men of the 1st kept moving toward the enemy lines. After seven rows of the regiment had been wiped out, the last row broke formation and began to retreat. The men were not running because of fear – they knew it was over before it had started – they were retiring in an effort to save their fallen comrades. Men were carrying and dragging the wounded in an attempt to salvage anything from this massacre and still the Maxims punished them.

As the seventh row of men fell, Terry and George realized they had somehow come through untouched. There was no point in piping anymore so they began helping injured men back to the St. John's trench, then went back for more.

Major Winsted was yelling orders and waving his arms around, but there were few left to hear his commands. He had moved back to the seventh row and, as his men dropped around him in a hail of bullets, he, too, lurched backward in a spasmodic dance of death. Bullets ripped through his body, putting an end to his mad charge and quest for glory.

≈

The advance had been a complete disaster of unthinkable proportion – a tragedy of uncommon courage and unprecedented folly. The regiment had been wiped out with its men dead or dying before they even reached the British advanced trenches. The slaughter took less than fifteen minutes.

Hartwig Bier took his finger off of the trigger of his gun, and the 08 lurched to a stop. His feeder looked at him questioningly, but Hartwig looked straight ahead. He shook his head as he looked at the horrific carnage before him – the result of his efforts. They were all destroyed and for what purpose?

"Lions lead by donkeys," he muttered, and turned his Maxim back toward the advanced trenches of the British to resume his duties with a profound feeling of disgust.

≈

As the trickle of survivors made it back to St. John's trench dragging or carrying wounded comrades, an officer who had survived stopped the men from returning to the field for more wounded. His decision to resume the retrieval of wounded under cover of darkness was met with protest by those brave survivors. The orders were firm and the men had to wait for darkness.

It was only 10:15 in the morning. Both Terry and George went to the commanding officer -– a sergeant –and implored him to let them go and continue the retrieval, inasmuch as they were trained to be bearers – and George was almost a doctor. The sergeant insisted that there be no retrieval.

"No more Newfoundlanders will needlessly die today," he said solemnly. But the pipers were quick to remind him that they were not from Newfoundland and that to leave the men wounded on the field could, in fact, needlessly allow those who could be saved to die. They badgered him like teenage girls trying to get their father to allow them to go to a dance and, as is usually the case, he broke down and allowed them to go.

"I want no more death in this regiment today!" he commanded. "I will permit you two to go out and field-dress the wounded now, and our parties will go out and retrieve them after dark."

Terry and George ran to get some medical supplies and deposit their pipes in a safe place. They knew that they had to leave quickly before the sergeant could change his mind.

≈

Back above the trenches, the two crawled around the sloping field, moving from body to body until they found a wounded man. Then they would stop the loss of blood as best they could and move on. They dispersed morphine and allowed those that were beyond hope to slip away peacefully and painlessly.

This slow process of crawling from man to man went on for several hours until they had run low on supplies. Terry volunteered to run back for more medical provisions and George stayed to tend to his current patient. The two of them tirelessly toiled throughout the afternoon, patching up the wounded and retrieving supplies.

By dusk they felt they had located and stabilized those that could be saved. The wounded soldiers who were to be picked up were fixed with a long streamer of gauze to identify their location.

≈

Back in the St. John's trenches, George informed the sergeant that they had found nearly four hundred wounded men who were ready for pick up and the man broke down.

"We owe you two men more than we can ever repay," the sergeant said. "Because of your heroism, many lives have been saved today. You will be remembered for your bravery." He hugged them both.

As darkness fell, the parties of eager survivors formed up and brought back hundreds of wounded men. In all three hundred eighty-five men were counted as wounded.

≈

The next day, after a tireless group of volunteers had worked throughout the night, the sergeant took roll call for the 1st Newfoundland Regiment. Only sixty-eight men answered the call. More than 700 were dead, wounded, or missing.

The young sergeant looked old now, with a pale color and dark rings deeply encircling his eyes. He had been laboring all night with his men and was completely spent. His uniform was covered with both mud and blood. He and his men had borne more than any young men should ever be asked to bear, and they were drained and devoid of emotion. He held out the roster with the sixty-eight checks and turned to his men and the two pipers and gave thanks for their safe return.

Terry and George had recovered their pipes and played "Amazing Grace" for all the fallen men. They played the tune three times and stopped. There was neither clapping nor cheering this time, just a sad and tired "Thank you."

"OLD CHUM"

TO MY CHUM
No more we'll share the same old barn,
The same old dugout the same old yarn,
No more a tin of bully share,
Nor split our rum by star shell's flare,
So long old lad.

What times we had both good and bad,
We've shared what shelter could be had,
The same crump hole when the whizz-bangs shrieked,
The same old billet that always leaked,
And now – you've "stopped one."

We'd weathered the storm two winters long,
We'd managed to grin when all went wrong,
Because together we fought and fed,
Our hearts were light; but now you're dead.
I am mateless

Well, old lad, here's peace to you,
And for me, well there's a job to do,

For you and the others that lie at rest,
Assured may be that we'll do our best,
In vengeance

Just one more cross by strafed roadside,
With it's G.R.C., and a name for guide,
But, it's only myself who has lost a friend,
And though I may fight through to the end,
No dug out or billet will be the same,
All pals can only be pals in name,
But we'll all carry on to the end of the game,
Because you lie there
—Wipers Times, unknown author

≈

By 08:30, the 1st German trench had been reached and breached. The objective of the 36th was to take the three main enemy trenches and move south of Beaumont-Hamel to capture the Beaucourt Station. It was a tall order considering how well the Germans had fortified this area. The St. Pierre Redoubt and the infamous Schwaben Redoubt were protecting the ground between them and their objective, and neither stronghold seemed to be weakened by the week long bombardment.

Hundreds of Irish had fallen in an effort to reach the first trench and now even more were charging into the onslaught running past the bodies of their dead comrades.

Bill, Sean, and I had marched across No Man's Land, playing around craters and dead men. The stink of death and smoke from exploding shells was so profound that I had to breathe exclusively through my mouth to avoid gagging and retching. Puking and piping does not work well together.

Sean was leading our small band through the muck and we played "Wearing of the Green" as we crested the first German trench. Waves of Irishmen continued past us and down the bank of the barbed wire trench.

We couldn't believe what we saw, other than the paths cut by the 36th, the entanglement trench seemed almost entirely intact. The large paths through the treacherous wire were a testimony to the sacrifices required of being the first to reach and cut through such a barrier.

The sides of each path were strewn with the bodies of brave young men, now being used to weigh down the wire and keep it back so the still-living could charge through in an effort to kill their enemy and avenge their comrade's deaths. The amount of dead was appalling especially at the eastern end of the entanglement paths. The German gunners focused their guns at the openings and simply mowed down the men as they ran through.

Thankfully, by the time Sean, Bill, and I arrived and marched through the entanglement trench, the bombers had taken out many of the machine guns. The heaviest fighting had moved into the second trench, but over the fifty meter stretch of land between the trenches there was still plenty of hand-to-hand action.

A German aeroplane flew over us, very low. It seemed to be moving slowly and I could see very plainly the faces of the pilot and his gunner/bomber behind him. The man in the back seat leaned over the edge of the aircraft and dropped a hand bomb on a group of advancing Irishmen.

The young men were focusing on their objective and never saw the threat looming overhead. As I watched the event, I instinctively shrugged up my shoulders and winced my face in anticipation of the impending explosion. In a flash, the explosion sent dirt, debris and men flying in all directions. Out of the fifteen or so men that had been advancing, just one remained. He stood stunned, unsteady, and looking around trying to comprehend what had just happened to him and his fellow mates.

His helmet had been blown off of his head and some of his tunic and webbing was torn, but all in all, he seemed unharmed. The cloud of confusion was lifting as he saw all his friends dead and dying all around him. The unmuffled noise of the low-flying aeroplane finally caught his attention and he looked in its direction now realizing what had just happened.

I watched curiously as the young soldier leaned over and retrieved a rifle from the body of one of his comrades. He calmly pulled the bolt back and ejected the spent shell from the chamber replacing it with a new bullet, raised the gun to his shoulder and fired it at the retreating aircraft.

I could still clearly see the bomber in the back seat of the aeroplane smiling as they flew farther from the destruction of his attack. The young Irishman fired only one shot and I knew that it was ridiculous to think that he could actually hit the plane, but I looked at the aircraft to see if he might possibly have gotten lucky. The bomber still looking back at his handy work suddenly snapped back, a brief puff of pink spatter blew by and his head rolling back, then forward. He hung limply over the edge of the cockpit with his arms flapping in the slipstream as the pilot sharply banked the aircraft away from the battle and toward his home field. It was a remarkable shot, either highly skilled or extremely lucky.

Both Sean and Bill had stopped playing and had joined me in watching this stunning battlefield duel and its astounding outcome. The entire event – from attack of the aeroplane to the revenge of the rifleman – had not taken more than forty-five seconds, but for some reason that seemed like a long time.

I looked back to where the young man had been standing and he was gone. The rest of the battlefield, which had seemingly stood still while this played out, was now active again and the noise and confusion of war had returned. We had only progressed some twenty feet when the aeroplane attacked, with still about thirty feet to go before we entered the second trench. The three of us once again refocused on our mission and began playing.

There was still a remarkable amount of fighting going on all around us, but it was clear that the Germans were retreating. I looked around at the landscape, there were hundreds of gray and khaki bundles strewn about the battlefield like so many piles of dirty laundry, each one representing someone's son.

Then, seemingly from nowhere, a German soldier ran toward us with his rifle held high over his head and its bayonet pointing right at me. I assume he must have been out of ammunition, or else he would have shot me.

He looked deranged as he charged us screaming something in his native tongue. We stopped playing and braced helplessly for the attack. Then, inexplicably, the German stumbled forward and fell face down in the muddy earth at our feet. Twenty meters away I saw the Irish rifleman who had killed the aeroplane bomber just minutes before with his gun pointing at the dead German. He glared at the body of our attacker then looked at me. Then, with a slight nod, he spun around and fired at two other Germans killing them both.

My heart was pounding wildly as just moments before I thought I was a dead man. My mind and body had not caught up with the quick turn of events. Sean looked at me wide-eyed and then at Bill who was equally wide-eyed. Looking at each other in disbelief we all seemed to let out a collected sigh of relief and then began to play "The Minstrel Boy" again.

My hands were shaking rather noticeably and I was having some difficulty with my playing when my right shoulder was abruptly punched back with such a force that my hand flew off the chanter and the blowpipe popped out of my mouth. I stumbled one or two steps, but was able to plug my blowpipe back into my mouth and raise my right hand back to the chanter. I fell back into place with Bill and Sean and resumed the tune afraid to think about what had just happened to me.

Both my friends realized, as it soon occurred to me as well, that I had just been wounded. They seemed to be more interested than I was as to the extent of the wound. Sean was looking at me across Bill as we continued to play and march. I kept on playing, looking straight ahead not wanting to acknowledge having been shot. The pain had elevated from dull to intense as my nerves recovered from shock and began to send me the message that something bad had happened to me. I grimaced and my eyes began to water as the pain continued to build.

Bill was keenly aware of my deteriorating condition and, in mid-tune, his right arm came up across my chest with his hand held out flat.

"Hold on there buddy boy," he said. "I think it's time to take a look at you, eh."

I was in no condition to argue and, in fact, was quite relieved that someone had made the decision to stop me.

Blood had soaked the right arm of my tunic and was dripping down my hand and off of my pinky finger. It had been interfering with my burls – I remember being very annoyed at that. As men continued to run past us and flood the German trenches, I stood unsteadily letting my friends open my tunic and search for the source of the scarlet flow.

"Bingo," Sean said. It was a clean shot, he said, through the shoulder muscle just outside the joint. Judging from the blood flow, no major blood vessels had been hit, only tissue.

"Very lucky," Bill said as he began to wrap the oozing wound with gauze from his small field dress kit. I was lightheaded, but immensely relieved.

"We must press on. These men need our support," I said.

"Okay, then press on we shall!" Sean agreed. Bill smiled and muttered something about tough guys, but I didn't really hear his full comment. We pressed on. The time was 10:00 and the 36th Ulster's men had fought their way through the third German trench. It had taken two-and-a-half hours to make six hundred meters, and at what cost? The battle, which at the onset was projected to be a decisive and easy victory, had turned into a costly and devastating miscalculation.

Unknown to the men of the 36th, their advances had been among the greatest of the day. The German command, however, was well aware of that fact and responded with a massive and focused artillery bombardment. The result was the killing of hundreds of Irish and German soldiers alike. Waves of Germans rushed the breach created by the Ulstermen and were met with well-placed Vickers and Lewis machine guns exacting some well-deserved revenge.

The fighting was everywhere around us, and we continued to pipe as ordered. Right in front of our trio lay a wounded Ulster soldier. He had been shot but was trying unsuccessfully to stand and continue the fight. The gunman who had shot him was thirty feet away and running at the wounded soldier with his gun held out in the bayonet thrust position. The wounded man was too focused on trying to stand to notice the charge of the German and only saw him at the last second.

Bill yelled, but it was too late. The Irishman spun and fell on his back, his arms held out in a vain effort to stop his attacker, but it was of little use. The German plunged his bayonet through the helpless young man's chest causing his victim to curl into a fetal position. The pain was so intense, he couldn't even scream, all he could do was look horribly surprised.

Bill Lewis cast off his drum and charged wildly at the German who was standing over the dead soldier. The Boche was too involved in watching the young soldier die to notice the rapidly approaching danger.

Bill hit the man at a full sprint, as he had many times on the Queen's rugger field. This time though, instead of trying to yank the rugby ball out of the arms of his opponent, he grabbed the German's head around the neck and under the chin. As Bill would have with a rugby ball, he pulled and snapped the man's neck twisting it grotesquely, one hundred-eighty degrees from its original position. The result was instant. The man fell dead next to the dead Irishman with Bill standing over both of them. His breathing was tight from the anger that had driven him to kill without mercy.

When Sean and I arrived moments later, Bill was still staring menacingly at the man he had just killed.

"He should never have killed that wounded boy," he said in a low growl. I put my hand on his shoulder. That seemed to help bring him out of his rage.

"Where's my drum?" he asked. He was concerned about having left it behind.

"I have it, Bill. I brought it," I assured him.

Bill nodded, took his muddy but undamaged instrument and clipped it to his harness. The dead German lay stomach down on the muddy ground, his head twisted, looking up at his killer with unseeing eyes. We walked past him with no pity or remorse and started to play another tune.

By 1400 hours, six-and-a-half hours after we had started the advance, our reserves were running dry. Lieutenant McDonnell had ordered us back to the third German trench, which was being adequately held. He feared that the B.E.F. had horribly underestimated its enemy and, as a result, there would be few if any reinforcements coming.

A small group of Ulstermen had fought up to the Beaucourt Station, but the resistance was so intense and the support so inadequate that they were unable to hold on to the position.

The three of us had stopped our piping and drumming to help retrieve the wounded – our other very important duty. It seemed to be an endless task. Trip after trip, we would go out and collect the wounded and return to the newly set up field station.

It had become very apparent to me that the number of injured men moving back toward our lines far outnumbered the soldiers coming from behind our lines. The waves had completely stopped by 1800 hours and we were ordered to fall back to the second German trench.

≈

The three of us were preparing to withdraw when Sean realized that he had placed his pipes in a temporary aid post that had been set up in one of the third German trenches being evacuated. Bill and I had moved our equipment back to the German first trench earlier.

"I have to get my pipes before darkness sets in," Sean announced. There was a hesitance in his voice. Bill and I tried to reason with him – it was still too dangerous to leave the relative safety of our position – but it was to no avail.

"I'll be right back," he yelled over his shoulder as he trotted toward the now poorly held location of his pipes. Ten minutes later Bill and I had just off loaded a badly wounded man at a new aid post and were returning to the battlefield when Sean reappeared with a gravely wounded man draped over his back.

"That doesn't look like your pipes to me," I said, relieved to see my friend had safely returned.

"I couldn't just leave him suffering there, could I? Will one of you take him from here? I need to get going." We agreed to take the wounded man and Sean turned once again and ran off to retrieve his beloved pipes. "I'll be right back," he called again.

Bill hollered to him over the constant noise of the front. "You haven't got much time before dark."

I don't know if he ever heard Bill's warning.

≈

Machine gun teams were repositioned so as to protect our troop retirement, but the task left to them was a difficult one.

As our troops retreated, the gunners had to take care not to shoot their own men. With the approaching darkness, their job would soon become impossible.

Sadly, too many men who fought bravely against the enemy were mistakenly gunned down by their own troops as they retreated to a safer position. Our runners were being sent with desperate requests for support, but there were few reserves. Moreover, the command was in a state of total shock, confusion, and denial.

Nightfall was upon us now and the fighting had subsided from continuous to sporadic. There was still no sign of Sean. Both sides were reeling from their losses. It was too stunning to comprehend. Bill and I were now employed completely as stretcher-bearers. We had been collecting the wounded for several hours and were beyond the point of exhaustion. Yet neither of us would dare speak of resting or quitting. There were too many men still out there and one of them could be Sean – although neither of us would voice our concern out loud.

The Germans had taken back all but the last of their trenches and were again securing their positions and tending to their own wounded. As we stumbled around the shell-riddled area between their position and ours, we occasionally had to dive for cover as a star shell illuminated the landscape.

Our enemy wanted to make sure that no raiding parties were coming their way and would communicate that desire with several bursts of machine gun fire. What they didn't realize was that we had only enough manpower to collect our wounded. We soon discovered that the warning shots were just that – warnings – and not aimed at any of us, but fired high.

There was a good reason for that. As with our own side, teams of German stretcher-bearers were roaming around in the darkness looking for their own injured colleagues, so this gave us a degree of relief.

With that realization, we became bolder when the star shells lit up the night using the luminescence to help find the fallen men. They were everywhere.

In the blackness, we heard a moaning coming from a crump hole several meters away. We were manning a four-man stretcher, having been joined by two mildly injured men from the 9th Irish Fusiliers. Moving cautiously in the direction of the moaning we finally saw the man deep in a crater thanks to the light of another star shell. The phosphorus light revealed that our wounded soldier was a German lad, not more than 19 years old.

We were as stunned as he was and we all just stood looking at each other for several moments. The young fellow had no fight left in him and resigned himself to his fate – no doubt he believed we would kill him. But, he was just another wounded man to us and we went to work dressing his wounds as he moaned to us in German.

He was ready to transport for further attention and we were carrying him out of the shell hole when another star shell lit the sky. Not more than ten meters away stood a German bearer team and we all froze.

I was the first to move. I pointed to our passenger and called out to them, "Hey, this guy is a comrade of yours!" The Germans looked at one another, the white of their eyes in brilliant contrast to the dirt and filth covering their faces.

They spoke softly to each other and then began to cautiously move toward us. Their eyes never left our eyes as they came closer. Bill comforted the wounded German as his comrades moved closer to our team. We set the stretcher down and stepped back.

The lead man from their team abandoned any caution he had been exercising and proceeded to inspect the injured soldier. He soon concluded that we had dressed the lad's wounds and had cared for him as if he were one of our own.

He looked up at us searchingly from his kneeling position. He saw no anger or malice in our eyes; we were all pawns in this mess. He motioned his crew to approach and they transferred the young man onto their stretcher. The lead then stood and came face to face with us. He was tired and worn looking, and he smelled awful.

"Danke," he whispered looking deeply into our eyes with an emotionless expression. Bill put his hand on the man's arm.

"You're welcome," he said. As he held the German's arm, he pulled out of his tunic pocket a flask of rum and gave it to him.

The German was momentarily puzzled, but then realized what Bill was offering. He took the flask, uncorked it, smelled it, and then held it up to the injured man's lips.

The soldier took two large gulps and sighed, "Ja, das ist gut."

The German stretcher team helped themselves to the rum and handed it back to Bill empty. It should be noted that the Germans were not given rations of rum as the B.E.F. were, so it was an invitation they wouldn't refuse.

The men picked up their injured comrade and began walking back toward their lines, but then stopped after several steps. There was a brief discussion between them as we watched curiously. The lead came walking back to us, he pointed at my kilt and blood soaked sleeve then pointed at his injured man and then in the direction of their lines.

"Comrade," he said and pointed again toward their line. It was clear to us that he was telling us of the location of one of our own wounded.

My heart pounded – could it be Sean? "Let's go," Bill said. "Ja, kommen sie hier," the German replied. We followed him into the muddy darkness. Twenty meters later, he pointed to his right with his free hand. In the darkness, we could make out a figure curled up in a crump hole.

The Germans stood motionless as we scurried to the aid of the khaki figure who was laying as still as dead. In the blackness, he had no way of knowing whether we were friend or foe, so he lay unmoving until I asked, "Are you alive, man?"

The man began to sob. "Thank the Lord, oh Lord, thank you, I am alive." I recognized the voice. The figure slowly rolled over; he was clutching something. In the darkness I could now see that it was his set of pipes. Sean was alive.

We looked up out of the small crater at the German team. The lead stiffened up, snapped his muddy hobnailed boots together and tilted his head forward in a salute to us. I stood up and returned the honor. Then they moved quickly into the night with their cargo. Bill had been busy inspecting and bandaging Sean and I noticed he was now administering a heavy dose of morphine. I looked at him curiously to see why he was drugging our friend so heavily. Bill looked up into my eyes. His face pale and hard. He shook his head almost imperceptibly. I had seen that look too many times before.

I turned back to Sean. My throat was tightening up but I choked out, "You'll be okay old chum."

I couldn't hold back my tears as our friend quietly drifted off to sleep. We loaded our gravely injured comrade on to our stretcher along with his pipes and carried him back to the aid station, where he died of his wounds twenty minutes later.

≈

The eastern sky was beginning to show signs of dawn. There had been little killing for six or seven hours.

"Perhaps both sides have had enough of this," I said to no one, but I knew that would not be the case. Like two exhausted prize fighters late in the tenth round, both sides were resting on each other's shoulders, almost hugging, trying to regain enough strength to continue to pummel their opponent into submission, it was just a matter of time.

Nonetheless, the brief expression of humanity we had just experienced, in a place where inhumanity seemed the rule, was an event we would remember for the rest of our lives along with the loss of our good friend.

≈

When we returned to our trenches, the Lancasters and the Yorks had joined us to relieve what was left of the 39th. When roll call was taken that morning it became clear that no one had realized the magnitude of our losses.

The 9th Irish fusiliers lost all of its officers and had five hundred-twenty casualties out of six hundred-thirty men. The Royal Irish Rifles had five hundred ninety-five injured or killed.

Sadly, Lieutenant McDonnell, for whom we had great regard, was also gravely injured and died in the field with his beloved Irishmen. The 36th Ulster had suffered more than five thousand casualties on the first day of the battle. Somme was a fight that would continue for another five months.

Bill and I had somehow survived the worst catastrophe in British military history with minor injuries. My shoulder wound was not enough to get me sent home, but it was enough to require some time away from the Front. We were given a week to recuperate and ordered to billet in a small town by the name of Albert about five miles west southwest of the Beaumont-Hamel and the Front and about three miles from Auchonvillers, where George and Terry had been billeted.

Before we left for Albert, Bill and I made sure that Sean was given a proper burial and that his family was notified of his heroism. His funeral was an emotional event. I piped one of the best bagpipers I had ever known into the grave to the tune of *Flowers of the forest*. We buried him along with his pipes.

FINDING AN OLD FRIEND

The main road to Albert was a mess. With so many ambulances coming and going, and an endless train of supply lorries in transit, things were almost at a standstill. We decided to walk. Though we were exhausted and had some distance to cover, it didn't matter. The fighting had churned up again and every step away from that hell was a step in the right direction. As we distanced ourselves from the Somme battle, the landscape began to transform from a wasteland back into a French countryside. The color green was so beautiful to see, it almost overwhelmed me. Bill and I lazily walked the five miles as if we were on a summer stroll on Wolf Island. Neither of us spoke much. I think we were just trying to avoid thinking at all. We were accompanied by the distant but ever-present noise of the war, which we chose to ignore. When we arrived at the square of Albert, we went straight to the hotel, checked in, had our clothes cleaned of lice, deloused ourselves and took very long, very hot baths. That night we joined up with some jocks from the London Scottish and found a pub that was happy to exchange our money for far too much beer. We all got roaring drunk and laughed and cried, and then went our separate ways. Bill and I somehow found our way back to our hotel and slept for a day and a half. After a week, we received orders that we were to rejoin our countrymen to the north in a city called Arras. We were being attached to the Canadian 42nd highlanders, and they needed pipes and drums.

The distance from Albert to Arras is about twenty-five miles and parallels the western front rather closely. It is a well-traveled route. The orders gave us three days to make the one-day trip so we were in no big hurry.

But, as always, it seems that when you are in a hurry you can't find a lift, and when you have all the time in the world everyone wants to give you a ride.

We hopped a lorry and were in Arras by that afternoon. When we got to the city it was evident that the war had arrived before us. This beautiful and ancient city had been laid waste by German artillery. Some of the most magnificent churches and buildings in France had been reduced to rubble, but the city was still very much alive.

The British Command firmly held the city now and had moved the fight further to the east by several miles to Vimy Ridge, a location that provided the Germans with high ground. It gave them a tactical superiority which they took full advantage of.

Despite the severe damage inflicted on the city, we were able to secure lodging at the Hotel de L'Universe, which remained fully open.

This particular afternoon Bill and I had just purchased a baguette and a half-wheel of brie near the center of the city and were dividing it up with a small bottle of red wine when we heard a familiar sound – bagpipes.

"I can't seem to get away from that confounded sound," Bill joked. After a few mouthfuls of bread, cheese, and wine we agreed to go in search of the piper. We walked down several very narrow, winding streets but couldn't get a fix on the location of the unknown piper.

Finally, in front of us was a huge cathedral that had been badly damaged on one side. We were getting closer to the sound. At the end of the block we could see that the other side of the cathedral was still fully intact. There was a huge assembly of men in a large courtyard that were gathered around a stage, a kilted regiment. On the stage were four Scotts preforming the Scottish sword dance and a lone piper.

The piper was playing a familiar tune, "The Rakes of Mallow." The song is normally a two-four march, and it's a peppy tune, but this fellow was ripping through it. The dancers were having a terrible time keeping up and the crowd was howling with laughter at their difficulty.

The faster he played, the faster they danced, and the louder the crowd laughed. It was just the medicine these lads needed after a week-and-a-half on the Somme.

"No one can play 'Rakes' that fast, eh?" I said to Bill.

"I know someone who can," Bill said in feigned annoyance, "and I'll bet my 6 pence a day pay it's Manning." He wasn't fooling me – I knew he was as happy to see our old friend as I was. We rushed over.

Terry hadn't noticed our arrival yet. He was poised in a classic piper stance and fighting off a laugh as he put the dancers through the paces.

Bill yelled, "Hey pal, what you need up there is a good drummer." Terry turned to see who the rude heckler was. His mouth piece fell out when he realized who had yelled.

"Bill! Ian! Am I ever glad to see you fellows." He hopped off the stage as his drones groaned to a stop from lack of air and the crowd protested his departure. We all embraced and exchanged greetings.

"Where is that big lug McKee?" Bill asked.

"He was wounded the night before day one so he is loafing in the 5th Canadian hospital. George and I billeted with some muckety-muck from the Royal Army Medical corps just prior to the big show. He pulled some strings and the Doc is working for the RAMC now. It seems he's worth more as a medic than as a piper," Terry said.

"And you, young Macdonald, I see you're wounded. Not a blighty, I take it."

"No such luck," I said. "I'll be good as new and piping in no time."

"Now where's my old pal Sean?" Terry asked, although I suspect he somehow sensed the answer. Bill and I looked at each other with sad eyes to see who would break the bad news to our friend.

Bill cleared his throat, something that so many people do when they are about to deliver sad news. "I'm afraid that we have lost our chum on day one."

"What? What do you mean?" Terry knew exactly what Bill was saying; he just didn't want to grasp a hold of the idea yet.

"He went back to retrieve his pipes when we were pulling back," Bill continued. "We found him later that night in a crump hole clinging to his pipes, barely alive. We got him back to the aid station but, he died shortly thereafter."

"He was a fine piper and a good friend," Terry said. He reached into his tunic and produced a flask. "Here's to our old chum, may he rest in peace and pipe us through the pearly gates when our time comes."

We all drank to the toast and reflected on our friend for several moments.

"We had a tough go the first day." I said. "The 36th suffered five thousand casualties – almost half its men. Is this your group?"

"No," Terry replied solemnly. He explained that his regiment was all but wiped out so senselessly in a matter of minutes.

We had all seen the horrors of war and the slaughter of the battlefield and were different now. Changed men that now knew that this was no great adventure. We also realized that we couldn't run away, we had to see this thing through – not for some lofty ideal or love of country, but for our friends who lay in the battlefield.

The crowd of Scotts were getting louder and louder, chanting "Piper! Piper!" Terry hopped up on the stage and held up his hand.

"Gentleman, we have the possibility of being treated to another piper and a drummer if they can be convinced properly."

The men roared to life hooting, yelling and whistling. We couldn't say no. Despite the pain from my wound, for the next thirty minutes we entertained the troops as they coaxed us on. Neither they, nor we, thought about the war for that half hour.

THE 5TH CANADIAN STATIONARY HOSPITAL, JULY 1ST (09:00HRS)

By 09:00 the influx of injured was so steady and massive that the personnel were becoming overwhelmed. The orderlies stared out at the line of ambulances clogging the road and searching for an end. There was none to be seen. In the past, when there were assaults, the hospital always received waves of injured with lulls in between. This was different.

Dan McKee wheeled his chair over to the opened door and looked out at the buzz of activity outside. Sheila rushed past.

"Hey, toots!" Dan yelled. "What's cooking?"

"Oh, my god," Sheila spoke quickly. "This is horrible. I've never seen so many incoming at such a steady rate. We're already swamped!" She was gone before her words had faded.

Dan's hands grabbed the wheels of his chair, his knuckles white. He needed to do something, but what could he do? His jaw muscles knotted in frustration.

"I can't just sit here," Dan said. "This is ridiculous!"

The doctor's warning flashed through his mind – "Keep your leg elevated, stay off it, and you may just be able to keep it." Dan grunted angrily.

Perhaps survivor's guilt was setting in. He wheeled his chair to a different vantage point, his leg sticking straight out like a ramming rod. An orderly scurried by.

"We took your bed, Dan. Sorry, but there was just no choice. Too many new injuries requiring beds now, old man." The orderly appeared to be from a well-to-do family, judging by his accent.

"No sweat, pal," Dan replied, faking a smile. Alan Macdonald was standing across the room watching the activity but staying well out of the way so as not to add to the confusion. Dan saw him and yelled out "Hey, Alan come here, eh?"

Alan was getting slowly used to his real name and was recovering more and more of his memory every day. This comfort of knowing his real name and the flashes of personal recognition helped ease the level of frustration that plagues those with memory loss.

"Ya, Dan. What's up?" Macdonald asked. He had a new found degree of confidence only made possible after he and Dan had spent hours together going over and over what personal information Dan could recollect about him.

"I feel as useless as tits on a bull here, Al! We need to help somehow."

"Look at us. What can we do?" Alan asked. Dan looked around the ward. There was a closet full of uniforms and hats belonging to wounded officers that had been brought in at one end of the room. They had been cleaned and were awaiting the day that they would be reunited with their owners.

"Wheel me down to that closet," Dan commanded. Alan did as he was told. "Grab the biggest and most high ranking tunic and hat you can find for me, will you Al, old buddy."

Alan rifled through the tunics and hats and came up with a very ample jacket and lid.

Four chevrons on the sleeves indicated the rank of Major and the hat had plenty of gold rope and leaves. Dan threw the tunic over his shoulders like a shawl and plopped the cap on his head then looked up at Alan.

"How do I look?" he asked Alan, who only shrugged his shoulders in confusion.

"What this place needs is someone in charge!" Dan said. "It needs someone to direct the flow and bark out orders."

There was an ornate walking cane in the closet that Dan decided would top off his transformation, people respond better to a man waving a stick.

"Okay James, drive me into the courtyard and I shall create order from chaos. He pointed the stick toward the door and Alan pushed him out.

≈

The noise and confusion were so great that it was no wonder things were getting bogged down. "You there!" Dan pointed his stick at an ambulance driver. "Move that vehicle over! We will be unloading three lorries across now! So form three lanes."

The driver jumped in his truck and moved it over enough to allow two others to come up alongside. McKee had an analytical mind and enjoyed this type of challenge. "Unload the ambulances three across," he boldly ordered three Red caps that had been idly standing nearby. "The groups will be staggered five paces apart so as to allow access to all three without interfering with each other!"

The man was fearless in his impersonation and so convincing that these fellows snapped to attention and did as they were told. The orderly that had informed Dan that his bed was taken pushed a wounded man past the new officer on deck and his eyes popped out in astonishment. Major McKee smiled and winked, then continued to orchestrate an efficient offloading of the wounded.

"All those who can walk will walk toward the front of the ambulances parked behind you and then form an orderly line into the ward!" He yelled at the back of the ambulances. These men were used to taking orders and responded to the Major's orders.

Things were beginning to flow nicely when the orderly who knew Dan returned with Sheila in tow.

"What on earth are you doing? You can be court marshaled for impersonating an officer!" she whispered to him.

"I was cold and couldn't find a blanket, so I put this on," he said. "Besides, this place needed someone in charge and there was no one taking up the reins."

She stood back, looked at him with exasperation and went off to help more wounded.

The orderly looking down said "Sorry, Dan I thought ..."

"Listen young man, I'll demote you if you try a stunt like that again!"

"But you're not a real major," the orderly whined.

"I've been a major for years, young man – a major pain in the ass!" As always Dan laughed at his own joke. "Now off with you."

There was still work to be done. "The five pace areas will be divided into three lanes, the inside closest to the ambulance door will be for stretcher bearers and gurneys," Dan ordered. "The next lane is for wheelchairs and those needing assistance to walk, and the outside for those who can walk unassisted."

A small crowd of hospital personnel were taking in all the orders and setting up the new system that this commander was promoting.

Doctor Bradley, Sheila's friend, was attending to a patient. He had seen Sheila talking to this new take-charge fellow and stopped her.

"Y'all know who that officer is? We've needed that kind of discipline and orderly thinking around here for a long time and he looks kinda familiar."

"Oh, well, I just met him today, doctor," she replied nervously. "I think he's from the Canadian forces and is... uh... moving out tomorrow. I don't think you know him."

"Well, he's a welcome addition, even if it's just for a day! A welcome addition, indeed. We can all learn a lot from that type of leadership," the doctor said admiringly.

Sheila nodded, her eyebrows raised high in disbelief and relief that Bradley had not recognized her friend.

Meanwhile, back in the fray, Dan was barking out orders and being pushed by his associate from hot spot to hot spot. The volume had increased, but so had the efficiency, so things were moving far better than they would have had Dan not interfered.

Alan leaned over and spoke into Dan's ear "I can't believe the amount of wounded!"

"Yes," Dan replied. "It's not a good sign. We tried to warn them but, it appears they didn't listen. Terry and George got through to command as far as I know."

A flood of fear pumped through McKee at the thought that they may not have made it. He never even made an effort to find out. A soldier shuffled past them. He had a bewildered look on his face, his arms hung slightly in front of him and his hands were shaking uncontrollably.

"I've seen that before – it's shell shock." Alan made the statement without thinking. Dan looked up at him, wondering if Alan realized what had just happened.

"Really? Where? Where did you see that?" he pressed. Alan's expression became strained as he searched for more of his suppressed memory. He didn't know where.

≈

One of the Sunbeam ambulances let out with a backfire as it pulled away from the offloading area. Everyone jumped at the noise except the shell shocked man, who began to walk in a jerky disjointed fashion. His eyes became huge dark holes that displayed total unbridled fear. He began to howl like a cornered dog looking around at everyone but seeing nothing. The entire area stopped, all activity came to a halt.

Doctor Bradley, who was some fifty feet away, looked up from his patient and assessed the scene. "Attend to this fellow, will you?" he asked the nurse next to him. "I'll be right back."

He walked toward the howling man standing just six feet away from the wheelchair-bound mock Major. Bradley wound his large right arm back and came across the shell shocked man's face with a stunning slap that staggered the man. He immediately stopped his howling and coherently looked at Bradley, rubbing his reddened face.

"What was that for?" the now awakened man said.

"I'll need y'all to go over and join those men in line and quietly wait your turn. Can you do that?" the doctor asked.

"Yes, sir," the man said sheepishly.

Bradley turned toward the take-charge Major. He wanted to introduce himself. As he and Dan made eye contact, the doctor withdrew his outstretched hand and pondered the imposter for a moment. "I shoulda known you weren't the real McCoy," he said in his strong southern accent. "Most officers aren't so damn organized." Then he became serious. "You better wrap this thing up, son, before y'all get your backside in a sling." Bradley walked back to his waiting patient shaking his head.

VIMY RIDGE

The next several months were relatively quiet in our sector. To the south, the Somme raged on until November and then fizzled out leaving the western front line essentially unchanged except for the addition of the seventy thousand men unaccounted for who were probably now part of the landscape. In all the activity between Somme and Verdun it seemed that both sides had forgotten about Arras and Vimy Ridge, and that was just fine with us.

We were assigned to the Third Canadian Division, Argyle and Sutherland battalion and were settling in very well. We were regularly giving concerts in the courtyard of the Cathedral Arras and, other than the trench raiding parties, the hostilities were light. This was all about to change.

It started with the arrival of the royal engineer corps. They went right to work cutting into the chalk sub strata carving out tunnels that would lead to multiple mines under enemy territory. Then all four Canadian divisions slowly began to arrive.

The Royal Air Corps began numerous flights over Vimy Ridge for reconnaissance. Twenty five squadrons with a total of three hundred sixty-five aeroplanes were employed to survey the enemy. To counter the build-up of British aircraft, the Germans called on the well-equipped and highly experienced Jasta 11, the Royal Prussian Fighter

Squadron, led by none other than "The Red Baron," Manfred von Richthofen himself. He and his squadron promptly downed over a hundred British aircraft in a little over one week.

It was starting to look like we were about to undertake another major assault, only this one seemed to be primarily Canadian and far better planned.

≈

In January 1917 Lieutenant-General Sir Julian Byng took command of the Canadian forces and began formulating a strategy for the assault on Vimy Ridge. The plan was to involve the four Canadian Divisions and the British 5th Infantry Division for a total of one hundred seventy thousand men, of which ninety-seven thousand were Canadian. There had been some costly but very valuable lessons learned from the battles Somme and Verdun and this command was not about to make the same mistakes.

The plan was simple. First, place and detonate mines in such a way as to create a huge trench across No Man's Land providing shelter and cover for the advancing troops.

Next, four hundred British eighteen-pound field cannons would lay down a creeping barrage to clear the path for the infantry. The troops would advance in a leap frog manner every hundred yards the first wave would dig in and the second wave would pass them advancing another hundred yards. The heavy and medium howitzers were to pound the known points of German defense.

And finally the "Stokes Sticks" would clear out any strong holds with their deadly effectiveness. At just eleven pounds, the Stokes Mortar was a lightweight, portable weapon that could easily move along with the advancing troops and lay down cover or take out machine gun nests. One could fire twenty-five rounds per minute and achieve a range of over twelve hundred yards.

Probably the most important consideration of Lieutenant-General Byng's plan was the extraordinary amount of communication cable laid out for field phone and telegraph. He was determined that the total breakdown of communications experienced during the first days of the Somme would not be repeated here on Vimy. Reliable communications are an integral and essential part of effective command.

≈

The troops were being trained over and over again to insure their readiness for the offensive and to secure their success. We, on the other hand, were left mostly to our own recognizance. We all realized that this was indeed going to be a well-orchestrated event.

The date chosen for the assault was 9 April – Easter Sunday – but the French requested that we postpone the operation by one day to 10 April in respect for the holy day. Our command agreed and the new date was set.

Excitement was in the air and we were caught up in it. It had been almost nine months since the Somme and, although we still missed Sean – and all those we lost in that battle – the anticipation of the upcoming campaign was almost intoxicating.

There is an inexplicable feeling about being a part of something that is so much larger than you are. We had no illusions about war now, and we had seen its outcome. Given the choice to stay and fight or leave, most of us would have chosen to stay. I believe we felt obligated to our dead comrades to carry through to the end.

≈

Two weeks prior to the date of the assault the artillery began to shell the enemy strongholds. We had seen this same artillery attack at the Somme, but in this case the strategy would be to increase and then decrease the intensity of the barrages in an attempt to confuse the enemy. It would be two weeks of hell for the Germans because they'd expect an attack every time the artillery slacked off, only to be pounded again in earnest shortly thereafter.

Because of the intensity of the artillery attack the German command kept their reserve troops well away from the front by some twenty miles. Consequently, they ran short of supplies and fresh troops and by 9 April those on the front were hungry, demoralized and mentally broken.

In the early morning hours of the tenth, the first waves took up position in the advanced trenches. At 05:30 all hell broke loose. The land mines blew up in unison and the artillery began to lay down a walking barrage a hundred yards ahead of us.

The whistles blew. We played the pipes and our troops charged forward. The forward movement of the men had to be halted periodically so as not to run into the creeping barrage.

Compared with the Somme, Vimy Ridge had a remarkable first day, with minimal losses and all objectives met. The whole battle lasted only three days with fewer than four thousand Canadians lost and many more German prisoners taken.

PART NINE

GOING HOME

Guelph Veterans Home. Present day

Mr. Macdonald abruptly stopped his story and reflected on where he was in his recollection. Mike and I sat leaning forward and impatiently waited for him to give us more of his remarkable tale, but he seemed to have somehow lost his train of thought.

Perhaps this was the time for some insightful interviewer-type questions, I thought.

"So, Mr. Macdonald, where did you and your fellow pipers go from there?" Not the most prying question, but it seemed like a natural one.

"From where?" he asked, somewhat confused. I looked at Mike then back at the old man.

"Well, from Vimy Ridge, sir," I gently reminded him. After all at 109 years old, you're entitled to lose your train of thought every once in a while.

"Oh, yes," he said. "Forgive me, sometimes I am forgetful. We went back to Arras after five days and remained there for two more months."

He stopped. The reliving of these terrible events was taking its toll, he was emotionally exhausted. "Boys," he said, "I think I need to rest, may we resume this tomorrow?"

"Of course," I said. "We've taken up a great deal of your time and we appreciate your valuable insights." Under other circumstances that might have sounded patronizing, but I really meant it.

I needed to get home anyway. It was already two in the afternoon and the family Thanksgiving dinner began around four. I asked Mr. Macdonald if he would join the gathering, and after a little coaxing, he agreed. He then retired to his room for a little rest.

A little bit before four o'clock, I returned to the Veterans home to pick him up. He was standing at the front desk dressed in his best suit and leaning on a walking cane. I helped him into my parent's minivan, a far better choice of vehicles than my Datsun for such an occasion and we headed to my parents' house.

He was obviously looking forward to escaping his depressing surroundings. I thought about the man's age again, he must have outlived all his friends and most, if not all, of his family – a curse of longevity.

He was very talkative, obviously the nap had revived him and the invitation had invigorated him. My folks were great–they realized that having this gentleman join us was quite an honor and they welcomed him warmly.

Before dinner we sat around the living room talking, and our guest was nursing his glass of wine. You could tell that he was savoring every sip. I don't believe the veteran's home serves any alcohol.

His face became mildly flushed as he began to speak of his experiences again. He spoke in broad generalities this time, not as graphic or detailed as before. I assumed this was because of our mixed company – very old school. Mr. Macdonald did speak of his reunion with his brother Alan.

"We were on a several day leave when we ran into George Cohen. He had been permanently assigned to the Medical Corp. It seemed a sensible move – very uncustomary of the B.E.F.

George said he had gone to the 5th Canadian Stationary Hospital and had run into Dan McKee and a nice nurse we might know named Sheila Lougheed. We were overjoyed at the news. He slyly kept the real news until last.

"Oh, yes," he said. "There's one more bit of news you might find interesting, they have a patient that has been recovering for quite a while from head injuries. His name is Alan Macdonald – any relation?"

We looked at each other open-mouthed and unbelieving.

George just stood there with a big toothy grin waiting for his statement to sink in. I grabbed him by his shoulders and stared hard into his eyes. "George, what are you saying?"

"Alan is alive and well, except for some memory loss," George said, smiling. I almost fainted. I had given up and resigned myself to the idea of his death. I thought I was going to vomit, but took several deep breaths and suppressed the urge. It was decided that we would all hook a ride on an ambulance that day to go and visit the 5th Canadian and surprise Alan.

≈

The ride was quite nice, except for the condition of the road. The weather that day was warm and spring like. As we passed a small village, we noted a gathering of some fifty French military personnel. I didn't realize at first, but it soon became apparent that it was a French firing squad.

They had ten or twelve men in chains and were allowing them a final smoke. The men looked like someone had let the air out of them, all stooped over, deflated. They lined half the men up against a building leaving the other half to watch the cold fate that was about to befall them. It was one of the most horrific and haunting scenes I'd ever seen.

I have witnessed the look on scared men's faces before battle, but none as desperate as those of the condemned men there. What an awful state, to know that you are to be killed by your fellow soldiers and almost as bad, would be getting the order to execute them. I noted no officers were pulling the triggers. The driver of the lorry explained that morale was so low in the French army that they were experiencing mass desertions and this was their way of deterring it. For the rest of the two hour trip, I couldn't stop thinking about that awful scene.

≈

My family sat quietly listening to the old man tell his story. The thought of seeing the firing squad was appalling and this was supposed to be one of his less graphic accounts. Wow!

My dad cleared his throat which thankfully disrupted the mental images that we all were conjuring up in our minds.

"What of your reunion with your brother?" Dad asked.

"Well," Mr. Macdonald continued, "it was one of the most joyful moments of my life. Alan recognized me at once. We hugged each other for ten minutes. I cried like a baby. Alan never returned to battle, his memory loss was too great for him to ever be reinstated and he was sent home within six months. After the war, he and Sheila were married. They lived on Wolfe Island for the remainder of their lives, doubling the population on the island."

He finished his tale with a warm smile and polished off his wine. It was an upbeat moment and my mother seized the opportunity to coax the crowd into the dining room for dinner.

≈

After my father gave thanks, we gorged ourselves on turkey, candied yams, mashed potatoes, lima beans, and a host of other side dishes. It was a wonderful Thanksgiving knowing that we could share it with Mike and Mr. Macdonald. Before I dropped him off at the Veteran's home, he must have thanked me five times and confirmed that he had a wonderful time. I made him promise that he would fill me in on what happened to Dan, Bill, Terry and George. He agreed to if we would come back in the morning.

≈

At nine o'clock the next morning, I arrived once again at the Veteran's Home. I came alone this time, as Mike was still sleeping off the effects of massive turkey ingestion. Mr. McDonald had just finished his breakfast and was sitting in his favorite chair looking out at the courtyard.

"Good Morning, Sir" I greeted him.

"Alone today, eh? Well, then, I have one more story to tell you and then I'll stop boring you."

I assured him I was far from bored. He started talking without any persuasion.

"We had been on the Western Front for well over a year and we were considered old veterans. The flow of young men being sent into this slaughter seemed to have no end. We became numb to death. The Somme had ended by November with more than a million combined Allied and German casualties, and the front had not moved more than several kilometers at the most during that entire time.

Field Marshal Haig had turned his attention back to the north. The Ypres Salient, where Alan had been wounded, was now embroiled in a new offensive. The intention of our high command was to pressure the German army, which was thought to be near collapse, and then to move North to destroy the German sub bases in Belgium that were pounding the British Maritime.

We were given orders to join the Canadian 3rd Division, it was mid-October and the offensive had begun in mid-July. The heaviest rains in thirty years had plagued the battle from the beginning turning the low lying land into a soupy, muddy mess.

Tanks, trucks and field cannons were useless because of the deep mud and their getting stuck so often. The trenches were knee-to waist-deep in muck, yet the men were ordered to go forward to capture a town and its ridge called Passchendaele.

We didn't do much piping on the battlefield, the conditions were too difficult. Instead we retrieved the wounded carrying them through cold mud until we were exhausted. Dan McKee was wounded and died just before we were relieved in early November. Bill was never the same, they were very close. In fact, before Dan died of his wounds, he told Bill to take anything of his he wanted. He took his pipe. Terry, Bill, and I played pipes and drum at countless mass burials that November, including Dan's.

The Canadians did capture Passchendaele and its ridge and in a period of sixteen days suffered almost sixteen thousand casualties. Bill Lewis eventually became one of those casualties when a mustard gas shell exploded nearby as he was helping another stretcher-bearer carry a wounded Canadian lad through the mud. Mustard gas was a terrible blistering agent and caused scarring on the linings of his lungs.

And because his hands were full, Bill never covered his mouth with a wet rag to protect against the gas. Instead he continued to carry the young man to the aid post. He didn't die that day, but he was sick for some time after that and continued to have upper respiratory problems for the rest of his life.

Bill did go back to Queens University after the war and earned a degree in Engineering. He lived in Kingston and worked as a design engineer for the Kingston Locomotive Company until 1950. Then he and his wife retired to Tampa, Florida, and he quietly passed away just over twenty years ago at age 86.

His wife sent me a package several weeks after his death with some things in it that he wanted me to have. One of those things was the pipe that Dan had given him years earlier at Passchendaele. I smoke it from time to time as a reminder of my old friends and our trials during the Great War.

≈

He sat for some time holding the ornate pipe, rubbing the ivory bowl absentmindedly with his thumb.

"What about your other friends? What happened to Terry and George Cohen?" I asked.

"Oh, yes, Terry," he said, awakening from his trance. "He was highly thought of by the command of the B.E.F. for his heroism. Not only was he awarded a Victoria Cross for extraordinary valor, but he was also made an honorary member of the Black Watch Pipe and Drums Band and performed before the King and Queen.

"After the war he returned to Queens, but died a year later from the Spanish influenza. It was so sad and ironic that he made it through some of the worst battles of the war only to die from that horrid disease. They say that the Spanish flu killed as many Canadians as the war, but in half the time. It was a frightening time," Macdonald said.

"George went back to McGill and became a doctor. He practiced until he was seventy years old and then moved to Tampa where he and Bill Lewis would visit regularly."

"And you, Mr. Macdonald? What did you do after the war?" I asked.

"Well, I went back to Queens and five years later graduated as a doctor of internal medicine. I made the decision to open a general practice in Kingston and live on Wolfe Island. My wife and I lived there for fifty years," he said.

I was stunned. I never knew he was a doctor. "I'm sorry Doctor Macdonald, I would have been calling you doctor had I known! My apologies."

"Nonsense!" he said, smiling. "I gave up my practice thirty-five years ago. Anyone who knew me as Doctor Macdonald has long since died. I've become comfortable with just being Mr. Macdonald."

Then his smile faded. "I did lose one of my two sons in the Second World War. It seems that we humans just can't help ourselves."

He began to pack the ornate pipe he had inherited years earlier, struck a blue tip match and puffed it to life. Blowing out a sweet cloud of smoke, he winked and said, "I'm 109 years old. They're not likely to throw me out on my ear for smoking inside."

We sat there for some time smelling the sweet aroma and looking out at the courtyard. Staring at its neatly trimmed hedges and still quiet green lawn, both of us became lost in thought, not saying a word. It was time for me to go.

QUEENS UNIVERSITY

Several weeks had passed since my conversations with Dr. Ian Macdonald, and I was once again engrossed in my studies. One afternoon, my cell phone vibrated in my pocket, so I inconspicuously pulled it out to see who would be bothering me during class. "Mom" was spelled out on the screen. The class had fifteen more minutes, so I had to call back after class. She probably wants to congratulate me on receiving "the Pulitzer Prize" for my paper, I thought.

The professor ended her lecture and I put the cell phone up to my ear to listen to message that Mom left.

"Hi, sweety," she said. "Mom here." Why do parents think that their kids can't recognize their voices on the phone?

"I have some sad news," she continued. I covered my other ear with my hand and pressed my phone closer to my ear to drown out the background noise.

"Mr. Macdonald, from the veteran's home, passed away last night. The newspaper said that his funeral services will be this Saturday at nine o'clock. Call me. Love you."

I sat back down, took a deep breath and let out a long sigh. The last one was gone, just like that.

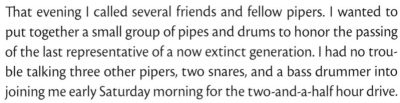

That evening I called several friends and fellow pipers. I wanted to put together a small group of pipes and drums to honor the passing of the last representative of a now extinct generation. I had no trouble talking three other pipers, two snares, and a bass drummer into joining me early Saturday morning for the two-and-a-half hour drive. It was early November and the days were getting cool. We arrived at the grave site after the service. You could still see your breath as we assembled and made ready for Doctor Macdonald's casket.

Our mini band was fully dressed in Military garb, Royal Stewart tarten, plade, horsehair sporran, spats and glengarry. We never looked sharper. As the hearse drove up, we played "Maple Leaf Forever" and then "Highland Cathedral," followed by "Amazing Grace" as they lowered the coffin.

I then played "Flowers of the forest", a tune that Ian Macdonald had played over the graves of countless soldiers almost ninety years earlier. There were about twenty people there, which I thought was a good number given that, as he said, everyone that ever knew him had long since died. There were several people from the Veteran's home, including staff, and my family also came to pay their respects.

It was a fine ceremony. The casket was draped with both Union Jack and Maple Leaf flags. After, as we were putting our pipes and equipment away, the receptionist from the Veteran's home came over to me.

"When you and your friend came to see Doctor Macdonald, that was a real high point for him and inviting him for Thanksgiving – well, he spoke of it all the time. He asked me to see to it that you received several of his belongings. I have them here." She produced a fine handmade wooden case. On the side of the case, below the handle, was inscribed – Ian Macdonald "42nd Canadian Black Watch."

I was impressed – apparently, he had forgotten to tell me that story. Inside was a beautiful, very old set of Mcgregor pipes. Pinned in the lining was a Victoria Cross and lying next to the bagpipes was his carved ivory smoking pipe.

My parents were standing next to me, as were my fellow band members and they all were impressed with the gifts, as was I.

My mother asked about the story behind the items. I told her what I knew from Ian Macdonald's story. The pipes were his from childhood, the case was made by his grandfather. I thought the Victoria Cross was Terry Manning's, but I didn't know anything about the inscription on the case though.

"And, what about the pipe?" she asked reaching in and picking it up.

I told her that it was owned by a stretcher bearer who died while saving an officer. It was given to Ian's friend who passed it on to another friend upon his death, and it was eventually passed on to Ian Macdonald after that man's death. The pipe, I said, had quite a history.

My mother gasped. She had been looking at the inscription on the side of the pipe, when her mouth fell open and the color ran out of her face.

"What's wrong?" I asked worriedly.

"The inscription says Leslie Greenhow," she said softly. "That was the name of your great uncle who died as a stretcher bearer in 1916."

HISTORICAL CORRECTIONS

THE OLYMPIC

In 1915 the Olympic had not yet been used to transport Canadian forces to England. It was in-fact in service transporting troops to the Southern front.

The battle with U103 actually took place in the English channel in 1918.

THE 1ST NEWFOUNDLAND

Although the recollection of events was historically correct, it does need to be explained that Major Henry Winsted is my fictional character. The real commander of the 1st was faced with a monumentally difficult decision and I think the results show that he chose poorly.

"HIGHLAND CATHEDRAL"

It was not a tune used in WW1. It is, however, one of my favorites.

20100871R00199